The Civilization of the American Indian Series

AN INDIAN CANAAN

AN INDIAN CANAAN

Isaac McCoy
and the Vision of an Indian State

by
GEORGE A. SCHULTZ

FOREWORD BY ROBERT E. BELL

UNIVERSITY OF OKLAHOMA PRESS
NORMAN

Library of Congress Cataloging in Publication Data

Schultz, George A   1925–
    An Indian Canaan.

    Bibliography: p.
    1. McCoy, Isaac, 1784–1846. 2. Indians of North America—
Government relations—1789–1869. 3. Indians of North America—
Indian Territory. I. Title.
E93.M122S3   970.5   72–863
ISBN 0–8061–1024–4

to
Vi Schultz

Foreword

by Robert E. Bell

This chronicle, more than a biography of Isaac McCoy, presents a scene of westward expansion by whites into Indian territories of the frontier during the early portion of the nineteenth century. The scene is both refreshing and sorrowful. It is refreshing in that military conquest, treaty-making, and political maneuvering are not the primary focus; somehow, the Indians' story and predicament emerge as the dominant theme. Yet I would hardly accuse either McCoy or his biographer of being a romanticist. The scene is sorrowful in that it recounts the Indians' sufferings and frustrations which McCoy hoped to alleviate by the creation of an Indian Canaan—an impractical and unrealistic plan.

Isaac McCoy was a Baptist missionary who started his work with frontier whites and Indians in the Old Northwest territory, now Indiana. His activities were supported by mission boards, though he was often criticized and was bypassed in important appointments, some of which were of great concern to him. His aggressive character often alienated individuals, but his knowledge of conditions on the frontier provided his superiors with important information. McCoy frequently made trips to the East (which he regarded as lounging in luxury) in order to apprise both mission boards and influential politicians or members of Congress of problems in the West. He was convinced that ignorance of the situation often prompted what he considered to be improper action.

In his early work with Indian tribes, McCoy witnessed the impact of white frontier culture upon the Indians' way of life. He noted the disintegration and resulting impoverishment, both culturally and morally. He viewed the contacts with whites and the expansion of the white frontier as a cancerous disease which, in spreading to the Indian populations, would render them destitute. The situation, of course, disrupted his own work as a missionary so that he was unable to function as he wished. McCoy established boarding mission schools, as far away from the whites as possible, but these were finally engulfed by the expanding frontier.

McCoy believed that the only solution was the establishment of an Indian state in the Far West beyond the Mississippi River. Here, in a territory of their own, the various Indian tribes could be isolated from the whites and develop their own nation. McCoy worked toward this goal, and as pressures for Indian removal beyond the Missouri became felt, he made numerous trips to the West to survey and evaluate a prospective Indian Canaan. He became involved with Indian Territory and the placement of tribes within that region; he fought in all the ways he knew for the Indians' welfare and support. Somehow, however, the removal and creation of an Indian Territory in the West did not work out as McCoy had visualized. Too many tribes were involved, lands were too limited, and already the regions were tainted by white intruders. Although it is not stated in specific terms, I think that McCoy probably realized the futility of what he had hoped to do—isolate the Indians from advancing "civilization," which he saw only as a deleterious effect upon them.

McCoy emerges as a supporter of the Indian at a time when

support of the Indian was a minority and unpopular position. He
had no special favorites among the tribes but helped all of them
in any way that he could. He had personal contact with many
different groups, and he maintained a sincere interest in their
way of life—even to the point of recording customs, beliefs, and
the like. I believe that as a missionary he would have been considered a failure by his contemporaries. As a humanitarian sincerely concerned with the Indians' welfare, today there can be
no question about his worth.

xi

Preface

The desire to plant a garden in the wilderness or to build a paradise in the desert has played a long and varied role in both secular and religious history. In the story of American development, wilderness and desert suggest metaphoric themes comparable to the frontier. When the Puritans first came to the forests surrounding Massachusetts Bay, they spoke of their colony as a refuge from the strife and religious dissension of England. It was to be a place of purification as well, just as the ancient land of Canaan had been a place of refinement for the children of Israel. The trek of the Mormons to Utah again suggests the epic of the Exodus. They came to the arid and desolate wastes in the valley of the Great Salt Lake. It was not quite a paradise that Brigham Young and his followers constructed in the desert, but it was a fairly reasonable facsimile.

Another man in the early years of the nineteenth century also dreamed of a kind of paradise in the American wilderness, but the people of this exodus were to be the Indians residing east of the Mississippi River. Isaac McCoy, a Baptist missionary, proposed to lead them to the vast empty region between the borders of Missouri and the Rocky Mountains. Having given up hope of Christianizing the Indians within the settled areas of the country, McCoy wanted to get them as far away as possible from the contaminating influence of the white trader and settler in order to work for their Christianization and civilization unhampered. The main purpose of this book is to show how the idea of an Indian Canaan emerged in McCoy's thinking and to interpret his career in the light of it. It is not a biography in the usual sense.

McCoy's missionary career was devoted almost entirely to the Indians of the Old Northwest. The missions he founded in Indiana and the Michigan Territory were some of the first missionary projects sponsored by Baptists. He was one of the few missionaries who actively supported Andrew Jackson's Indian policy. Consequently, when removal became an actual fact, McCoy was involved in a northern "Trail of Tears," an aspect of emigration not so well known as its southern counterpart.

In Baptist hagiography, McCoy is overshadowed by such contemporaries as Adoniram Judson, missionary to the Burmese, or John Mason Peck, missionary to the American frontier and builder of schools in the wilderness. McCoy escaped the biographer until 1895 when Walter N. Wyeth published *Isaac McCoy: Early Indian Missions*. It is an uncritical, laudatory work, in which McCoy is portrayed as "one of the most loveable of men . . . children loved him." No other major study of McCoy has appeared in print. And yet Carl Coke Rister, a Baptist layman but better known as a historian of the American West, writes, "Isaac McCoy ranks with Adoniram Judson and William Carey as one of the greatest American Baptist missionaries, if he were not one of the greatest missionaries of all times and of all nations."[1] Despite such encomiums, the most recent history of Baptist missions, Robert G. Torbet's *Venture of Faith*, contains only two short references to McCoy.

Like most histories of Indian-white relations, this book relies on the white man's description of the native's reaction to what was often an unsolicited concern for his welfare. Anthropolo-

[1] Carl Coke Rister, *Baptist Missions Among the American Indians*, 38–39.

gists have developed techniques to interpret Indian-white relations in terms of cultural contact or acculturation, but they too depend heavily on the kind of information historians use. It is hoped that this work will afford some insight into acculturative processes, although the topic itself has limitations for this type of approach. The tribes to which McCoy directed his missionary endeavors were almost completely demoralized and their numbers decimated when he began his work. Agencies of cultural disintegration, other than Christian missions, had been at work. It became McCoy's intent to help the Indian reconstruct his society, which he did, at times, with a breadth of vision; often, with considerably less. In either circumstance, there were undoubtedly some Indians among those whom McCoy tried to help who reacted as Quequeg did in Herman Melville's *Moby Dick*. The Indian harpooner of mysterious South American origins, after his first brush with the white Christian civilization of early-nineteenth-century Massachusetts, concluded that "We cannibals must help these Christians."

GEORGE A. SCHULTZ

Winnipeg, Manitoba
January 17, 1972

Acknowledgments

The bulk of the research for this book was accomplished at the Kansas State Historical Society Library in Topeka, Kansas. I am deeply indebted to its staff, particularly Mrs. Lela Barnes, who was, until recently, curator of manuscripts. I wish also to express my appreciation to Professor Allan G. Bogue, now at the University of Wisconsin, under whose direction this study was initiated.

Lastly the author must acknowledge the help of his wife. She has gotten to know Isaac McCoy as well as I do.

The publication of this book was facilitated by a grant from the Research Board, University of Manitoba.

George A. Schultz

Contents

Illustrations

Maps

AN INDIAN CANAAN

Chapter 1

The Making of a Missionary

Among those who participated in the settlement of the trans-Appalachian West were a number of frontier preachers with minds of great natural capacity. Denied the opportunity of formal education and isolated from the world of thought, they injected a dynamic factor into organized religion and into frontier life. Making use of the intellectual materials at hand they acquired a prodigious Biblical knowledge and developed a homespun variety of philosophical and theological speculation. They preached what they understood of the Christian message in the widely scattered cabins of the pioneers. Self-taught, they resented the presumption of the eastern churches in sending out young college-trained ministers to undertake missionary work within their boundaries. The lack of education was a matter of little importance either to the frontier preacher or to the frontier congregation, for above all prerequisites ranked the "call" to preach.

Unlike the Methodists, who together with the Baptists dominated the religious life of the frontier, the Baptists had no powerful national organization with selective and licensing authority. When a Baptist layman felt that God had called him to become a preacher, he announced the fact to his church, and the members listened to a sample sermon. If it turned out well, he was given a license to preach locally, and if he continued to improve, his church allowed him to become a full-fledged minister authorized to "smite the Devil" anywhere in the nation. When a Baptist preacher wished to found a church in the wilderness, he simply did so, asking leave of no one. Since most Baptists believed that God had ordained the Gospel to be dispensed free of charge, the typical Baptist minister was self-supporting. Usually he was a farmer who wrestled with rocks and roots during the week and then took on Satan on Sunday.

Isaac McCoy started his religious career as a Baptist frontier preacher, and in most respects his early years fit the typical pattern. He had no formal education, not even the opportunity to attend the most rudimentary schools. Many influences were ultimately to shape his thoughts and actions, for his career spanned a formative period in American Protestantism and the missionary movement. In the immediate sense, however, McCoy was a product of the western frontier, and throughout his life he shared its values and prejudices, its handicaps and opportunities.

McCoy grew up in a restless, westward-moving family which uprooted no sooner than it had settled. The spread of white civilization from the foothills of the Appalachians to the regions beyond the Mississippi River can be traced in the movements of grandfather, father, and son. James McCoy, a Scotch-Irish emigrant orphan boy, is said to have arrived as a stowaway in the colony of Maryland in the 1730's.[1] He eventually made his way to western Pennsylvania, and his son William took the McCoy name farther into the West. In 1789, William McCoy and his family, including Isaac, who was about five at the time, joined the throng of adventurers who were moving to the Kentucky frontier. The McCoys floated down the Ohio River on a flatboat

[1] The descendants of John M'Coy, Isaac's brother, have had an active clan interest in genealogy. See William H. McCoy, Notes on the McCoy Family, and Elizabeth McCoy Hayward (ed.), *John M'Coy: His Life and Diaries.*

and landed near Louisville, then a small town with its back to the wilderness. Here they remained for three years before moving on to Shelby County, Kentucky, where settlement had just begun.[2]

The Scotch-Irish emigrants were usually Presbyterians, but somewhere in their journeying the McCoys became Baptists. Shortly after moving to Kentucky, William McCoy felt the call to preach. Since other Baptist ministers had already established themselves in Shelby County, McCoy itinerated in a region across the Ohio River, outside the state but not far from his homestead. Here he founded the Silver Creek Baptist Church, thought to be the first Protestant church in the Indiana Territory. There were some advantages in growing up in a frontier preacher's family, for when John M'Coy,[3] Isaac's brother, reflected on his home environment, he remembered that his father's library contained the larger part of all the books in the community, even though it would not have much more than filled "an ordinary portmanteau."[4] There were disadvantages too, apparently; for when Isaac reminisced about his younger days, he recalled many bitter arguments with his father on matters of religion.

Baptist ministers of Calvinist traditions had long dwelled on themes of original sin, election, and predestination. It was natural, perhaps, that some, like William McCoy, concluded that it was interference with divine prerogative to attempt to convert the non-Christian world. This was God's work and he would do it in his own way. McCoy opposed proselytizing even in his own family. That too was "the work of the Lord." Isaac McCoy, in his memoirs, recalled that as a youth he had vigorously objected to his father's beliefs and strongly suspected his "orthodoxy."

[2] John M'Coy, "Isaac McCoy," *Annals of the American Pulpit: The Baptists*, VI (ed. by William B. Sprague), 541–647.

[3] He preferred this spelling of the family name.

[4] M'Coy, "Isaac McCoy," *Annals*, VI, 542.

But he was looking backward from the perspective of a missionary who had frequently crossed swords with obstructive hyper-Calvinists. The "unorthodoxy" of his father may well have been the orthodoxy of the time and the region. Whatever the true situation, there can be little doubt that Isaac was a religiously precocious youngster whose views sometimes conflicted with those of his elders. At the age of sixteen, having decided that human instrumentality was necessary to convert the world to Christianity, McCoy debated the issue with the local Baptist minister in a church meeting. It seems that no one else agreed with him, so McCoy, a minority of one, stormed out in full view of the congregation.[5]

When John M'Coy wrote his story of growing up with father, he remembered William McCoy's concern about the "wild and wicked" tendencies of his sons. They may have been guilty of nothing more than taking part in a shooting match or dancing to the music of a fiddle, but such activities were proscribed for Baptists, particularly preachers' children. Baptist churches were most assiduous in policing the morals of their members. In business sessions local churches considered a great miscellany of infractions of approved conduct. A session might, for example, take cognizance of "hard sayings" or express disapproval of short-haired women and long-haired men.[6] Being a Baptist in the churches of the frontier was serious business, and this was exactly how young Isaac McCoy regarded it. He wrote that in his younger days "my morality and particularly my ad-

[5] From an unpaged manuscript entitled "Autobiographical Statement," dated 1817, in the Isaac McCoy Collection, Kansas State Historical Society Library.

[6] Some of the early records of the Silver Creek Church are held by the Indiana University Library and extracts are quoted in R. Carlyle Buley's *The Old Northwest: Pioneer Period*, II, 464–65. Not all of the judicial business of the church was taken up with minor infractions. On one occasion, a James McCoy was excluded from the church for shooting "Bro. Perry."

version to dancing, induced my associates, by way of derision to call me a Methodist, which I considered a reproachful epithet, and a grand insult, and altho I stood alone, I was determined to resent it even to blows."[7] John M'Coy, obviously, cannot have had Isaac in mind when he recalled the waywardness of his brothers.

In view of Isaac McCoy's preoccupation with matters of religion, it is not surprising that he felt a call to preach. The tide of settlement had moved into a part of the Indiana Territory known as Clark's Grant, but McCoy felt directed toward Vincennes,[8] a military and trading outpost on the edge of the Indian country and the seat of government for the territory. At the turn of the century the town had about seven hundred inhabitants, a mixed population of French, Americans, Indians, and a few Negro slaves.[9] One unfriendly English tourist to Vincennes in the early nineteenth century described it as an "antique lump of deformity . . . an old, worn out, dirty village of wooden frame houses, which a fire might much improve . . . the inhabitants principally French Canadians, and the rest the refuse of the east."[10] McCoy set out for Vincennes in 1803 despite his father's warning that it was foolhardy for a mere boy to preach in such a "strange and wicked place." McCoy was somewhat apprehensive, but just before striking out on his own, he married and made note of the occasion in candid, if unromantic, fashion. "As I had been un-

[7] McCoy, Autobiographical Statement.

[8] In 1803 the only areas in the Indiana Territory cleared of Indian claims was the region adjacent to Vincennes, and Clark's Grant, a tract that had been conveyed originally to General Rogers Clark and his soldiers in 1780. These cessions were confirmed by the Treaty of Greenville in 1795. C. J. Kappler (ed.), *Indian Affairs, Laws and Treaties*, II, 41.

[9] Clarence E. Carter (ed.), *The Territorial Papers of the United States*, vii; *Indiana Territory*, 24–25.

[10] William Faux, *Memorable Days in America*, Vol. XI of *Early Western Travels, 1748–1846* (ed. by Reuben Gold Thwaites), 207–208.

accustomed to living among strangers, I at length concluded that it would be better for me to marry and have a home of my own, I now began to look out for a companion, who might lighten my difficulties."[11] The girl he married, Christiana Polke,[12] was sixteen and he was nineteen. They settled near Vincennes. There were no Baptists in the community who suited McCoy's tastes, and he found little encouragement to become a preacher. Fortunately he received an appointment as the town jailor, which at least provided housing. His father, with undisguised sarcasm, wrote, "While I expected you were proclaiming liberty to the Captives I hear that you are keeping the keys of the prison." Eventually, an opportunity to preach did come to McCoy, and he was asked to minister to a small Baptist congregation at Maria Creek, eight miles from Vincennes. He was ordained by this church in 1810.[13]

Because he had been denied the opportunity for any formal training, McCoy's ministry at Maria Creek can be regarded as the apprenticeship period of his career. His interests were not confined to the one church, for, from the beginning, he was constantly involved in various projects. He fancied himself a poet and a hymn writer, and so he set out on an itinerary of churches in Kentucky and Ohio to try to collect money for the publication of his works. A more successful and perhaps constructive undertaking was a plan he conceived for the formation of "societies for domestick missions." These societies were to be formed by associations or groups of Baptist churches. They would receive contributions and employ persons to carry on organized missionary activity among the settlers on the frontier.

[11] McCoy, Autobiographical Statement.
[12] The father of President James K. Polk and Christiana Polke were cousins. See James Polke, "Some Memoirs of the Polke, Piety, McCoy, McQuaid, and Mathes Families," *Indiana Magazine of History*, Vol. X (March, 1914), 84.
[13] McCoy, Autobiographical Statement.

McCoy had expected to become permanently engaged in missionary work among the pioneers, but when he returned from his tour, he found that the men in the Long Run Association who had promised support for his plan of "domestick missions" now planned to channel their funds through the Board of Foreign Missions, an agency of the General Missionary Convention of the Baptist Denomination in the United States of America for Foreign Missions. Heathen were heathen wherever they could be found, and so this newly formed organization had decided to extend its activities to the American frontier. Most western local associations of Baptist churches refused to co-operate with the eastern-centered board, but the leaders of the Long Run Association concluded that the advantages of a national missionary agency outweighed those of many small ones. McCoy was disappointed. He was convinced that his plan for locally controlled societies would find greater acceptance. Furthermore, he was reluctant to resume the role of a self-supporting pastor. He found it an intolerable position. "When I go to meeting some think I neglect my business at home. If I attend to my business at home, I am charged with indifferency in religion." That there was some justification for the first criticism is indicated by his admission that for a year he had earned almost nothing to support his family. In the spring of 1817, McCoy heard that the Board of Foreign Missions planned to begin a mission in St. Louis. He overcame his reservations about the organization, for the time being, and offered his services. He had now to wait for the General, or Triennial, Convention, meeting in Philadelphia in May, to make a decision on his application.[19]

McCoy had an immediate stake in the outcome of the first

[18] Isaac McCoy, Journal, March 21, 1816, to May 29, 1816, unpaged MS in the Isaac McCoy Collection, Kansas State Historical Society Library.

[19] McCoy, Journal, June 10, 1816, to April 3, 1817.

Triennial General Convention, but once established, the convention represented a trend toward centralization that he would oppose. Some Baptist leaders had long advocated such a body. An awakened interest in foreign missions, owing largely to the activities of two Congregationalist missionaries turned Baptist, had finally provided the catalyst. To support the work of Adoniram Judson and Luther Rice in Burma, and to commission other foreign missionaries, representatives from a number of local Baptist constituencies, ignoring a long tradition of local autonomy and paid ministries, had formed the General Missionary Convention of the Baptist Denomination in the United States of America for Foreign Missions. They also had set up the Board of Foreign Missions in Boston to "manage" the affairs of the convention.[20] Without waiting for the first meeting of the convention, the board proceeded to commit the denomination to schemes not only to promote foreign missions but to further education and home missions.

Despite concerted opposition, a majority of the delegates to the first Triennial General Convention approved the actions of the board. Plans were set in motion to establish a school to train teachers, ministers, and missionaries which resulted in the founding of Columbian College (now George Washington University) in the District of Columbia. The convention also accepted the board's recommendation to set up a mission in St. Louis. Ignoring McCoy's application, it commissioned John Mason Peck of Connecticut and James E. Welch of Kentucky to preach to the pioneers, and to devote some attention to the Indians.[21] Subsequently, the board instructed them that it was "particularly

[20] *Proceedings of the Baptist Convention for Missionary Purposes*, 4–5.
[21] *Proceedings of the General Convention of the Baptist Denomination in the United States at the First Triennial Meeting, Together with the Third Annual Report of the Baptist Board of Foreign Missions for the United States*, 172–75.

desirous that Fox, Osage, Kansas and other tribes engage your peculiar zeal."[22] With little more awareness than that these must be the tribes in the St. Louis area, and with no realization that the problems of preaching to the white man and the red man might be totally dissimilar, a Baptist missionary organization had, for the first time, expressed an interest in the religious welfare of the Indians.

Meanwhile, the world all but tumbled in on McCoy when he learned that others had been appointed to St. Louis. Characteristically, he had the whole universe participating in his disappointment. When he received the news, "a thundergust darkened the scene, by loud peals of thunder and flashes of lightning, by the darkened sky, the flood of rain, it seemed as if nature was testifying against me and declaring the displeasure of God."[23] To add to his distress he became gravely ill, the first bout of a continuing struggle with a disease which he described variously as some "strange malady" or "malevolent malignancy," but which today probably would be diagnosed as tuberculosis. Thinking that he might not survive, McCoy felt he owed the world an account of his life. Somewhat absurdly, he wrote out an autobiographical statement of 479 closely written pages in the form of a letter addressed to his brother-in-law, William Polke. He looked back on his life with bitterness, for although he believed himself destined for greatness, he had little to show but a recital of misfortune and small accomplishments; and now his life, it seemed, was about to be cut short at the age of thirty-three. Yet he was determined to write an autobiography despite the incongruity of it all.

Men who have risen to emminence [sic] on the theatre of life,

22 *The American Baptist Magazine and Missionary Intelligencer*, Vol. I (September, 1817), 189.
23 McCoy, Journal, June 29, 1817.

frequently add a feather to the wing of fame at the close of the scene, and give us a history of their good fortune . . . . But astonishing indeed for one who is unknown to fame, and indeed little known to the world by any occurrence, to give extracts of his life.[24]

McCoy recovered. Fame continued to elude him, but then he was never tempted to write another autobiography. His spirits and fortunes also revived, at least temporarily, for he received word from William Staughton, the corresponding secretary of the Board of Foreign Missions, that he had been appointed to missionary service for one year among the settlers in certain specified counties in Indiana and the Illinois Territory. He was to extend his efforts to the Indians "as far as practicable."[25] For his services, he was to be allowed five hundred dollars. "I would rather my appointment had been permanent, but this teaches me to live more by faith."[26]

For reasons he did not explain, McCoy decided to devote himself exclusively to the Indians. In the late fall of 1817 he visited General Thomas Posey, agent for the Weas, Miamis, and Kickapoos, with headquarters in Vincennes, and asked for information about these tribes and for the General's approval and aid in setting up a mission among them. Many years later when McCoy wrote his *History of Baptist Indian Missions*, he stated that he had always felt himself called to preach to the Indians, and that in fact he proposed an Indian mission to the board. Nothing in McCoy's writings to this point indicates that he had any other ambition but to get an appointment to work among the settlers in Missouri Territory. Perhaps, McCoy's sympathy for the Indians

[24] McCoy, Autobiographical Statement.

[25] Staughton to McCoy, June 23, 1817, McCoy Correspondence, MSS in the Isaac McCoy Collection, Kansas State Historical Society Library.

[26] McCoy, Journal, October 22, 1817.

had recently been aroused after witnessing the degradation and suffering in their camps around Vincennes. Easy prey for shop-keepers and traders, many of the tribesmen had been systematically stripped of their annuities and property. Since the managers of the board had expressed interest in Indians, and since he was not being sent to St. Louis, McCoy apparently decided to draw the board into a permanent Indian mission in Indiana.

McCoy's involvement in Indian missions added a dimension to his life that was lacking in most frontier-trained ministers. He made many trips to the East where he met with denominational leaders, and although he had a traditional westerner's suspicion of the eastern-bred and college-trained missionary executives sitting in comfortable offices in Boston, these were broadening experiences. As his horizons widened, McCoy became concerned about the whole problem of Indian reform, and this concern took him repeatedly to Washington, where he became acquainted with a number of government leaders. The sophisticated legislative bills he drew up for the friends in Congress who supported his views are in marked contrast to the crude style and parochial outlook evident in his early journals and correspondence. Further evidence of his widened interests is found in the library he accumulated. Upon accepting an appointment from the Board of Foreign Missions, McCoy became accreditable to it for all his assets, and he regularly listed his books. He moved a sizable library with him into his Indian Canaan, despite acute transportation problems, a library which included books on many topics outside the realm of religion.[27] On one trip to Washington, he noted with great satisfaction that he acquired all of the *Trans-*

[27] "Bill of Articles Taken by McCoy and Lykins on going to Westward, for which they are accountable to Board," October 1, 1828, McCoy Correspondence. Also see John Francis McDermott, "A Frontier Library: The Books of Isaac McCoy," *Bibliographical Society of America*, Vol. LII (Second Quarter, 1958), 140–43.

actions of the American Antiquarian Society.[28] Without a day of formal schooling in his life, the education of Isaac McCoy had advanced considerably beyond the books in his father's portmanteau.

[28] McCoy, Journal, April 15, 1838.

Chapter II

The Beginning of a Venture

The scene of Isaac McCoy's missionary activities in the Old Northwest had long been a favorite haunt of the Indians. The forests and treeless prairies to the east and south of Lake Michigan in what is now southern Michigan and central and northern Indiana provided a highly desirable environment for a semi-sedentary life of hunting, fishing, and farming. Until the time of white settlement, the region was, by Indian standards, a densely populated area.[1]

Tribal locations shifted in response to pressures of war and the development of the fur trade with the Europeans. Throughout most of the historic period, the Potawatomis pushed hard on the Miamis from the north. By the nineteenth century the greater part of the Miami tribe had consolidated on the Wabash and Maumee rivers. Two Miami bands on the lower Wabash, the Weas and Piankashaws, had come to be regarded as separate tribes. According to native traditions, the Potawatomis, Ottawas, and Chippewas reached the upper Great Lakes in company from a region farther east. The Potawatomis, as "keepers of the fire," formed the vanguard and moved southward, while the Chippewas headed westward to both sides of Lake Superior. The

---

[1] W. B. Hinsdale, *Distribution of the Aboriginal Population of Michigan,* Occasional Contributions of the Museum of Anthropology of the University of Michigan, No. 2, 5–10.

17

Ottawas remained more or less residual. By 1800, the Potawatomis had dispossessed the Miamis of the whole country around the head of Lake Michigan. Some of the Potawatomi bands spread out over the plains of Illinois and took on a separate identity as the Prairie Potawatomis. The Ottawas, meanwhile, occupied much of the lower Michigan peninsula, and expanded eastward to the southern shore of Lake Erie. The Grand River formed an inconclusive boundary between the Ottawas and the Potawatomis.[2]

By the nineteenth century there had arisen among the Potawatomi, Ottawa, Miami, and other tribes in the western Great Lakes region a uniformity of tribal culture brought about by prolonged contacts with the white fur traders and the change in native economic systems caused by the fur trade. Bands of various tribes frequently established joint villages. It was not thought desirable or necessary to maintain pure blood, and there was a long-standing habit of intermarriage not only with members of other tribes but with the white traders. The appearance of such names as François and Louison as signatories for the Potawatomi tribe at the Treaty of Chicago in 1821,[3] indicated that persons of mixed Indian and white blood had risen to positions of leadership. In one of McCoy's first contacts with the Miami Indians he noted with considerable interest that "among the tribes there were many who are somewhat related to the

---

[2] Henry R. Schoolcraft, *Historical and Statistical Information Respecting the History, Condition, and Prospects of the Indian Tribes of the United States*, 308; John R. Swanton (ed.), *The Indian Tribes of North America*, Bureau of American Ethnology *Bulletin No. 145*, 238–39, 288–89.

[3] C. J. Kappler (ed.), *Indian Affairs, Laws and Treaties*, II, 201. Joseph Francis Murphy discusses the difficulty in tracing the origins of Potawatomi bands through the maze of intermarriage in "Potawatomi Indians of the West: Origin of the Citizen Band" (Ph.D. dissertation, University of Oklahoma, 1961), 17–19.

whites, and all such feel more dignified than full blooded Indians."[4]

Pushed out from the hospitable environment of the region surrounding Lake Michigan, the Miamis felt the full pressure of white settlement before the Potawatomis or the Ottawas did. In the 1790's the Miamis led in forming a confederation to attempt to hold the line at the Ohio River. In contrast to their vehement opposition to the encroachment of the white men, the Miamis allowed tribes of dissimilar backgrounds to settle on their lands with little protest. They permitted the Kickapoos to occupy much of what is now eastern Illinois and to establish a number of villages on the Wabash itself. Charles C. Trowbridge, amateur student of the Indians and private secretary to Governor Lewis Cass of Michigan Territory, reported in 1825 that considerable assimilation in customs and language had taken place between the Miamis and the Kickapoos.[5]

Of equal significance was the presence of Delaware and Shawnee tribesmen in the Wabash country. Remnants of the Delawares, unfortunate victims of the Iroquois conquests, made their way to the Ohio country and there staged a strong recovery. By 1800 the Delawares, with the permission of the Miamis, had expanded into the region between the Wabash and the White Rivers in the Indiana Territory.[6] These Delawares, in turn, invited a number of Shawnee bands to live with them. The Shawnees, the "Bedouins" of the North American tribes, after years of wandering, also found new strength and prestige in the

4 McCoy, Journal, June 17, 1818.

5 Trowbridge to Cass, March 6, 1825, in Charles C. Trowbridge, *Meearmeear Traditions* (ed. by W. Vernon Kinietz), Occasional Contributions from the Museum of Anthropology of the University of Michigan, No. 7, 2.

6 W. Vernon Kinietz, *Delaware Culture Chronology*, Prehistory Research Series, Indiana Historical Society, Vol. III, 9–12.

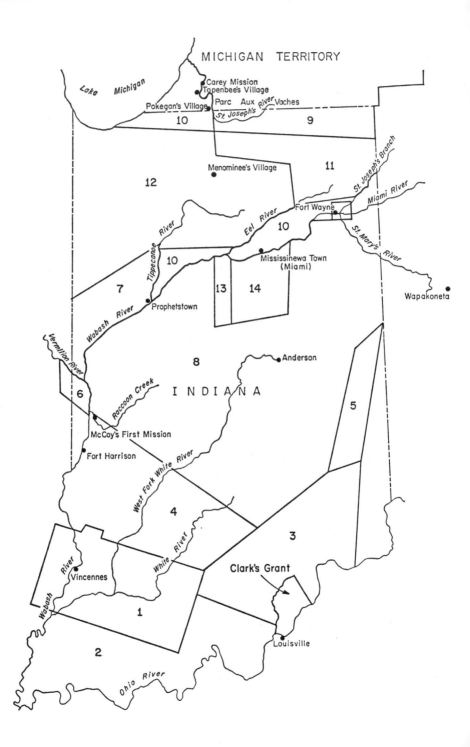

MICHIGAN TERRITORY

Lake Michigan

Carey Mission
Topenbee's Village
Pokegan's Village
Parc Aux River Vaches
St. Joseph's

10   9

Menominee's Village

12   11

St. Joseph's Branch

Miami River

Eel River   Fort Wayne

10

Tippecanoe River   St. Mary's River

10   Mississinewa Town
(Miami)

7   13   14   Wapakoneta

Prophetstown
Wabash River

8   Anderson

Vermilion River   I N D I A N A

Raccoon Creek

6   5

McCoy's First Mission

Fort Harrison

West Fork White River

4

White River

Wabash River   Clark's Grant

3

Vincennes

1

Louisville

2

Ohio River

INDIAN LAND CESSIONS IN INDIANA, 1795–1840

1. Ceded by the Indians in Anthony Wayne's treaty at Greenville on August 3, 1795.

2. Lands ceded by the Delawares to the United States by the treaty of August 18, 1804, at Vincennes. This cession was concurred in by the Piankashaw on August 27, 1804. The Potawatomi, Miami, Eel River, and Wea, on August 21, 1805, at Grouseland, acknowledged the right of the Delawares to sell this land.

3. By treaty of August 21, 1805, at Grouseland, the Delawares, Potawatomi, Miami, Eel River, and Wea ceded this area to the United States.

4 and 5. On September 30, 1809, at Fort Wayne, the Delawares, Potawatomi, Miami, and Eel River ceded this land to the United States.

6. Ceded by Kickapoo by treaty at Vincennes, December 9, 1809.

7. Ceded on October 2, 1818, at St. Mary's, Ohio, by the Potawatomi to the United States.

8. On October 6, 1818, at St. Mary's, Ohio, the Miami Nation of Indians ceded to the United States this area of 6,789,831 acres, besides 297,600 acres in Ohio.

9. Ceded August 29, 1821, at Chicago, by the Ottawa, Chippewa, and Potawatomi to the United States, besides other land in Michigan.

10. Ceded by the Potawatomi by treaty negotiated near the mouth of Mississinewa upon the Wabash, October 16, 1826.

11. Ceded to the United States by the Potawatomi by a treaty made on September 20, 1828, at Carey Mission.

12. Ceded by the Potawatomi in a treaty made October, 1832, at Tippecanoe River, Indiana.

13. Part of the "Big Reserve," ceded with numerous smaller reserves, by the Miami by treaty of October 23, 1834, made at the Forks of the Wabash in Indiana; which provided also for patenting ten sections of Miami land to John B. Richardville.

14. "The Residue of the Big Reserve," made at the treaty of St. Mary's in 1818, ceded by the Miami, November 28, 1840, by treaty made at the Forks of the Wabash, "being all their remaining lands in Indiana."

Ohio country. Of all the Indians in the Old Northwest, they were the most consistently hostile to the expansion of the white man. Accompanying the Shawnees who went to live with the Delawares below the Wabash were two brothers, Tecumseh and Tenskwatawa.[7] Here, Tenskwatawa, better known as "The Prophet," began to preach a new doctrine which exhorted the Indians to return to the communal life of their ancestors, and asked them to abandon all customs derived from the whites. Tenskwatawa and his followers were well aware that profound changes had taken place in their way of life. They blamed the white settler and his greed for land. But long before the settlers came the native economic systems had been greatly affected by the fur trade, which had reduced the various tribal cultures to common levels.

It was a pan-Indian culture that was breaking up when Mc-Coy first appeared on the scene. The fur-bearing animals were becoming scarce, and the fur traders were moving farther to the west. This scarcity meant that many Indians lost their livelihood, and could no longer purchase the tools, weapons, utensils, clothing, ornaments, and even food upon which they had become dependent. They were not totally unprepared, however, to take up agricultural pursuits, for during the spring and summer they had usually set up agricultural villages. Nor were the Indians necessarily averse to learning better agricultural methods. As early as 1742, a company of Potawatomi chiefs, visiting Montreal on official business, had asked the French to send them a blacksmith so that they might have better agricultural tools.[8] But because they were swamped by an onrush of white settlers in the early nineteenth century, the Indians did not have an oppor-

[7] Charles C. Trowbridge, *Shawnese Traditions* (ed. by W. Vernon Kinietz and Erminie W. Voegelin), Occasional Contributions from the Museum of Anthropology of the University of Michigan, No. 9, xi–xiv.
[8] Murphy, "Potawatomi Indians," 11.

tunity to make the kind of major economic adjustments they had made in the past.

Other factors led to a rapid disintegration of Indian cultural life. One of the most demoralizing problems was liquor. It was readily accepted by the Indians, perhaps initially for religious reasons. It had been customary to obtain religious experiences from dreams and visions brought on by fasting and fatigue. Whisky could, conceivably, provide a convenient short cut to hallucinations. It was the chief stock in trade for the trader, but in the spirit of American free enterprise, a class of whites emerged on the fringe of settled areas who made a precarious living by supplying liquor to the Indians. McCoy developed a wide range of expletives for these parasites.

Accompanying the deterioration of tribal culture was a decline in population. Wars and introduced diseases exacted a heavy toll. In 1817, Major Benjamin F. Stickney, the Indian agent at Fort Wayne, estimated the population of the Miamis to be about 1,400.[9] One seventeenth-century French explorer had judged the population of that tribe to be about 24,000.[10] The latter figure was probably an exaggeration, but a dramatic decline is, nevertheless, indicated.

The decrease in the number of Indians in the Old Northwest coincided with a rapid shrinkage of their territory. In the first decade of the nineteenth century the Miamis, Piankashaws, and Weas had the misfortune to cope with William Henry Harrison,

[9] Stickney, to T. L. McKenney (superintendent of Indian trade), August 27, 1817, quoted in W. A. Brice, *History of Fort Wayne, with a Biography of the Late Hon. Samuel Hanna*, 291. James Mooney gives the same figure for the Miami population in 1825, including Weas and Piankashaws. *The Aboriginal Population of the American Indians North of Mexico, Smithsonian Miscellaneous Collections*, Vol. LXXX, No. 7.
[10] Nicholas Perrot, "Memoir of the Manners, Customs, and Religion of the Savages of North America," in *Indian Tribes of the Upper Mississippi Valley and Region of the Great Lakes* (trans. and ed. by Emma H. Blair), Vol. I, 223.

newly appointed governor of the Territory of Indiana. He employed a great talent in separating Indians from their ancestral lands, and called conferences almost yearly at Fort Wayne, Vincennes, or Grouseland. He convened some to correct alleged wrongs done the red man, and the Indians insisted on calling others to protest illegal cessions, but the result was always the same. The tribesmen signed away millions of acres for miserly annuities and the distribution of goods. Realizing that they were rapidly losing their lands, being deprived of much of their aboriginal culture, and suffering under a badly depressed economic situation, the Indians of the Old Northwest staged their last important resistance under the leadership of Tecumseh and Tenskwatawa. McCoy began his missionary career in the aftermath of this uprising.

The futile but bloody attempt to delay white settlement hastened the processes of cultural disintegration and discredited movements similar to the one led by "The Prophet." McCoy lived to see the day when a disillusioned Tenskwatawa gave his approval for a Baptist mission on a Shawnee reservation west of the Missouri River.[11]

The region west of the Missouri was still far from McCoy's mind, however, when he attempted, in 1818, to open his first mission with the Miamis living in west-central Indiana. As yet he knew little about the over-all problems that faced the Indians. Although he had lived near Vincennes for fifteen years, he appeared to be almost completely ignorant of the tribesmen who lived in the immediate vicinity. The "managers" of the Baptist Board of Foreign Missions had even less comprehension, for when they gave McCoy a one-year appointment, they expected him to begin immediately to preach to white settlers and Indians

[11] Isaac McCoy, *History of Baptist Indian Missions*, 404–405.

alike. McCoy at least simplified the problem when he decided to devote himself exclusively to the Indians.

Thomas Posey, the Indian agent at Vincennes, whom McCoy had approached for help in setting up a mission, died before he could be of any assistance. Benjamin Parke, his successor, showed no enthusiasm for McCoy's plans, but did nothing to obstruct them. In the spring of 1818, McCoy went to Fort Harrison, near Terre Haute, to talk to the Miamis who had gathered there to receive their annuities in the form of goods, which were heaped in a pile and divided. McCoy noted that the Indians had no opportunity to compare receipts with invoices; quantity and price depended entirely on the honesty of the agents who delivered the goods.[12] Thomas Jefferson once observed that any civilization program must begin with teaching the Indians arithmetic so that they could keep accounts.[13] McCoy, after witnessing the distribution of annuity goods, quickly came to the same conclusion.

McCoy soon realized that to reach the Indians at all he would have to live with them. But first he would need the permission of the agent and the consent of the Indians themselves. McCoy hoped to get the agreement of the Indians and the agent by proposing the establishment of a school where native children would be fed, clothed, and educated without charge.[14]

As McCoy formulated his plans, the pieces fell quickly into place, at least in his mind. Presumably, a mission school would require some knowledge of the tribal languages, but McCoy did not intend to wait. He would hire as a teacher a half-blood Frenchman, who besides French, would be able to speak the

12 McCoy, Journal, May 29, 1818.
13 *The Writings of Thomas Jefferson* (ed. by H. A. Washington), V, 440.
14 From an undated memo in the McCoy Correspondence entitled "Plan for Introduction of the Gospel to Wabash Indians."

Indian dialects and English, all without profanity, for twenty dollars a month. The mission would include a farm, which would make it partially self-sustaining and which, at the same time, would afford the opportunity to teach the native children the arts of agriculture and homemaking. White children would be taken into the school to help defray expenses. McCoy hoped, also, to solicit funds from the "publick."[15] Conspicuously absent were any plans for continued reliance upon the Board of Foreign Missions. It would be his mission. The object of his labors would be to make out of the Indian "a farmer, a citizen of the U.S., *A Christian*."[16] In short order, McCoy arrived at the goals that separately or together characterized Indian reform and Indian missions in the nineteenth century. Ordinarily, the amorphous term *civilization* implied all three.

Since the United States was overwhelmingly rural, it was not unusual that agriculture was chosen as the key to the good life for the Indian by politicians as well as missionaries. Henry Knox, the nation's first secretary of war, in his capacity as superintendent of Indian affairs recommended that the government send missionaries to reside among the Indian nations, who besides their religious duties would introduce farm implements and domestic animals and cultivate a love for property.[17] During Thomas Jefferson's presidency there were further appeals to provide the Indians with training "in agriculture and the domestic arts."[18] Unlike Knox, Jefferson was critical of the "ancient and totally ineffectual plan of beginning with religious missionaries." He outlined a scheme that could well have been plagiarized from Thomas More's *Utopia*. The Indian men would raise cattle, and

[15] *Ibid.*
[16] McCoy, Journal, March 30, 1818.
[17] *American State Papers: Indian Affairs*, I, 9, 66.
[18] "Second Inaugural Address, March 4, 1805," *Jeffersonian Cyclopedia* (ed. by John P. Foley), 982.

the women would spin and weave, and for their enjoyment, they would sit around in the evenings and read *Aesop's Fables* and *Robinson Crusoe*.[19] Succeeding administrations urged Congress to devise plans for promoting civilization among the Indians by the introduction of "husbandry." There were, therefore, precedents for McCoy's triple objectives.

Throughout the summer of 1818, McCoy went back to Fort Harrison repeatedly to attempt to get the consent of the Miami chiefs to build a mission school. A novice in negotiating, he resorted to blandishments. He assured them that while their children would be receiving an English education, his would be getting an Indian one. The students would not be asked to give up any customs, and they would not be required to alter the fashion of their dress. He appealed to the pride of the chiefs by telling them that through schools the southern tribes had risen to great dignity and happiness. All these assurances helped little. The chiefs were more interested in discussing the next annuity payment than schools.[20]

Another element in McCoy's plan went awry. He had hoped to gain financial support from the western churches, particularly those in the Long Run Association in Kentucky where he was well known. He made a tour of these churches and found them seething with antimission sentiment. A Baptist minister by the name of Daniel Parker was largely responsible. John Mason Peck, usually broadminded and generous, described Parker as a man "without education, uncouth in manner, slovenly in dress, diminutive in person, unprepossessing in appearance, with shrivelled features and a small piercing eye." Whatever his personal and physical defects, Parker was able to mount a crusade that split the Baptist denomination in the West. He denounced mis-

[19] Jefferson, *Writings*, V, 440.
[20] McCoy, Journal, June 7, 1818.

sions, Sunday Schools, Bible societies, and similar facilities as
men's contrivances to take God's work out of His hands.
Parker's books, pamphlets, and sermons were full of bitter dia-
tribes against "money begging missionaries" and "Judases with
the bag."[21] In time, more sophisticated men, such as Alexander
Campbell, who left the Baptists and founded the Disciples of
Christ, lent their support to an antimissionary movement that
brought an end to most local missionary societies; but as early as
1818, McCoy found that "the contempt that was poured upon
me was rather more than I could comfortably bear."[22]

While McCoy was on his tour in Kentucky, his eldest daughter died. A true descendant of John Calvin, McCoy attributed
her death to divine providence. He had been particularly concerned about the child's education once they settled with the
Indians.[23] With this impediment removed and with his one-year
appointment slipping away, McCoy decided to act. Since he had
not yet received permission to establish a mission on Indian soil,
McCoy purchased a small tract of land on Raccoon Creek,
sixteen miles north of Fort Harrison and immediately adjacent
to the Wea Reservation. Here he began the erection of two log
cabins, one for his family, and one for a school. McCoy and
his family left the Maria Creek community in the fall of 1818
and settled in their wilderness home.[24]

McCoy's first concern was to get pupils for his school. He

21 Peck, *Forty Years of Pioneer Life*, 109.
22 McCoy, Journal, August 12, 1818. Campbell took with him a number of
former Baptist churches, including the Silver Creek Church. John M'Coy
described "Cambelism [*sic*] and Parkerism as two sore conflicting warfares."
Hayward, *John M'Coy*, 57-58.
23 McCoy to William Staughton, September 21, 1818, McCoy Correspondence.
24 McCoy to Peck, September 17, 1818, McCoy Correspondence.

intended to work mainly with the Weas, and to some extent with the Kickapoos residing nearby on the Vermilion River, but he could not have chosen a more inopportune occasion. The process of land cession had resumed in the Northwest. About the time McCoy moved to Raccoon Creek, a large number of Indian chiefs had gathered at St. Mary's, Ohio, and in a feverish round of treating, placed their X's or thumb prints on documents which ceded land were not usually required to move until the line of the English and the Americans, they now had to deal on only American terms, and the United States commissioners acted with directness. The Weas, for their part, surrendered all of their land except a small reservation at the forks of Raccoon Creek and the Wabash River, while their kinsmen, the Miamis, gave up most of their land below the Wabash. In a few months, the Kickapoos on the Vermilion and Wabash would meet with Benjamin Parke at Fort Harrison and agree to leave Indiana.[25] Given these circumstances it is not surprising that the Indians showed little interest in McCoy's school.

The cessions of 1818 did not necessarily preclude missionary work with the Weas and Kickapoos, however. Indians who ceded land were not usually required to move until the line of white settlement reached them. This could take years. When they were finally forced to leave, it would often come as a complete surprise to them to learn that the land they were living on was not theirs. But McCoy soon realized that any missions with the Weas and Kickapoos would be very temporary. Their condition was deteriorating rapidly. Reduced to wards of the government and dependent on annuities for livelihood, McCoy observed that many of them spent their time in a decidedly inebriated condition. Stone-eater, the principal chief of the

[25] *Statutes at Large of the United States of America*, VII, 186, 189, 202.

Weas, who appeared at the mission on several occasions begging for food, was himself killed in a drunken brawl.[26]

Because of the discouraging prospects at Raccoon Creek, Mc-Coy decided to look for another location. Leaving his family behind in unfinished cabins, he set out, in midwinter, to visit the Delaware and Shawnee villages in eastern Indiana. He pushed through the wilderness, passing through a number of Indian villages. He recorded an interesting description of the sociology and architecture of one such village, called Langlois Town, inhabited by the Eel River Miamis. Set out in the open prairie, it was made up of eighteen families, living in box-shaped affairs made of sticks and bark. "Nature has formed the floor and mostly the seats." Where once villages had been located on favorable sites for hunting and farming, the only factor that gave this village any cohesion was a trading post operated by a Frenchman, Pierre Langlois. Here the villagers could conveniently spend the annuities upon which they had become dependent.[27]

Near the site of the present-day city of Anderson, Indiana, McCoy came upon the village of the principal chief of the Delawares, William Anderson. Of mixed Indian and white ancestry, Anderson had rejected white manners and customs.[28] He refused to speak English and communicated with McCoy through a Negro interpreter. Courteously, but firmly, Anderson informed McCoy that the Delawares wanted nothing of his religion.[29] Years later, when the Delawares were living on a reservation west of the Missouri River, McCoy found the chief just as

[26] McCoy, Journal, December 3, 1818.

[27] *Ibid.* Langlois, a native of France, served with Anthony Wayne, and then settled in the Wabash country. See *The John Tipton Papers* (comp. and ed. by Glen A. Blackburn, Nellie A. Robertson, and Dorothy Riker), I, 477n.

[28] Tipton, *Papers*, I, 438n.

[29] McCoy, Journal, November 30, 1818, and December 3, 1818.

adamant in his opposition to Christian missions. In a conversation with one of McCoy's assistants, Anderson related that as a youth he had witnessed a murderous affair at Gnadenhutten in the Upper Ohio River Valley in 1782 when an American militia unit wiped out a community of Christian Delawares because of unfounded rumors that they were helping the British. The pagan Delaware bands had fled, but the Christian bands stayed behind. They had felt they had nothing to fear from their fellow Christians. "No persuasion could overcome his abhorence of that transacting, nor soften his feeling in favor of the 'whiteman's religions' .... As long as the name and influence of Anderson is remembered by the Delawares, their sin will 'follow after' and be thrown in the face of the missionary."[30]

With no better mission site in prospect, McCoy on his return to Raccoon Creek, opened a small day school, attended mostly by pupils from nearby white settlements. An opportunity to become more significantly involved presented itself when a number of destitute and foot-loose Indian families camped in the vicinity of the mission on unoccupied but ceded land. McCoy hoped to help them settle down to agricultural pursuits, but when the white settlers got wind of this plan, they rounded up the Indians and in "an unauthorized and cruel proceeding" ordered them to leave.[31]

The mission at Raccoon Creek served as McCoy's headquarters for almost two years, although he was seldom there. Despite constant laments about the rigors of travel and its effect on his health and disposition, McCoy undertook frequent, extended tours. The purpose of his trips was not always clear, although the overriding concern was to find a permanent loca-

[30] Johnston Lykins, Journal, July 18, 1831, MS. in the Kansas State Historical Society Library.
[31] McCoy, *Baptist Missions*, 55.

tion for a mission. A logical site was the main Miami Reservation about two hundred miles upstream on the Wabash, but neither the chiefs nor Dr. William Turner, the new agent at Fort Wayne, offered any encouragement.[32]

In any case, it was the Delawares who had a particular fascination for McCoy. He hired a Delaware guide to assist him in his peregrinations, and from him learned enough of the language to be able to converse about matters of religion with members of the tribe. The Delawares in Indiana were primarily pagan as distinguished from elements of the tribe still living in the East who were largely Christian.[33] From McCoy's observations it was apparent that the native religion of the pagans had not been entirely impervious to Christianity. McCoy noted, for example, that the concept of a literal hell had entered their doctrines, although they had added novel ideas of their own. They believed that the only drink available in the future abode of the damned would be melted pewter.[34] Evidently, the tribesmen had had some bitter experiences with counterfeit pewter money.

During McCoy's many absences, his wife was largely responsible for everything in and out of doors. In lieu of a pious half-blood teacher who could speak Indian, French, and English without profanity, McCoy managed to hire a young frontiersman by the name of Corbly Martin. He also became McCoy's first convert. Martin came to the mission claiming to be a Deist, but left in a year an ardent Baptist and a firm believer in the doctrine of predestination.[35] McCoy hoped that Martin might

[32] Turner to McCoy, September (n.d.), 1819, McCoy Correspondence.
[33] Kinietz, *Delaware Culture*, 10.
[34] McCoy, *Baptist Missions*, 70. Vernon Kinietz, in a study of Delaware remnants living in Oklahoma and Canada in the 1930's, noted a number of unusual concepts of immortality in their native religion. "European Civilization as a Determinant of Native Indian Customs," *American Anthropologist*, Vol. XLII, (January–March, 1940), 118.
[35] McCoy, Journal, June 28, 1819.

develop into a missionary after his conversion, but the young teacher in rare candor confessed he lacked nothing but "talent, influence, opportunity and courage."[36] Johnston Lykins, a product of a frontier community in Ohio and not yet twenty, came to replace Martin as a teacher. He, too, came as an unbeliever and ultimately emerged as a Baptist, but the process was slower.

The mission school grew to twenty students, ten of them Indian and one a Negro. The young Negro lived with the Mc-Coy family, and it was McCoy's hope that he would some day go to Africa as a leader of freed Negro slaves. McCoy had added Negro colonization to his list of causes and actively supported the Indiana Auxiliary of the American Colonization Society. Conceivably, McCoy's familiarity with the purpose and program of this organization later suggested colonization as a solution for the Indian problem.

The Board of Missions continued its support for McCoy's school beyond the first year. McCoy's real hope, however, was to lay an independent financial base for his operations. In the fall of 1819, he received a circular from the War Department inviting churches and benevolent societies to seek subsidies from a "Civilization Fund," which Congress had created. With uncontained enthusiasm, McCoy hurried to Vincennes to claim his share. However, the wheels of officialdom simply did not work this way, as McCoy soon found out.

Despite urgings from presidents and cabinet officers, Congress in the past had made few appropriations for education programs for the Indians. What funds were voted for "civilization" were used mainly to entertain tribal delegations and to buy gifts for annual distribution among the "friendly Indians." Through arrangements with separate tribes, there was scattered provision for instruction in agriculture and the mechanical arts. The first

[36] Martin to McCoy, June 9, 1821, McCoy Correspondence.

treaty which mentioned a more formal type of education was a treaty signed with three New York tribes in 1794. It provided, among other things, that the government would pay $1,000 for the erection of a church for the purpose of promoting religious instruction.[37] In a treaty with the Kaskaskias in 1803, the United States agreed to make an annual appropriation for seven years for the support of a Roman Catholic priest, who besides his religious duties, would provide a "literary education" for the children of the tribe.[38] It is apparent that up to the first part of the nineteenth century at least, the philosophy of the separation of church and state did not seem inconsistent with the support of Indian missions from public funds. Jefferson had expressed some reservations about government-sponsored missionary programs, but as president, he made three recommendations for appropriations for Gideon Blackburn's mission with the Cherokees.[39] There were practical considerations involved in aiding the missionaries. No administrative machinery existed to undertake education projects. The mission societies were already involved. Since there was precedent, and since a purely government-sponsored plan would probably have cost much more, it was not surprising that when Congress created a $10,000 annual "Civilization Fund" in 1819,[40] the Secretary of War turned to the missionaries to implement a civilization program.

The Civilization Fund provided no large windfall for any society or mission. It was doled out sparingly and carefully on a ratio based on the number of students enrolled in the mission schools. The House Committee on Appropriations in recommending the fund had summed up its arguments with a note of

[37] *American State Papers: Indian Affairs*, I, 145.
[38] *Ibid.*, I, 687.
[39] Oliver W. Elsbree, *The Rise of the Missionary Spirit in America, 1790–1815*, 73.
[40] *Statutes at Large*, III, 516–17.

urgency. "In the present state of our country one of two things seems to be necessary. Either that those sons of the forest should be moralized or exterminated."[41] In view of the alternatives, it was ironic, perhaps, that the Department of War was to administer the fund and that it was a year before its secretary, John C. Calhoun, applied any part of the appropriations. As carefully used as it finally was, the fund provided an incentive to private groups to continue the Indian schools already in existence and to start others. These organizations then poured in much more than they received. Calhoun subsequently informed the mission societies that if the government had the means and approved the arrangements, it would bear two-thirds of the cost of erecting new buildings.[42] This announcement provided an added inducement. More immediately, Calhoun's deliberate policy precluded the possibility of any quick aid for McCoy's mission.

After two discouraging years at Raccoon Creek, McCoy was convinced that he must move deeper into Indian territory. The Delawares were still uppermost in his mind. He heard that the Delawares in Indiana, who constituted the major body of the tribe, had decided to move west if they could get a "paper" which would give them sure title to land in perpetuity. For the first time, McCoy's attention was directed to the regions beyond the Mississippi. He immediately applied to the Secretary of War for permission to establish a mission with the Delawares when they moved from Indiana. The Delawares, as a tribe, were not unfamiliar with the trans-Mississippi West. A sizable migration to the area around Cape Girardeau had taken place when the region still belonged to Spain. From there the Delawares scattered into Texas and other parts of the West. In 1818, the

[41] *American State Papers: Indian Affairs*, II, 151–52.
[42] From a copy of a supplementary circular issued by the Department of War, February 29, 1820, in the McCoy Correspondence.

remaining tribesmen at Cape Girardeau received permission to join the Western Cherokees in the Arkansas country.[43] John Mason Peck, aware of McCoy's interest in the Delawares, suggested they begin a mission there.[44]

After exploring the possibility of a mission in Arkansas Territory, McCoy decided that it would be more feasible to concentrate on tribes closer at hand. The condition of the Miamis had evidently deteriorated to the point where their principal chief, Pishewah, better known as Jean B. Richardville, reached the conclusion that missionaries could do no harm and might do some good. He now asked McCoy to begin a mission. McCoy proposed that he settle in the main Miami village, Mississinewa, but Dr. William Turner, the Miami agent, insisted that he locate at Fort Wayne. The garrison had been removed in 1819, and the agent offered McCoy free use of the "Old Fort." He also pointed out that Fort Wayne was ideally located to reach not only the Miamis, but the Potawatomis and the Shawnees as well. In May, 1820, a large "batteau" containing the McCoy belongings and manned by Indian students from the abandoned mission school, pushed up the Wabash toward Fort Wayne. Meanwhile, McCoy and his family made their way overland, driving cattle and hogs in front of them.[45]

[43] Charles C. Royce, The Cherokee Nation of Indians: A Narrative of Their Official Relations with the Colonial and Federal Governments, Bureau of American Ethnology Fifth Annual Report, 221.

[44] Peck to McCoy, February 10, 1820, and March 3, 1820, McCoy Correspondence.

[45] "Missionary Intelligence," American Baptist Magazine, Vol. IV, (May, 1824), 330–36.

Chapter III

A Mission at Fort Wayne

Fort Wayne in 1820 was a small village inhabited mainly by traders, government employees, and interpreters. Most of the residents were of mixed French Canadian and Indian descent and nominally Roman Catholic, although there had been no missionaries or schools in the area since the departure of the French Jesuits.[1] Major Benjamin F. Stickney, Indian agent at Fort Wayne until 1819, described the place as a "resort for discharged soldiers and others of the refuse of the human race." He added, "I could wish there were some civil Government."[2] Judging from his subsequent accounts, Isaac McCoy would have agreed with this appraisal.

The fur trade was the principal commerce of Fort Wayne. Some of the traders had become quite wealthy. Jean B. Richardville (Pishewah), chief of the Miamis and a licensed trader, had amassed a fortune and was reputed to be the wealthiest Indian in North America.[3] The trappers portaged the hides and pelts across from the Wabash, and at Fort Wayne the traders placed

[1] Brice, *History of Fort Wayne*, 4–5. Hanna arrived in 1819 and became a wholesale supplier to the traders.

[2] Stickney to Lewis Cass, December, 1818, *Letter Book of the Indian Agency at Fort Wayne, 1809–1815* (ed. by Gayle Thornbrough), Indiana Historical Society *Publications*, Vol. XXI, 242.

[3] Frederick W. Hodge (ed.), *Handbook of American Indians North of Mexico*, Bureau of American Ethnology *Bulletin No. 30*, II, 235.

them in pirogues and reshipped them to Detroit by way of the Maumee River. Flatboats, coming down the St. Mary's, brought in provisions from Ohio.[4] Supplies were very expensive, adding to McCoy's already perplexing financial problems. He reported that corn meal, which sold in white settlements for twenty-five cents a bushel, cost from $1.50 to $2.00 a bushel at Fort Wayne.[5]

The Board of Managers of the Board of Foreign Missions approved McCoy's move and assured him continued support. Persuaded by McCoy that the prospects of a successful mission were promising, the board recommended that John Mason Peck become his assistant.[6]

Peck and McCoy had corresponded frequently from the time of their first appointments. Peck had a happy facility of not taking himself too seriously, a quality lacking in McCoy, and could refer to the sober business of winning Indian converts as taking "prisoners & Scalps."[7] Both missionaries had a common grievance against the board because they felt that it was so absorbed "in sending the Gospel to Burmah" that it neglected their work. The board had already discontinued its financial aid to Peck, for the managers had concluded that Baptist ministers had probably migrated to the St. Louis area along with other settlers and there was no need, therefore, to support missionaries.[8] Peck became so impoverished that he began "composing & delivering a course of lectures on ancient and modern history to a class of gentlemen who had subscribed for that purpose."[9] He had little confidence

[4] Brice, *History of Fort Wayne*, 285.

[5] McCoy, Journal, December 22, 1820.

[6] "Proceedings of the General Convention of the Baptist Denomination in the United States at the Second Triennial Meeting, Together with the Sixth Annual Report of the Baptist Board of Foreign Missions for the United States," *Latter Day Luminary*, Vol. II (May, 1820), 133.

[7] Peck to McCoy, August 19, 1818, McCoy Correspondence.

[8] "Sixth Annual Report of the Baptist Board of Foreign Missions for the United States," *Latter Day Luminary*, Vol. II (May, 1820), 125.

in the uneducated and untrained Baptist frontier preachers, upon whom the board was prepared to rely, who could "rattle off words . . . and foam at the mouth, and yet not communicate one Scriptural idea."[10] Already he had decided to found a seminary in the West to help remedy the situation, and so he refused to join McCoy at Fort Wayne. This decision offended McCoy, whose own work seemed the most important in the world.[11]

As it had been at Raccoon Creek, the major concern of Mc-Coy's mission at Fort Wayne was the school. In spite of the general predilection for the Roman Catholic faith among the village inhabitants and continued misgivings on the part of the Indians in the region, McCoy soon collected a fairly large school of Miami, Potawatomi, and half-blood children. One young pupil, Abraham Burnett, was related to the family of Topenebee, principal chief of the Potawatomis, and was a grandson of William Burnett, a trader who had come to the St. Joseph area when it was controlled by the British.[12] Abraham became Mc-Coy's interpreter on his trips into the Indian country. Some parents suspected that in the end they would have to pay for their children's education, or even that their children might not be allowed to return to their homes once they were through school.[13] The immediate prospect of some relief in the burden of family support was appealing, however, and by the end of the first year, McCoy had a school of about forty Indian students. They ate at the same table with the McCoys and received their clothing and lodging.[14]

[9] Peck to McCoy, February 10, 1820, McCoy Correspondence.

[10] Peck, *Forty Years of Pioneer Life*, 151.

[11] McCoy, Journal, April 26, 1821.

[12] Blanche M. Haines, "French and Indian Footprints at Three Rivers on the St. Joseph," *Michigan Pioneer and Historical Collections*, Vol. XXXVIII (1912), 395–96.

[13] McCoy, Journal, August 12 and December 30, 1820.

[14] Isaac McCoy, *Baptist Missions*, 98.

Missionaries had used the boarding-school principle in most Indian mission schools since colonial times, when Eleazer Wheelock first conceived the idea of removing children from parental influence as a means of speeding up the process of civilization.[15] In the early national period, Gideon Blackburn organized a boarding school for the Cherokees in Tennessee, the first located on tribal lands, because parents and agents opposed schools which took students away from the reservations.[16] McCoy also believed that it was necessary to take the young people out of their native home environment if they were to be properly educated. At Raccoon Creek he had not had the facilities to operate a boarding school, but this was no longer a problem at Fort Wayne. Because of the proximity of the school to the tribal lands, McCoy encountered few objections from parents who might otherwise have been reluctant to allow their children to get too far from home.

According to McCoy the teaching in his school was patterned on the Lancasterian plan. This was a system devised by Joseph Lancaster, an English scholar, to be used in the poorer parts of London. Using student monitors, it supposedly made possible the instruction of hundreds of students under a single trained master. Prelates and government officials on both sides of the Atlantic acclaimed the system as solving the problem of educating the poor.[17] Its advantages lay in that it carefully regimented the learning process, for Lancaster worked out a systematic arrangement of subject matter and a method of grading students according to achievement. The curriculum consisted almost

[15] Hildegard Thompson, "Education Among American Indians: Institutional Aspects," *Annals of the American Academy of Political and Social Science*, Vol. CCCXI (May, 1957), 95–96.

[16] Blackburn to Jedidiah Morse reprinted in the *Panopolist*, Vol. III (June, 1807), 85.

[17] Some American political leaders, such as Henry Clay, looked upon the

entirely of reading, writing, and arithmetic.[18] The use of monitors as subordinates, the carefully worked out methods and materials, the emphasis on rewards and punishments, suggested a military orientation. Understandably, the Lancasterian system appealed to missionary educators, who, like McCoy, operated on small budgets and worked with indifferent students.

The Lancasterian plan offered no simple solutions to the operation of the Fort Wayne mission school. McCoy had encountered serious problems of attendance and discipline at Raccoon Creek, and he came no nearer solving them at his new school. Keeping students in the classrooms, even after their parents agreed to have them there, was as difficult an undertaking as before. Interspersed in McCoy's journal entries were such comments as "The boy we received yesterday, has run away today." Getting the students who did attend classes to exert themselves was next to impossible. McCoy wrote that they were so "jealous of freedom" that "the course of conduct we must observe . . . must be such as will not in their estimation breathe the slightest appearance of an infringement on their liberties.[19]

In view of McCoy's objectives, and they were similar to those of most other missionary educators, it was not surprising that he encountered these difficulties. He was attempting to bring to the Indians knowledge and skills of a non-Indian culture. The education that he offered made little sense in their lives. To add to the frustration of the students they were taught in a foreign language. Directives from the War Department and instructions from missionary societies often insisted that the English language

Lancasterian system as a panacea for the nation's educational problems. *Niles' Weekly Register*, Vol. XVII (January 15, 1820), 322–26. When Lancaster visited the United States in 1819, he was enthusiastically welcomed in Congress as a special guest. *Ibid.*, Vol. XVI (April 24, 1819), 148.

[18] Edward H. Reisner, *Evolution of the Common School*, 250–55.
[19] McCoy, Journal, December 23 and 30, 1820.

be used, apparently to attempt to speed up the integration of the Indian into American life. Frequently, an Indian child was forced to accept an English name. Usually it was the name of a prospective donor, who was thereupon informed of the existence of his namesake, with the hope that this honor would appeal to his pride and largesse. One young lad in McCoy's school with the majestic name of Muh'quohkonongg became simply Francis Pringle.[20]

If McCoy's main concern at Fort Wayne was the school, he did not ordinarily spend his time in the classroom. His wife and a succession of young men hired as teachers, five of whom came and left during the first year, assumed these duties. Matters of finance occupied most of McCoy's time. His credit was soon exhausted in Fort Wayne, and so he made frequent trips into Ohio and Kentucky to raise money to pay debts nearer home. He was responsible for a community of between fifty and sixty people, including students and his family. The burden of providing food and clothing, usually at exorbitant prices because of transportation costs, was an onerous one. And yet he busied himself trying to find more pupils. He wrote to a Quaker mission at Wapakoneta in Ohio and offered to help educate some Shawnees at a time when he claimed not to have enough money to buy a barrel of flour. He apparently felt that the school had to expand constantly to impress the Baptist constituency and the Indians. "My greatest fears are . . . that the institution will become contemptible in the eyes of the natives."[21]

The Board of Managers expressed surprise at McCoy's expenditures. He was authorized to draw $500 annually, but this amount did not begin to meet his expenses. The financial pressures built up to such an extent that on one occasion he sold

---

[20] *Ibid.*, January 30, 1821.
[21] *Ibid.*, August 12, October 24, November 25, 1820.

drafts on the board to a Dayton, Ohio, merchant to the amount of $1,100. The board honored the draft and spared McCoy from possible imprisonment, but issued a mild reprimand. McCoy felt affronted. "I cannot divest myself of the thought which has haunted me ever since I was appointed a Missionary under the patronage of the Bapt. B.F.M. That is . . . they expected my services to close in a short time."[22]

To add to McCoy's problems, antimissionary Baptists now singled him out for attack. The movement captured the Wabash District Association, which then expelled the Maria Creek Church, McCoy's former charge, because of its continued interest in his work.[23] The tactics of the antimissionary leaders could become abusive at times. A man who had purportedly visited the mission at Fort Wayne circulated a letter that McCoy was living in luxury. He reported that the mission tables were "spred with the most superfluous dainties, and especially that of Liquors, that the U.S. could afford," and claimed that McCoy presided over the mission company like "a little God."[24] Knowing that any honest visitor to the mission would have "blushed at our poverty and savingness," McCoy felt acutely the sting of such slander. He became disillusioned with Baptists in general. "I find the most friendship for our cause among the Presbyterians, and among persons professing no religion at all."[25]

McCoy was unduly pessimistic about public interest in his work. When Lewis Cass, governor of Michigan Territory and superintendent of Indian Affairs, heard of McCoy's plight, he furnished $450.00 worth of clothing and food for the mission school and promised future aid.[26] William Staughton, the cor-

22 *Ibid.*, March 24, May 26, 1821.
23 Hayward, *John McCoy*, 53–54.
24 Benjamin Archer to McCoy, May 3, 1821, McCoy Correspondence.
25 McCoy, Journal, April 13, 1821.
26 *Ibid.*, February 11 and 24, 1821.

responding secretary of the Board of Managers, graciously re-
minded McCoy that what he thought to be indifference on the
part of the board members was actually inexperience in support-
ing a mission boarding school. Although some of the members
believed McCoy's expenditures excessive, Staughton was convinced the board would not permit McCoy "to suffer."[27]

Administering and financing the mission school occupied Mc-
Coy so completely that he had little time to circulate among the
Indian villages to preach and to gain converts. To be effective
this type of work demanded a knowledge of the Indian languages. In his initial enthusiasm, McCoy attempted to master
Delaware, Miami, and Potawatomi dialects all at the same time,
but he could not keep it up. And as for seeking converts, he
developed some distinctive attitudes of his own. Had they been
widely known, they undoubtedly would have shocked many of
his Baptist supporters. After about one year at Fort Wayne, he
wrote, "I have never yet conceived that the time had come when
it was proper for me to go among the Indians on a tour of preaching." He further stated that most missionaries to the Indians in
the past had "begun at the wrong end of their business." Filled
with zeal for preaching but unacquainted with the Indian's character, they had put in motion all of the "rude enthusiasms" of the
Indians, "and for a while it would seem the whole forests were
about to burst forth into praises at once." But the Indians, being
"rude in the arts & sciences . . . return to their huntings, and their
wanderings & their wars, and the promising prospects end in
disappointment." Every such failure added additional obstruc-
tions to succeeding missionaries.[28]

Superficially, it appeared as though civilization and Christianity had become synonymous in McCoy's mind, but this would

[27] Staughton to McCoy, July 2, 1821, McCoy Correspondence.
[28] McCoy, Journal, April 9, 1821.

be too simple an explanation. His thinking never was this rational or uncomplicated. He expended most of his energies on what might be called "civilization projects," but he would have been the last to deny that a conversion experience was necessary. "Salvation" was to be sought above everything else. It took the form of a concrete and ascertainable experience. McCoy continued to lament that his eldest daughter, who had grown up with all the benefits of a civilized Christian home, had left no outward signs of "a gracious state" when she died. The need for help at the mission was always acute, yet McCoy refused to accept one man who offered himself as a missionary; for although he seemed genuinely dedicated, the account that he gave of the "work of grace in his heart" was unsatisfactory.[29]

McCoy conducted preaching services every Sunday in his home. A number of local citizens attended, and at times unexpected outsiders stopped by. His residence was often mistaken for that of a trader, and on one occasion two Indian women, though disappointed in not being able to secure liquid refreshment, consented to stay for the sermon. It turned out that their thirst for liquor was greater than their thirst for religion. They interrupted the morning service with a loquacious discourse on the greater merits of whisky drinking.[30] There were some converts, however. The first was the Indian wife of the agent, Dr. William Turner. He threatened to kill her when he heard of her conversion, and so she took refuge with the McCoys until the agent's composure was partially restored.[31] Not so violent but equally disturbed was the Roman Catholic husband of another convert. He was horrified to learn that his sickly wife was

29 *Ibid.*, March 29 and August 28, 1821.
30 *Ibid.*, November 24, 1820.
31 *Ibid.*, June 16, 1820. Turner was removed by John C. Calhoun in the summer of 1820 for "unsatisfactory conduct." See Thornbrough, *Letter Book*, 256.

to be baptized in an icy stream in the middle of winter, nor was he altogether reassured when McCoy informed him that he had "never known any one injured by it."[32]

The membership requirements to join the small Baptist group in Fort Wayne were obviously quite rigorous. Yet it was with some conviction that McCoy wrote, "I have never thought it expedient to make innovations on the customs of the Indians."[33]

McCoy had at least an amateur interest in Indian culture and occasionally took time to write out lengthy descriptions of certain practices employed by tribes in the vicinity. He was particularly interested in their methods of interring the dead. He observed that no one method of burial could be identified with an individual tribe. Some natives entombed their dead in hollow logs, and then piled other logs alongside to resemble a cord of wood. Other tribesmen interred corpses in small huts, with narrow apertures, through which twists of tobacco could be inserted by passers-by. The mourners, in lieu of tobacco, sometimes provided liquor, although McCoy observed that the offerings set aside for such purposes seldom reached their destination. McCoy came upon one dead woman tied in an upright position in a log enclosure with a small window on the east so she could behold the rising sun. He had a greater appreciation for this "expressive emblem" than for tobacco or whisky. McCoy found other bodies wrapped in blankets and fastened to forks of trees, or placed on scaffolds eight or ten feet from the ground.[34]

While on the subject of burial practices, McCoy noted that the bereaved frequently adopted a person in place of the deceased. He described some of the elaborate adoption ceremonies, such as the burning of the adoptee's old clothes and the putting

[32] McCoy, Journal, December 12, 1820.
[33] *Ibid.*, August 3, 1821.
[34] *Ibid.*, May 5 and 9, 1822.

on of the clothes of the deceased. The adopted person was expected to make presents of clothing and tobacco to the near relatives of the dead man, but at the same time, the property of the deceased belonged to him. It there was a widow, she was part of the bargain. In such cases, McCoy observed, "a man's fancy" was not consulted.[35]

McCoy's description of menstrual rites was similar to those given by French explorers one and one-half centuries earlier.[36] He wrote that "at certain times" the women would retire and build a camp or go into an especially prepared hut. They could carry no fire to this place, but had to make a fresh one, and the flame from it could not be taken to any other place. They extinguished the fire when they left and destroyed all of the utensils from which they had eaten. McCoy did not elaborate on birth rites, but did express astonishment at what Indian women endured at childbirth. On one occasion, according to McCoy, the Indian wife of a trader asked her husband to stop while descending a flood-swollen river. She waded knee deep to a small dry spot of land nearby. After a brief absence she returned to the canoe with an infant in her arms, and they resumed their journey.[37] McCoy did not think it unusual, however, that his wife, with two or three of their youngest children in tow, should have to take an annual three-hundred-mile trip through the wilderness to Vincennes to give birth to another child. His chief lament was for himself. "I must now realize the toils, and anxieties of my forlorn situation, without the sympathies of a kindred bosom to console my griefs."[38]

Perhaps the main significance of McCoy's observations on Indian life while at Fort Wayne was that he was on hand to

35 *Ibid.*, May 9, 1822.
36 Trowbridge, *Meearmeear*, 37–41.
37 McCoy, Journal, May 20, 1822.
38 *Ibid.*, June 21, 1821.

witness the continuing processes of cultural disintegration in some of the tribes of the region, particularly the Miamis. It was not a pleasant picture, but one of strange diseases and death, of digging roots to keep from starving, and of drunkenness and crime. When the Miamis received their annuities at Fort Wayne in the fall of 1820, eight murders were recorded within the period of a few weeks.[39] During one of McCoy's absences from the mission, an Indian with motives of the "basest kind" assaulted his young daughter.[40] McCoy's hope for permanent improvement of the situation lay in educating the young. But more immediately, he had to contend with the sick, the economically destitute, and the drunkards.

McCoy found that there was little he could do for the sick. The natives were suspicious of any offers of help. At first, McCoy attempted to dispense some medicines, but on second thought discontinued the practice for fear that a patient die and he be accused of using poison. While the agents and other whites tended to believe that the Indians were naturally resigned to sickness and death, McCoy found that they usually had a lively interest in the outcome of an illness. He described a game which the friends of a patient sometimes played. They chose sides. One side played against the sick man and would hide a ball in one of many moccasins. The side playing for him would try to guess in which moccasin it was hid. The fate of the game was the oracle which decided the outcome of the case.[41]

There was little that McCoy could do for poverty-stricken Indians either. He tried to get them to plant crops and to raise livestock. On a visit to Detroit, he persuaded Governor Cass to employ a man to help some of the natives to get started in farm-

[39] *Ibid.*, May 7, 1821.
[40] *Ibid.*, February 12, 1822.
[41] *Ibid.*, May 13, 1821.

ing. No one was sent.[42] A further and perhaps more serious problem was a firmly fixed tradition that physical labor was beneath the dignity of the Indian male. When the red man observed the social distance between the traders and their hired hands, he saw that the white man also thought manual labor degrading.[43]

McCoy's answer to the liquor problem was to attempt to cut off the supply through an organization he founded, The Humane Abolition Society of Fort Wayne. Congress, in 1822, passed a law which forbade traders to take liquor into the Indian country under penalty of forfeiture of all goods.[44] It was never quite clear what was "Indian country," and in Fort Wayne the liquor trade continued to flourish. Members of the society dressed up as Indians and endeavored to buy liquor from traders suspected of selling it to the natives. They then placed the evidence in the hands of the proper civil authorities, although with little expectation that anything would come of it. They hoped, however, that some traders might be frightened into better conduct.[45]

At times obstacles to the temperance movement at Fort Wayne came from the most unexpected sources. In the spring of 1822 the Board of Managers appointed Peter Clyde, an easterner, as a missionary to Fort Wayne. The conditions at the mission so distressed Clyde and his family that he resigned almost immediately. He consented to stay for half a year, but even then, it seems, he needed extra fortification. McCoy suspected that it was not always medicine "the brother" was taking, but since he spent every evening "praying . . . and lecturing . . . mingling his complaints with ours at the intemperance of the Indians," Mc-

[42] *Ibid.*, February 24, 1821.
[43] McCoy, *Baptist Missions*, 111.
[44] *Statutes at Large*, III, 682–83.
[45] McCoy, Journal, June 28, 1822.

Coy gave him the benefit of the doubt. At his departure, however, Clyde was so thoroughly intoxicated that "fears were
entertained lest he would tumble into the river." Some Indian
spectators were amused, but McCoy considered it a "pernicious
stroke to the mission."[46]

If McCoy was a witness to the cultural breakdown among the
Indians living near Fort Wayne, he was also a witness to an
interesting attempt to create what one modern anthropologist
has called "Amalgamation Religion." Ruth Underhill classifies
most of the famous Indian prophets as reversion religionists.
Their goal was the disappearance of the white man and the return of the old life, either through magic or through successful
war. Other Indian prophets did not contemplate the conquest or
disappearance of the whites, but instead aimed at peaceful living
under new conditions. They would keep many old Indian customs, but "amalgamate" them with definite ethical teachings
from American Christianity, and hope thereby to control be-
havior in the anarchy of tribal breakdown and the loss of family
influence. The new preachers demanded total abstinence and
peaceful and upright living.[47] McCoy came to know a "prophet"
by the name of Menominee who fits the "Amalgamist" category
in most respects. Little has been written about Menominee, but
for a time he exerted considerable influence on the Indians living
in northern Indiana and the southern part of Michigan Territory.

When McCoy first came to Fort Wayne, the Indians were
already familiar with the "Potawatomi Preacher" who taught
that they should give up drinking, gambling, and idleness.[48]
With the memory of the Shawnee "Prophet" still fresh in their
minds, the Indians were wary and the whites were hostile.

[46] *Ibid.*, April 12 and 22, 1822.
[47] Underhill, "Religion Among American Indians," *Annals of the American Academy of Political and Social Science*, Vol. CCCXI (May, 1957), 135–36.
[48] McCoy, Journal, January 10, 1821.

Menominee and some of his followers came to Fort Wayne and asked McCoy to use whatever influence he could to reassure both the red man and the white man that their intentions were peaceful. That the "Potawatomi Preacher" and his company wore black-painted faces with small cross marks on each cheek and that before and after each conversation they crossed themselves did not seem to bother McCoy unduly. Menominee explained that what he knew about the Christian faith he had learned from Roman Catholic traders. Despite Menominee's obvious "unorthodoxy," McCoy gave him a written endorsement which stated that he had talked to him about matters of religion and was well pleased with his "sentiments." "This is therefore to desire all good people who are friends to the undersigned to treat the bearer with kindness, forebearance, and respect, and as a brother to Isaac McCoy, Missionary at Ft. Wayne."[49] McCoy apparently believed that he could build on Menominee's expression of Christianity. This attitude was in marked contrast to that of other Protestant missionaries of his era. Samuel Parker, missionary to the Oregon tribes, came upon a group of natives, who had gotten a few rudimentary ideas of Christianity from Roman Catholic Hudson's Bay traders, putting wooden crosses on some graves. Parker took the crosses from the Indians and destroyed them.[50]

McCoy's friendliness was reciprocated, and Menominee invited him to visit his village, which McCoy described as being close to St. Joseph of the Lake.[51] Here McCoy received an enthusiastic welcome, although it was somewhat disconcerting to

[49] *Ibid.*, April 9, 1821.

[50] Samuel Parker, *Journal of an Exploring Tour Beyond the Rocky Mountains*, 285–86.

[51] Menominee's village was later located in northern Indiana in Marshall County. See Charles C. Royce, *Indian Land Cessions in the United States*, Bureau of American Ethnology *Eighteenth Annual Report*, map No. 19.

him to discover that his host had two wives. Menominee confided that he too had come to believe in monogamy, but his two wives were sisters and were very reluctant to separate. He related that he had fasted to the point of physical exhaustion to produce a vision in which the "Great Spirit" might reveal which wife to dismiss, but he had received no response.[52]

On a later visit to Menominee's village, McCoy heard "The Prophet" expound on his version of the Virgin Birth. According to this interpretation, the Second Person of the Holy Trinity visited the Virgin Mary and told her she would have a son. She thought it impossible, whereupon the Second Person made a statue for her, out of clay and iron, of a boy about four feet tall. Mary forgot about the statue and it stood outside where the rains washed away the clay. She finally discarded it. The Third Person of the Trinity then appeared with a book in his hand and made two more statues, similar to the first. With a wing of a turkey he fanned the book, creating a stir of air which passed through the two statues and they became living persons. One of the boys was white and he was placed on one side of the sea, and the other was red, and he was placed on the opposite side of the sea. Upon completion of the sermon, Menominee duly recorded it with a series of notches on a square stick. According to Mc-Coy, the object was to record as many sermons as possible, not necessarily to spare the listener from hearing the same sermon again.[53]

McCoy's friendship with Menominee provided an entrée to the villages of Topenebee, Chebass, and Pcheeko, influential Potawatomi chiefs of the St. Joseph River region, where he was cordially received. The Potawatomis still held extensive tracts of land in Michigan Territory, and in Indiana and Illinois; there-

[52] McCoy, Journal, June 6, 1821.
[53] *Ibid.*, May 22, 1822.

fore, these villages were much more isolated than those of the Miamis on the Wabash. Because of this condition and because of Menominee's urging that he move to his village, McCoy decided to relocate his mission with the Potawatomis. It was known that the federal government was exerting pressure on a number of the Lake tribes to make further land cessions. McCoy hoped that when the negotiations were held he might somehow "contrive" to have the Potawatomis set aside a reservation for education purposes on which he would be invited to reside, and also to specify that part of the proceeds from the land sales be designated for school support.[54]

In the fall of 1821, United States commissioners met representatives of the Ottawa, Chippewa, and Potawatomi tribes at Chicago,[55] and acquired a large cession of land in the southwestern part of Michigan Territory. Besides cash annuities, the government agreed to pay $1,000 annually for fifteen years to the Potawatomis for the employment of a teacher and a blacksmith, and $1,000 annually for ten years to the Ottawas for the support of a teacher, a blacksmith, and an agricultural instructor.[56] Juliette A. Kinzie, daughter of John Kinzie, Indian agent and pioneer of Fort Dearborn, in her colorful recollections of the "Chicago Indian Chiefs," wrote that the chief My-Knose had confided to her that McCoy was largely responsible for the Potawatomis' getting a favorable treaty. According to the chief, McCoy had gotten them all down by the oak wood, on the lake shore, for an ox roast before the signing of the treaty, and there told them that if they wanted to please the commissioners and to get a good price for their lands and many presents they should

[54] *Ibid.*, May 26, 1821.

[55] Henry R. Schoolcraft estimated the total number encamped at the opening of negotiations at about three thousand. *Travels in the Central Portions of the Mississippi Valley*, 336.

[56] *Statutes at Large*, VII, 218.

say that they were not interested in money but "give us schools, and give us the Bible."[57] The story, unfortunately, is only that, a good story. McCoy was not there. Mrs. McCoy was in Vincennes to give birth to another child, and McCoy, in "solitary exile," had to remain in Fort Wayne to take care of the mission.[58] A likelier explanation for inclusion of the educational provisions was that the commissioners, Lewis Cass and Solomon Sibley, decided that the Potawatomis and the Ottawas should designate some of their annuities for civilization purposes, and it was done. At least some of the chiefs were completely bored by the negotiations and were probably unaware of their implications. According to Cass, Topenebee, the eighty-year-old principal chief of the Potawatomis, interrupted the negotiations with the constant lament, "We care not for the land, the money or the goods. It is the whiskey we want."[59] McCoy was thoroughly pleased with the treaty, for this was the first time that civilization measures had been included in a treaty with the Lake tribes. He was less pleased with the way it was achieved. The commissioners had supplied large amounts of whisky at the signing. Within twenty-four hours, ten Indians had lost their lives in drunken brawls.[60]

There was no guarantee that either McCoy or any other Baptists would be asked to fill the positions provided by the Treaty of Chicago. A movement got under way among the traders to see that Roman Catholics would be appointed. McCoy's plans called for the control of every one of the positions. They could not be looked upon merely as jobs for wages, but the potential means of

[57] *Bulletin of the Chicago Historical Society*, Vol. I (August, 1935), 105–16.
[58] McCoy, Journal, June 21, 1821.
[59] Cass to McCoy, July 16, 1822, McCoy Correspondence. Topenebee was a signer of the Treaty of Greenville in 1795. He was an ally of Tecumseh, and was present at the Fort Dearborn "massacre" in 1812. Otho Winger, *The Potawatomi Indians*, 95–98.
[60] McCoy, Journal, September 2, 1821.

support for Baptist teachers, smiths, and millers, who also happened to be missionaries. Determined to take every advantage of the stipulations of the Chicago treaty, McCoy decided to go to Washington to plead his case. The Board of Managers gave its consent, provided he preach and make collections on the way to pay for the expenses of the trip.[61]

With Mrs. McCoy back in charge of the oxen and milk cattle, the procuring of firewood and supplies, and the employment of help, with a teacher on the premises who was a stranger, and finally with a sick child whose recovery was not expected, McCoy set out on horseback for Washington in December, 1821. At the capital, McCoy met members of Congress and called on John C. Calhoun. He asked the Secretary of War for permission to nominate the teachers and smiths for the Potawatomis and the Ottawas, and a miller for the Miamis. Under the provisions of the St. Mary's Treaty of 1818, a mill had already been erected for that tribe. Calhoun informed McCoy that the responsibility of fulfilling the government's obligations under the Chicago and St. Mary's treaties had been delegated to Lewis Cass; therefore, he could make no commitments.[62]

While in the East, McCoy met with the Board of Managers in Philadelphia. The board was so deeply preoccupied with getting Columbian College established that McCoy felt he got an inadequate hearing for his problems and proposals. Because of the enlarged functions of the Convention, its name had been changed to "The General Convention of the Baptist Denomination in the United States for Foreign Missions, and Other Important Objects Relating to the Redeemer's Kingdom." Other Baptists felt as McCoy did that the "other important objects" detracted the Convention from its original purpose of missionary

---

[61] *Ibid.*, October 23, 27, and November 13, 1821.
[62] *Ibid.*, December 4, 1821, and January 10, 1822.

promotion. McCoy did get approval for his projected move to the Potawatomi country, but he could not get the permission he sought to spend whatever money he could personally collect for the mission as he saw fit. The board insisted that he keep within a budget of $3,000 a year, including government and denominational stipends and donations of food, clothing, and money.[63]

If McCoy's evaluation of his first exposure to cabinet officers, congressmen, denominational leaders, and easterners in general can be accepted at face value, he made a good impression. His own reaction to these same people was not always so kind. In his journal, he recorded his disgust with such things as eastern Christmas celebrations. "Old Meteor, A Putawatomie Chief, & his party, could not behave more ridiculous than these blockheads." While staying in the home of "a good old Baptist brother & sister," he complained of their constant prattle about "the smartness of little George who was going to school." Perhaps some of his sarcasm arose from his having been cheated in a horse trade by a Philadelphia "road jockey."[64]

Upon his return from the East, McCoy took up the matter of the government positions with Cass at Detroit. The Governor was obviously impressed with McCoy's ability and his plans, for in the summer of 1822 he appointed McCoy teacher to the Potawatomis, and asked him to superintend the civilization programs for both the Potawatomis and the Ottawas. McCoy was also given the privilege of naming the two blacksmiths. The annual salary for each teacher was set at $400, and $365 for each blacksmith.[65] Subsequently Cass indicated that he would allow McCoy to recommend a miller for the Miamis.[66]

McCoy now contemplated missions with the Ottawas,

[63] *Ibid.*, January 17 and 18, 1822.
[64] *Ibid.*, December 25, 1821, January 22, and February 2, 1822.
[65] Cass to McCoy, July 16, 1822, McCoy Correspondence.
[66] McCoy, Journal, July 17, 1822.

Miamis, and Potawatomis, to be supported largely by government funds, and under his control. To insure a unified missionary effort, he drew up an elaborate code entitled "General Rules for the Regulation of the Fort Wayne Mission Family." Since McCoy had already decided to leave Fort Wayne, it was apparent that the rules were not primarily intended for use there. The code provided for a written contract between the missionaries to put monies received from all sources into a common pot. A missionary would be entitled only to his current support and could not increase his own property. The missionaries were to agree to do any kind of work that circumstances required.[67] The man the board appointed teacher to the Ottawas was quick to object to the communistic implications in the rules.

John Sears, a college-trained minister from Philadelphia, arrived at Fort Wayne in time to accompany a commissioner appointed by Cass to the Ottawa country to locate a mission site. When Sears returned to Fort Wayne and had time to reflect on the problems involved in moving a family into the wilderness with no white settlements and physicians within two hundred miles, he began to have serious doubts about his calling. When faced with the "Family Rules," he resigned, for he thought them too degrading for a man who "had been raised as he had, and had received an education as he."[68]

Sears's resignation was a severe blow to McCoy's plans. He was completely disillusioned with board appointees. Peck had refused to come, and Clyde and Sears had quickly retreated. A number of frontier-trained ministers, in a momentary fit of missionary enthusiasm, had stopped by to offer their services, but had departed in a few days. The only persons he had found

[67] *Ibid.*, October 7, 1822. The editor of the *Latter Day Luminary* thought that the rules merited the consideration of all missionaries and reprinted them, Vol. IV (May, 1823), 152–53.

[68] McCoy, Journal, September 2 and November 13, 1822.

acceptable since he began his missionary career were two young men who came as hired help without any religious motivation, but who became converts. Corbley Martin had gone back to Ohio, and despite McCoy's entreaties, he refused to become a missionary. Johnston Lykins appeared at Fort Wayne intermittently to help out during times of emergency, but he was reluctant to become either a missionary or a Baptist.

With a setback in his plans for the Ottawas and no one to send to the Miamis, McCoy pushed preparations for the establishment of a Potawatomi mission. McCoy, with the help of Charles C. Trowbridge, a commissioner appointed by Cass, selected a site near Topenebee's village on the St. Joseph and about twenty miles from Lake Michigan. Building timber, firewood, and sugar trees were abundant, and springs were nearby.

In December, 1822, the McCoy family moved about one hundred miles through heavy snow to take up residence in five unfinished cabins. With them went eighteen of the Indian students of the Fort Wayne mission school.[69] Whatever their reasons for accompanying the McCoys, it was apparent that the school had had some impression on their lives, and perhaps vindicated McCoy's preoccupation with their education. The only other visible evidence of McCoy's work in Fort Wayne was an organized Baptist church, whose total membership included one full Indian, one half-blood Indian, and one Negro.

[69] *Ibid.*, December 9, 1822.

Chapter IV

Government Missionary

With an eye for the melodramatic, Isaac McCoy described for the Baptist public the removal of his mission into the Potawatomi country. It was a journey into the midst of "a tribe of unculti-vated savages, who had been second to none in hostilities against the whites . . . 100 miles from the nearest white inhabitants, and 200 miles from a settled country!"[1]

Actually, the Potawatomis in the past had been more willing than most tribes of the Old Northwest "to take white men's ways." They had been steadfastly loyal to the French. The process of transferring allegiance from the French to the English and then to the Americans created some upheavals, but for the most part the Potawatomis adapted quickly. When McCoy made his first trip to the St. Joseph River region, he found Pcheeko, the Potawatomi chief, flying a large American flag over his crude hut.[2] Moreover, the Potawatomis seemed gen-uinely pleased when the McCoys arrived. McCoy wrote:

> Chebass & Topenebee, chiefs, and other, men, women & chil-dren, about 40 in all, called in to congratulate us on the opening of the New Year. Shaking of hands and kissing are among the ceremonies which prevail among them on this day. In con-

[1] "Foreign Missionary Intelligence," *American Baptist Magazine and Missionary Intelligencer*, Vol. IV (May, 1824), 330–36.
[2] McCoy, *Baptist Missions*, 105.

forming to the former we felt no embarrassment. But we dispensed with the latter . . . . All appeared remarkably cheerful and well pleased.[3]

After the school and the blacksmith shop opened, Topenebee, the principal chief, moved his village closer to the mission.[4]

For sheer intrepidity, McCoy might better have described how thirty-two people, many of them children, moved into open cabins through which the snow was blowing and how a school commenced in a building with no floor, chimney, shutter, or door. He might have confided with the Baptists, through their periodicals, as he did with his journal, the "uneasy feeling" he had when the mission family, shortly after its arrival in the wilderness, sat down to breakfast and ate the last of its food.[5] Poor planning brought the mission to this point. Fortunately, some Potawatomi "Squantos" gave the missionaries what food they could spare. But to have publicized the poverty of the mission would have made it appear "contemptible" to the outside world.

The site of the new mission was contiguous to land the Potawatomis had ceded in 1821, although the nearest compact white settlements were a considerable distance away. St. Joseph, at the mouth of the St. Joseph River, had once been a thriving French settlement, but all that remained was Joseph Bertrand's trading post.[6] As a westerner, McCoy must have been aware that the frontier line could move rapidly. Since he was willing to endure

[3] McCoy, Journal, January 1, 1823.

[4] Irving McKee (ed.), in *The Trail of Death: Letters of Benjamin Petit*, Indiana Historical Society Publication (Indianapolis, 1941), 13–14, and Gilbert J. Garraghan in *The Jesuits of the Middle United States*, II, 176, have intimated that the Potawatomis were reluctant to accept McCoy's mission because they wanted Roman Catholic missionaries. The Potawatomis were simply not this discriminating.

[5] McCoy, Journal, January 12 and 27, 1823.

[6] Haines, "Footprints," 394–95.

the problems and privations of getting re-established near lands
to which the tribesmen had already given up their claims, it was
apparent that he had not yet decided that removal was the solution to the Indian problem.

McCoy's views on Indian reform at this juncture of his career
closely resembled those of Jedidiah Morse. Founder of the
Panoplist, the journal of the American Board of Commissioners
for Foreign Missions, Morse for a number of years had shown a
deep interest in the Christianization and civilization of the American Indians. In 1820, John C. Calhoun commissioned Morse to
make a thorough study of the condition of the tribes in the
United States. On his trip to Washington early in 1822, McCoy
had visited Morse and found him preparing his report.[7] This was
all that McCoy noted, but he undoubtedly had heard of Morse's
proposals for Indian reform before and probably was influenced
by them.

The key to Morse's views on reform was his concept of the
model community. He recommended that the Indians be gathered into a number of small communities in fertile regions under
the care of "education families," which would include ministers
of the gospel at the head, and teachers, farmers, blacksmiths, car-
penters, millrights, and women to teach sewing and cooking, all
working simply for their support. He envisioned no forced removal to some remote part of the country, but rather the gathering together of scattered bands in a favorable location where
there already was a fairly large concourse of Indians. Each of the
model communities would have its own schools and churches,
and after a time there would be a central college for all. Morse
hoped that these communities, if not too widely scattered, might
eventually join in an Indian state. Although not one of the designated purposes of the fact-finding tour for the War Depart-

[7] McCoy, Journal, January 11, 1822.

ment, it was Morse's private ambition to determine whether "education families" were feasible.[8]

When McCoy first contemplated a mission with the Potawatomis, he too thought in terms of a model community. All interested tribesmen would be invited to settle in a village favorably located for water, soil, and timber, where the houses would be wide apart and there would be room for feeding cattle and other livestock. There would be a gristmill and a sawmill, together with a church and a school. The missionaries would form a family, and according to McCoy's "Family Rules," they would receive only their subsistence.[9] The village would cut across tribal lines. Before moving to Michigan Territory, McCoy had contacted the Stockbridges, who had wandered into Indiana, and asked them to consider settling near his projected mission and become a nucleus in forming a settlement of civilized Indians.[10] The Stockbridges, a remnant of the Iroquois, and exiles from Massachusetts, had been deeded some land on the White River in Indiana by the Delawares. They began moving to the region in 1817, but by the time the greater portion arrived, the Delawares had ceded all of their Indiana lands. Morse had also included the Stockbridges in his plans. He thought them ideally suited for an "education family" experiment because they were already civilized.[11] Both McCoy and Morse believed that the example of one successful project would quickly lead to others, and eventually most American Indians would live in happy, planned communities. And so when McCoy took up residence

[8] Jedidiah Morse, *Report to the Secretary of War of the United States on Indian Affairs, Comprising a Narrative of a Tour Performed in the Summer of 1820, under a Commission from the President of the United States, for the Purpose of Ascertaining, for the Use of the Government, the Actual State of the Indian Tribes in Our Country*, 11–13, 76–79, 284–90.
[9] McCoy to Staughton, September 6, 1821, McCoy Correspondence.
[10] McCoy, Journal, September 14, 1821.
[11] Morse, *Report to the Secretary of War*, appendix, 112–16.

near the St. Joseph River, he thought that it was still possible to prepare Indians to live in nineteenth-century America without isolating them completely from the white man.

Many of McCoy's objectives at this point also coincided with those of Governor Cass, although Cass had difficulty in conceiving of a missionary in anything but a traditional role. Whatever obligations he might have to his denomination, Cass warned McCoy, he would have certain duties as a government teacher, and for these duties he would be accountable to a proper officer of the federal government. Cass used the term *teacher* in the broadest possible sense, and in detailed instructions he listed tasks which involved a good many things outside of the classroom. McCoy would be responsible for teaching the young and the old. He was to inculcate "a proper sentiment" towards the government and the citizens of the United States. His efforts should be unceasingly directed to the prevention of the introduction of liquor into the Indian territory. He was to observe the conduct of traders and report any infractions of laws. "To render them stationary," McCoy was to direct the attention of the tribesmen toward agriculture and to develop an appreciation for private property. Further, he was to educate the Indians in spending their annuities judiciously and to keep them from selling the implements and domestic animals provided by treaty agreements. Finally, McCoy was to persuade them to stay in their villages and keep them from wandering to white settlements.[12] McCoy apparently did not think these demands unreasonable. The only concern he expressed was for the paper work involved. There would be reports to Cass, to the Indian agent at Chicago, and to the War Department, as well as reports to the Board of Managers.[13] In addition, he would have to pre-

[12] Cass to McCoy, July 16, 1822, McCoy Correspondence.
[13] McCoy, Journal, July 16, 1822.

pare for an annual inspection by a commissioner appointed by Cass.[14]

That there might be a conflict of interest in the dual role of government teacher and missionary occurred to neither McCoy nor the Board of Managers, nor to the leaders of a denomination which supposedly was in the vanguard in advocating the separation of church and state. The editor of the *Columbian Star and Christian Index*, a Baptist journal, complimented the government on its "intelligent and paternal policy."[15] The antimissionary Baptists voiced criticism, but for different reasons. They now spread rumors that McCoy received an annual salary of $3,000, and that he was investing heavily in Indian lands.[16]

In spite of open endorsement of his schemes, McCoy's obsessive apprehension about his relationship with the board continued to plague him. The General Convention's periodicals gave his work considerable publicity and their editors reprinted large portions of his journals, but still McCoy felt ignored. When John Sears returned to the East and publicly upbraided McCoy to cover up his own hasty retreat, Staughton, the corresponding secretary of the board, vigorously defended McCoy. But when the board faced bankruptcy because it had over-extended itself in support of Columbian College, McCoy with some glee felt that this dilemma confirmed his past criticism of the board and vindicated his drive for government support. It never occurred to him, however, to dissociate himself from the Baptist missionary movement. He named the Potawatomi mission Carey, in honor of the well-known British Baptist missionary in Serampore, India, William Carey.[17]

At the outset, McCoy again attempted to master the Indian

[14] Cass to McCoy, July 16, 1822, McCoy Correspondence.
[15] *Columbian Star and Christian Index*, Vol. I (October 12, 1822).
[16] McCoy, Journal, November 27, 1822.
[17] McCoy, Journal, August 27, 1823.

dialects so that he could visit the tribesmen in their huts and preach to them in their assemblies. But as in his previous missions, problems of administration overwhelmed him.

Carey quickly assumed the appearance of a well-regulated establishment after the first months of privation. Major Stephen H. Long and his party stopped at the mission in June, 1823, on their way to the Red River country on an expedition for the War Department. William H. Keating, the mineralogist and geologist for the tour, noted that in seven months the mission had cleared fifty acres of forest, put up six dwellings, and placed a school in operation. He wrote:

> The Plan appears to be a very judicious one; to instruct them [the Indians] in the arts of civilized life; to teach them the benefits which they may derive from them without attempting to confuse their heads with ideas of religion, the value of which it is in their present state impossible for them to appreciate.[18]

With Carey on a fairly firm footing, McCoy turned his attention to the Ottawas. He visited their villages in the early summer of 1823 and found a great deal of dissatisfaction with the provisions of the Treaty of Chicago and with Kewagoushcum, their principal chief, for having signed it. The main body of Ottawas denied that they had authorized any sale of land and held the chief responsible for subverting their common interests. They felt that McCoy's efforts to furnish them with a school and a blacksmith shop merely constituted a stratagem to get them to accept the treaty provisions. The government would pay no salaries nor furnish any funds as part of its obligations to the Ottawas until a mission was in operation. McCoy soon realized

[18] William H. Keating, *Narrative of an Expedition to the Source of St. Peter's River, Lake Winnepeek, Lake of Woods, and Performed in the Year 1823, by order of the Hon J. C. Calhoun, Secretary of War, under the Command of Stephen H. Long, U.S.T.E.*, I, 149–56.

that it would take time and numerous contacts with the Ottawas before they would consent to one.[19]

McCoy again recorded observations on Indian customs and practices during his visit with the Ottawas. As usual his ethnological interests centered on burial rites. The Ottawa tribe was subdivided into a number of bands, for territorial and political purposes, and clans, made up of actual and assumed blood relatives distributed among all the bands. Each clan had a name, usually that of an animal, and McCoy noted that almost every grave had a post on one side with a picture of the animal by which the deceased's clan was identified. On the other side there was sometimes another post which attempted to show how the person died. If he had been killed in a battle, a number of men might be depicted without heads representing the warriors he had supposedly slain. Near the graves were sticks which visitors took and rapped on the posts to announce their arrival. At times the Ottawas carved posts to represent human faces, and McCoy discovered some "pretty well executed busts."[20]

McCoy had the opportunity to witness other Ottawa rituals and ceremonies. Tobacco played an important role in all of them. It was sprinkled on doorposts or in fires during religious rites and dances. In the "Feast of the Dead" each participant took tobacco and stuffed it through a small aperture into the coffin.[21] The Ottawas introduced other improvisations, and McCoy observed a dancer in one ceremony swallowing small bullets

[19] "Missionary Intelligence," 335–36.

[20] *Baptist Missions*, 194–95.

[21] "The Feast for the Dead" apparently underwent constant revision. Antoine de la Mothe Cadillac, in the late seventeenth century, described a feast to which the Ottawas brought in the bones of their relatives in small bags and offered sacrifices of dogs. W. Vernon Kinietz, *The Indians of the Western Great Lakes 1616–1760*, Occasional Contributions from the Museum of Anthropology of the University of Michigan, No. 10, 282–84.

"which apparently almost choked him, and gave him great uneasiness at the moment."[22] The older Ottawas, McCoy noted,
felt that tribal and religious observances had greatly deteriorated.
Although not unsympathetic, McCoy was more concerned
about what the innovation of liquor was doing to the life of the
tribe. Wagon loads of whisky could be seen going from place
to place.[23]

The sight of whole bands of Indians paralyzed by liquor and
the prospect of starting another mission had a melancholy effect
on McCoy. He wrote in his journal, "After all our labours to put
our missions into operation, we shall in a few years be driven
away ... or if we remain here, it will be only to witness the decline and ultimate ruin of the people of our charge, for no band
of Indians has ever thriven when crowded by white population."[24] He claimed that it was while he was camped along a river
on his return journey from the Ottawa nation that the idea of
colonizing the Indians in a country made forever theirs came to
him. In later years, as he looked back on the incident, it took on
something of the form of a supernatural revelation.

Characteristically, McCoy, upon his arrival back at Carey
Mission, immediately began a campaign for colonization. He
wrote to Governor Cass and Richard M. Johnson, United States
senator from Kentucky, to seek their support. Johnson had been
promoting education among the Indians by providing lodging
and schooling on his farm for Choctaw children under the aus-
pices of the Kentucky Baptist Missionary Society. McCoy urged

---

[22] *Baptist Missions*, 194, 208–11.

[23] Despite the law of 1822, most traders and the American Fur Company
itself continued to engage in the liquor traffic. Colonel Josiah Snelling in 1825
reported to the War Department that the American Fur Company that year
shipped 5,800 gallons of liquor to Mackinac, where it was diluted to fifteen
times the original amount. *American State Papers: Indian Affairs*, II, 661.

[24] Journal, June (n.d.), 1823; *Baptist Missions*, 196–97.

the two men to work for the creation of an asylum for "improved natives" somewhere in the extensive regions west of the Mississippi "no small distance beyond the frontiers of the White Settlement." Every such Indian of whatever tribe should be given a plantation, and all Christian denominations should have an equal privilege to settle their converts in that area. McCoy further urged the formation of a voluntary association to work for the approval of this plan in Congress.[25]

The burden of McCoy's concern at this juncture was for the Christian and educated Indians, and those who at least had become partly civilized. When he established Carey he believed that model communities of civilized Indians developed in the more populous aboriginal regions would provide examples for emulation, but he was no longer sure. He noted that the educated Indians and those who made a Christian commitment found little acceptance among their fellow tribesmen or in white communities. Often they became profligate or wandered back into the forest to resume their old habits.[26] A number of perceptive Indians had long since come to a similar conclusion and for this reason discouraged their children from frequenting the mission schools. Jean B. Richardville, chief of the Miamis, who initially invited McCoy to Fort Wayne, became a vigorous opponent of education because his son, who had been sent to school in Detroit, returned a misfit and a drunkard.[27]

McCoy, however, was not satisfied merely to write letters. By late 1823, he was on his way to Washington. The Board of Managers, which was meeting there, was still deeply engrossed in the affairs of Columbian College, although some members took time to listen to McCoy's colonization proposals. Staughton

[25] From a draft of a letter sent to Cass and Johnson in McCoy's Journal, June 23, 1823.
[26] *Ibid.*
[27] John Tipton to McCoy, December 20, 1826, McCoy Correspondence.

agreed to accompany him to present the plan to President James Monroe and Secretary of War John C. Calhoun. In a rare failure of ego, McCoy confessed, "I think I should find more pleasure in sitting on a bear skin or greasy Blanket in . . . smoky Bark huts than on their fine Sofas, in their ceiled houses." Ill at ease and yet anxious for his proposals to be heard, McCoy "preached along until I feared I should subject myself to a charge of a want of decorum." Calhoun seemed impressed, at least, although he argued that the area west of Lake Michigan would be a more suitable refuge for the Indians than the regions beyond the Mississippi River.[28]

The Monroe administration, as had its immediate predecessors, pursued an essentially contradictory policy toward the Indians, encouraging both segregation and assimilation. From the time of Jefferson's presidency, the government tried periodically to move eastern tribes across the Mississippi. Numerous treaties provided for immediate or ultimate removal. More than two thousand Cherokees had already migrated to Arkansas Territory. Some Shawnee and Delaware bands joined them there. The Piankashaws, who once roamed the regions around Vincennes when McCoy first went there, moved to the headwaters of the Black River in Missouri. The Kickapoos and the Weas, objects of McCoy's earliest mission, surrendered all of their lands in Illinois and Indiana by 1820, and most of them crossed the Mississippi River and made their way to western Missouri, where they became uneasy neighbors to the Osages.[29] The emphasis was on removal, not colonization. Little concern was expressed for the welfare of the Indians once they were removed. And yet while encouraging removal, the government at the same time

[28] McCoy, Journal, February 8 and 21, 1824.

[29] The Piankashaws gave up the last of their lands on the Wabash in 1818. Kappler, *Indian Affairs*, II, 182–84, 190, 1031–32.

subsidized civilization programs which would inspire the Indians to stay where they were and follow the white man's ways.

To the degree that the civilization projects succeeded and the tribesmen became cultivators and Christians, the government's claim of eminent domain over tribal lands was undermined. For the ordinary westerner the problem was simpler. The Indians were an encumbrance, and any talk of civilizing them aroused little sympathy.[30] While portions of some tribes had been moved beyond the Mississippi, and while almost every eastern tribe had already been pushed farther west, the course of events in the western and southern states picked up momentum. By 1823 there was growing sentiment for moving all of the Indians beyond the Mississippi and by force if they could not be persuaded to go peacefully. However, in the New England and mid-Atlantic states, now engulfed in a spirit of reform and where the Indian problem had been solved many decades earlier with firearms, there was increasing support for civilization and missionary programs, both government and private.

The larger considerations of government removal policy and sectional reaction meant little to McCoy as yet. He advocated segregation of only "improved Indians," and he had not thought about the many implications of general removal. On his return to Carey from Washington, McCoy, if anything, seemed intent on enlarging the scope of his missions in the Old Northwest, apparently to increase the number of civilized Indians who could be sent West.

The Potawatomis accepted the mission school with few reservations, and at its peak it had an enrollment of about seventy boys. The school made no provision for girls. As in Fort Wayne, the students boarded at the mission and ate with the missionary family. The regimen, as described by McCoy, was

[30] *North American Review*, Vol. VII (January, 1823), 44–45.

reminiscent of a medieval monastery. At four-thirty in the morning the bell called the students to morning prayers. They ate breakfast at six-thirty and then proceeded to their morning chores. School commenced at eight and continued until noon. It started again at two and dismissed at five, when there was another work period. Evening prayers began at eight, at which time there was also reading and exposition of the Scriptures and singing. Every Wednesday the teachers examined the youths on the chapter of the Bible which had been assigned the previous week for study. All activity ceased at nine in the evening. There was no school on Saturdays, when most of the day was allowed for recreation. On Sundays there was public worship at eleven and a "lecture" in the afternoon.[31]

The method of teacher and missionary recruitment continued to be haphazard. One of the chief purposes of Columbian College was to provide training in missionary leadership, but the school was in its infancy. The prime criterion for a missionary was still the "call." A number of young people, mostly without college education, who felt called, drifted into Carey. A few had the tenacity to stay and the capacity for self-education to become missionaries. If they could get along with McCoy, he recommended them to the board. If not, they had to establish their own connections if they wanted any formal recognition. In a real way, Carey became a training school for missionaries.

Johnston Lykins continued to be McCoy's heir apparent. He finally accepted baptism, and McCoy recommended him to the board as a missionary. But even then, one of Lykins' colleagues noted that he was a reluctant convert who needed "boldness" to take part in religious exercises.[32] Lykins' designated position was "school teacher," but he probably rendered his most valuable

---

[31] "Missionary Intelligence," 330–36.
[32] William Polke to McCoy, January 18, 1824, McCoy Correspondence.

service in superintending the procurement and transportation of supplies to the mission. Robert Simerwell, another of McCoy's loyal disciples, arrived at the mission in 1824. A native of Ireland and a cutler by trade, he had meager schooling but a great ambition to become a missionary.[33] Since he had been a cutler, there was perhaps some justification for getting him the government appointment of blacksmith. Others did the actual blacksmithing, but this arrangement assured the mission the government salary. Simerwell in turn got Jotham Meeker to come to Carey. Meeker had grown up in a pioneer environment in Ohio where he had little opportunity for formal education, although he had apprenticed as a printer.[34] He had an independent mind and soon came to doubt McCoy's whole approach to missions. Meeker concluded that missionaries must master the Indian languages and live in the native villages, and there preach to the Indians to bring about their conversion to Christianity.

As the missionary community increased, and as students were added, the problem of provisioning the mission became a formidable one. McCoy instituted a subsistence type of agriculture almost immediately. By 1827, Simerwell reported that 203 acres had been fenced in, about half of which were under cultivation, and that there was an orchard of over 400 trees. The mission also owned extensive herds of cattle, sheep, and hogs.[35] Nevertheless, a good many supplies had to be brought in.

Initially, Lykins transported the provisions in wagons over-

[33] Simerwell to R. W. Chessman (editor of the *Western Times*, Centerville, Indiana), May 14, 1829, Simerwell Correspondence, MSS in the Kansas State Historical Society Library.

[34] Meeker to Lucius Bolles, August 22, 1826, Meeker Papers, MSS in the Kansas State Historical Society Library. The Meeker Collection is divided into two parts, the "Papers," which include his correspondence and miscellaneous documents, and the "Journal."

[35] From a draft of a report prepared by Simerwell and sent to the War Department, October 1, 1827, Simerwell Correspondence.

land, and where the wagons could not get through he employed canoes. This method was slow and difficult. One trip from Ohio might take up to six weeks. Lykins also attempted to bring in supplies by lake vessels. He arranged with captains of schooners plying the lakes to bring cargoes to the mouth of the St. Joseph River. They had no accurate knowledge of the place to land, and the missionaries never knew when a vessel might arrive. Landing itself was difficult because of frequent high waters on the St. Joseph. Once it was accomplished, men from the mission transferred the cargoes to pirogues. They swamped easily, and the cargoes could be lost almost within sight of Carey. At times provisions were shipped to Chicago, and then brought overland to Carey. On one occasion, Lykins went to Chicago to salvage mission supplies from a ship that had run ashore. Sailing on the Great Lakes was equally hazardous to passengers. In the spring of 1824, McCoy returned from the East by way of the nearly completed Erie Canal and the lakes. Lykins laconically noted that McCoy never ventured on a lake vessel again.[36] Jotham Meeker a few years later took passage at Detroit for Sault Ste. Marie. The captain lost his course, spent a day searching for the mouth of the St. Mary's River, and finally ran the vessel aground.[37]

The problems of finance were no longer so acute at Carey, despite the temporary bankruptcy of the Board of Missions. McCoy's most recent trip to the East had been made to advance his colonization plan, but it also proved his ability as a financial promoter. While in Washington, McCoy had persuaded the War Department to increase his share of the Civilization Fund, and he also secured a promise that the government would pay 60 per

[36] Lykins, Journal, September 18, 23, October 2, and November 18, 1826.
[37] Meeker, Journal, October 17, 1832.
[38] McCoy, Journal, February 8, 1824.

73

cent of the building costs at Carey.[38] In New York, McCoy had stayed at the home of William Colgate, soap manufacturer and philanthropist, who was now a liberal supporter of his mission.[39] McCoy had also become acquainted with such influential Baptist ministers as Francis Wayland[40] of Boston and Spencer H. Cone of New York, and these acquaintances led to promises of support from their congregations. As a result of his six-month tour, McCoy received enough donations to pay off all debts and to purchase additional supplies. The Board of Managers issued a severe reprimand for keeping the contributions.[41] Solvent, and with an assured annual income from the government, McCoy declared his independence by no longer drawing on the board for funds, although he continued to submit accounts of all his financial transactions.

The unfinished business of establishing a mission among the Ottawas continued to plague McCoy. To make initial contacts, he arranged to have a temporary smithy set up and also to bring in some Ottawa youths to the school at Carey. Cass allowed Lykins to distribute the provisions and livestock provided by the Chicago treaty, and this function helped to broaden the acquaintanceship. All these tactics proved effective, and in the fall of 1824, Noonday, an Ottawa chief, not only requested that missionaries come, but offered a tract of seven hundred acres of land for their use.[42] Once again, McCoy faced the dilemma of having no one to send. None of the young men at Carey were mature enough to supervise the formation of a mission. McCoy persuaded his brother-in-law, William Polke, to undertake the

[39] Colgate to McCoy, February 19, 1824, McCoy Correspondence.

[40] Wayland, who soon became president of Brown University, corresponded with McCoy regularly, and usually requested detailed information about Indian life. See for example, Wayland to McCoy, March 9, 1825, McCoy Correspondence.

[41] Staughton to McCoy, n.d., 1824, McCoy Correspondence.

[42] McCoy, *Baptist Missions*, 242, 250–51.

project, and secured the government commission of teacher for him. A veteran of the Battle of Tippecanoe, member of the Indiana Constitutional Convention of 1816, former county judge, and state senator,[43] Polke had a wide range of experience, but none that qualified him as a missionary. He resigned after spending some months at Carey in preparation for the undertaking with the Ottawas. His family, he claimed, was too large to support on a missionary's salary. The Ottawa situation had become embarrassing. McCoy enjoyed a favorable relationship with Governor Cass, but he feared that his inability to get a mission started might reflect on his own competence.

While at Fort Wayne, McCoy had had frequent disagreements with Indian agents, but he seldom complained about government officials during his years at Carey. Cass regarded himself as something of a patron saint to the establishment,[44] and his commissioner, John L. Leib, who made the annual inspections, submitted glowing appraisals. Carey was within the boundaries of the Chicago agency,[45] but McCoy relied increasingly on General John Tipton, Dr. Turner's successor as Indian agent at Fort Wayne. A member of one government committee investigating Indian affairs once observed, "The eagerness to secure an appointment as Indian agent, on a small salary, manifested by many persons of superior ability, ought of itself to be a warning to Congress as to the objects sought by it."[46] This observation probably had some relevancy in the case of General Tipton. He accepted an appointment to an unattractive frontier post, and used it to build up large property interests through the

[43] McCoy to Staughton, February (n.d.), 1824, McCoy Correspondence.
[44] Frank B. Woodford, *Lewis Cass: The Late Jeffersonian*, 145.
[45] Alexander Wolcott (agent at Chicago) to Tipton, November 19, 1824, Tipton, *Papers*, I, 409–10.
[46] 39 Cong., 2 sess., *House Misc. Doc.* 37, 10.

acquisition of Indian lands.[47] But, whatever Tipton's motives, McCoy formed a lasting friendship with him. Tipton kept McCoy informed of intrigues among traders to get his government commissions taken away from him.[48] He urged the Miami chiefs to apply their education funds to Carey and to send Miami boys there to be educated.[49] He was instrumental in having Ramsey D. Potts appointed sub-agent for the Potawatomis. Potts was stationed at Carey.[50] Here he became a convert, married one of the teachers, and decided to become a missionary. McCoy, apparently, had a greater affinity for government officers than the managers of the Baptist Board of Foreign Missions.

Outwardly, Carey presented many visible signs of success. McCoy wrote, "I beheld a colony firmly settled, numerous, civilized, and happy." The Potawatomis were part-time agriculturists when McCoy first came to Carey. He estimated that the average family cultivated about half an acre of corn, beans, and pumpkins.[51] By 1825, about thirty Indian families had started to farm after the white man's fashion and had begun to build fences and houses and to raise livestock. The blacksmith, McCoy observed, could hardly keep up with the demands for axes, hoes, and plows.[52] The school had some promising students. A few natives had become converts. Yet McCoy increasingly realized that much of this achievement was superficial. Not far from Carey he had seen "children gathering weeds, to boil and eat. I have seen the mother in a swamp, digging roots for her half-starved children. I have seen them feed on animals that had died of disease and had lain until their flesh had become pu-

[47] Paul W. Gates, Introduction to *The John Tipton Papers*, I, 21–24.
[48] Tipton to McCoy, June 14, 1826, McCoy Correspondence.
[49] Tipton to Thomas L. McKenney (Bureau of Indian Affairs), February 24, 1827, *Papers*, I, 664.
[50] Tipton, *Papers*, I, 627n.
[51] "Missionary Intelligence," 334–35.
[52] McCoy, *Baptist Missions*, 262–63.

tride."[53] And, ironically, the very success of the missionary settlement attracted a class of white settlers who were always fond of being on the frontiers of civilization. The first harbinger appeared in the spring of 1825. Squire Thompson, a Hoosier, came to live at the station for a time, then built a hut on the other side of the St. Joseph, procured a barrel of whisky, and set up a liquor business.[54] McCoy began to push his colonization plan with renewed vigor.

[53] "Missionary Intelligence," 330–36.
[54] McCoy to Tipton, March 23, 1825, Tipton, *Papers*, I, 449–50.

Chapter V

On Indian Reform

By the spring of 1825 the federal government had decided on removal as a definite policy. This made Isaac McCoy's concern for Indian colonization seem very current. In the past, commissioners who treated with the Indians had often urged removal, but they were usually satisfied if they could persuade the tribes to accept small reservations in the corners of the ceded land. The rush of white population indicated that even these small enclaves would soon be absorbed. Most treaties made no provision for new homes for displaced Indians. Instead of cessions for stipulated annuities and other trifles, some government policy-makers felt that it was necessary to provide for an exchange of lands. In his message to Congress in December, 1824, President Monroe urged the adoption of a "well-digested" removal plan;[1] and early in 1825, he submitted to the Senate a number of concrete proposals. There would be no coerced removals, and if a tribe consented to go, it was to receive an adequate allotment of land in the country "lying westward and northward" of the acknowledged boundaries of the several states and territories. The government would undertake to connect the tribes in friendly relations, preserve order, prevent intrusions on their property, and teach them the art of civilized life.[2]

[1] James D. Richardson (ed.), *A Compilation of the Messages and Papers of the Presidents*, II, 261.

Accompanying Monroe's message to the Senate was a report prepared by the Secretary of War on the Indian population in the organized regions of the United States, the amount of land they held, and the problems and expenses anticipated in their removal. The number of Indians in Indiana, Illinois, Ohio, and Michigan Territory was placed at 42,345. In his discussions with McCoy, Secretary Calhoun had argued that the Indians, particularly the tribes of the Old Northwest, should not be sent beyond the Mississippi, but to the region west of Lake Michigan. This argument was now a main feature of his recommendations to the Senate.[3] Calhoun's political opponents charged him with a Machiavellian design to block free-state expansion, but there is little evidence to support this charge. The climate and the nature of the still very remote Wisconsin country were obviously more favorable to the habits of the eastern Indians. Limited Indian consolidation had already taken place there. The wandering Stockbridges and bands of New York Indians had settled in the Fox River area. Here the Reverend Eleazar Williams, a half-blood Indian, Episcopal missionary, delegate-at-large for the Oneidas, and self-proclaimed son of Louis XVI and Marie Antoinette, envisioned a grand confederacy of Indians with one supreme head.[4] Furthermore, Jedidiah Morse had included an extensive description of the region in his report to the War Department. It was not surprising that the area figured prominently in Calhoun's plans. During the congressional debates on the administration's recommendations, the delegate from Arkansas Territory, Henry W. Conway, offered a resolution for the organization of all the land west of Missouri, Arkansas, and

[2] *American State Papers: Indian Affairs*, II, 541–42.

[3] *Ibid.*, 542–47.

[4] Albert G. Ellis, "Recollections of Rev. Eleazar Williams," *Wisconsin Historical Collections*, Vol. VIII (1877–79), 322–52.

Michigan into an Indian Territory.[5] Calhoun sent McCoy copies of his own bill and other resolutions before Congress. McCoy thought it ludicrous simply to label the land west of the Mississippi "Indian Territory" without thought of more specific delineation. On the other hand, he did not think the Indian country should be limited to the fertile region west of Lake Michigan. These lands could not be held for the Indian for long. McCoy was unhappy that the emphasis of the proposals was on removal and not on colonization. What would happen to the Indian once he moved? But for the moment, McCoy did not voice his misgivings too loudly because he was pleased that Congress was at last discussing a permanent Indian Territory.[6]

To insure the success of any colonization scheme, McCoy believed it would be necessary to have Indian leaders trained in government, religion, and medicine. Some of the youths at the mission school had shown an aptitude for academic pursuits, and so McCoy decided that Columbian College would be a natural place for them to further their education. With eight boys in tow, McCoy set out early in 1826 to enroll them. Somewhat whimsically, he noted that one was not "religious," and if the Baptist school refused to admit him, he planned to take him to Princeton College.[7] The journal of Columbian College periodically published a census of the "pious students" at the various colleges in the United States. In 1823, for example, it listed Harvard University as having 302 students, 12 of whom were pious. Dartmouth College had a much better record with 64 pious students out of a total of 133.[8] Princeton, presumably, had one of the poorer ratios. The piety of the one Indian in McCoy's party of prospective students did not become an issue because

[5] *Niles' Weekly Register*, Vol. XXVII (December 25, 1824), 271.
[6] McCoy, *Baptist Missions*, 257.
[7] McCoy to Rice, December 17, 1825, McCoy Correspondence.
[8] *Columbian Star*, Vol. II (March 22, 1823), 15.

Columbian College declined to accept any of them. When they were about halfway to their destination, McCoy received a letter from Luther Rice, the former Burma missionary and now the general agent of the Board of Missions, instructing him to take his students to Senator Richard M. Johnson's Choctaw Academy in Kentucky.[9]

The Choctaw Academy was not properly a mission school, although it had loose ties with Baptists, but a venture in private enterprise which could hardly be construed as philanthropic. Senator Johnson had somehow managed to persuade the Choctaws to request that a $6,000 annual education annuity be given to him, even though the treaty required the money to be spent "in the nation."[10] Thus the Choctaw Academy was born, and at a time when Johnson was deeply in debt. "Fortune for the first time in my life seems to open some advantage to me by the providential friendship and confidence of the Indians."[11] The emphasis at the school was on the manual arts, and Rice argued that this training would be more beneficial to McCoy's students than the classical-oriented curriculum of Columbian College.

The urgency with which Rice, and also William Staughton, the corresponding secretary of the Board of Missions, attempted to head off McCoy's trip to Columbian College, suggests that they really feared racial problems. Not many months previously, a great furor had arisen in Protestant circles in the East when two Cherokee youths attending a mission school at Cornwall, Connecticut, married local white girls. An aroused citizenry burned the students in effigy, and in nearby Litchfield, Lyman Beecher denounced the marriages as an "outrage upon public

[9] Rice to McCoy, January 26, 1826, McCoy Correspondence.

[10] 26 Cong., 2 sess., *House Exec. Doc. 109*, Pt. 3, p. 9.

[11] Quoted in Leland Winfield Meyer, *The Life and Times of Colonel Richard M. Johnson of Kentucky*, 336–37.

feeling."[12] Whatever the reasons for the refusal to admit his students into Columbian College, McCoy could not be side-tracked by letters from board members. Although he valued Senator Johnson's friendship for practical reasons, he little appreciated his school; undeterred, McCoy continued on to Washington, got the promise of government support for each of the students, and then proceeded to Hamilton, New York, where he enrolled them in a Baptist college that had recently opened.[13] Subsequently, Lykins took two more Carey students to a medical school in Vermont to begin their training as physicians. Again the board objected.[14]

From the time of his first appointment in 1817, McCoy had frequently complained about the small group of ministers who managed the missionary enterprises of the General Convention of Baptists. In McCoy's mind these men took on a single identity as "the Board." Usually, McCoy lamented that the board members showed little interest in Indian missions. Occasionally he accused the board of obstructionism. His experience with the Indian college students seemed to justify the latter criticism, but he seldom kept Staughton fully informed about the changes in his plans. By the time the corresponding secretary had become accustomed to the operation of a large boarding school, McCoy had involved the board in Indian colonization. After 1826, the board paid more attention to McCoy's mission. He now complained about interference.

The General Missionary Convention of the Baptist denomination in the United States in its 1826 triennial session adopted a new course. Since the board's operation of Columbian College

---

[12] Clifton Jackson Phillips, "Protestant America and the Pagan World" (Ph.D. dissertation, Harvard University, 1954), 65–66.

[13] From a draft of a letter that McCoy submitted to the editor of the *Columbian Star*, March 17, 1826, McCoy Correspondence.

[14] Lykins, Journal, January 8 and February 10, 1827.

had emptied the denominational coffers, the Convention decided to break its formal connections with the school and limit its concerns to foreign and Indian missions. The delegates elected a new Board of Managers, and with one exception they were all from the New England states. The new board installed Lucius Bolles of Salem as corresponding secretary.[15] Bolles was an organization man who believed that the board's missions needed closer supervision and that loose connections, such as McCoy's, could no longer be tolerated.[16]

New directives soon emanated from Boston. Missionaries were to keep careful journals of their activities and submit them for periodic inspection. Since missionaries should expect no better education for their children than others, the board would no longer share the expense of educating them.[17] McCoy's two eldest sons were attending Columbian College, under the board's patronage, where both were enthusiastic students. Having grown up in the wilderness, they found even the most limited facilities impressive. Josephus wrote to his parents, "I was never in so advantageous a place for instruction. We can take two books out of the library every Wednesday, we have the opportunity of reading the history of any part of the world; on account of which we spend our leisure hours pleasantly."[18] Knowing that he would be hard pressed to educate his family without board support, McCoy, in a bitter rejoinder, informed Bolles that his sons would not be enslaved by a lack of education, no matter what the board decided, and then proceeded to lecture the college-trained easterner on the meaning of education.

[15] "Report on the Baptist General Convention at New York," *Columbian Star*, Vol. V (May 18, 1826); *American Baptist Magazine*, Vol. VI (May, 1826), 181, 208–10.
[16] Bolles to McCoy, November 28, 1826, McCoy Correspondence.
[17] Bolles to McCoy, June 17, 1826, *ibid.*
[18] Josephus McCoy to his parents, March 24, 1825, *ibid.*

The sons of Africa are not enslaved because they are black, but because of the absence of that talent and information which would elevate her character among the nations. Give to the African the requisite portion of talent, and it becomes as unpopular to enslave her sons as those of Asia or Europe.[19]

Carey had become largely self-sustaining, but Bolles kept adding to McCoy's growing resentment by such statements as "You did not explain your object in laying in *ten* tons of pork or why there is none raised on the missionary premises." The new corresponding secretary apparently placed some credence in the rumors of high living at the mission and went on to ask why the students had milk for breakfast and supper, and why corn should not be substituted for flour. Such "luxuries" as milk and flour, said Bolles, would endanger the character of the Indians.[20]

These tactics infuriated McCoy, but since he was no longer drawing on the board for funds, they could be ignored. Of much more serious consequence was a new policy which Bolles announced whereby all missionaries would be placed on a pay scale based on distinctions between ordained ministers, assistants, school teachers, farmers, and mechanics. By letters and by pamphlet, McCoy attempted to refute this plan. He argued that it reduced the missionary to the status of a hired laborer. Who could hire an unobtrusive Adoniram Judson to risk the horrors of a Burmese prison? The chief excellence of a missionary consisted in his becoming "disinterestedly benevolent" and in his enduring things which could not be explained in missionary journals. How was pay for such services to be reckoned? McCoy observed that little pay attracted men of little minds. Invariably, a petty office in a county tempted more candidates than a seat in Congress. Equally intolerable to McCoy was the

[19] McCoy to Bolles, September 27, 1826, *ibid.*
[20] Bolles to McCoy, November 28, 1826, *ibid.*

practice of making distinctions between missionaries, for all were equally deserving, no matter what their work. And furthermore, he concluded, if a missionary could not also be a bookkeeper, teacher, farmer, mechanic, and businessman, he would not be of much use on an Indian mission. McCoy's eloquent arguments could not hide the biases of a frontier-trained minister nor the fears that he might lose a measure of control over his missionary enterprises. That the board intended to assert its authority was equally clear. For the first time, it appointed a missionary to one of McCoy's stations without consulting him. McCoy willingly accepted Leonard Slater and put him to work, even though he refused to abide by the "Family Rules." From the beginning, Slater's only loyalty was to the board.[21]

In spite of the growing estrangement with the managers in Boston, McCoy had no intention of breaking his connection. He had built up a reservoir of good will in the Convention which he did not want to endanger. Meanwhile, a new spate of Indian treaties diverted his attention from his continuing controversy with the board.

The War Department, in carrying out the new Indian policy first announced by James Monroe and continued by John Quincy Adams' administration, prepared to provide a home for emigrating tribesmen. Under instructions from Washington, General William Clark, in June, 1825, convened representatives of the Osage and Kansa tribes at Castor Hill, Missouri, where the Indians ceded much of the territory which now constitutes the states of Oklahoma and Kansas. In the fall of the same year the government took the first step to prepare the Indians of the Old Northwest for removal. One thousand representatives of the northwestern tribes gathered at Prairie du Chien to meet with General Clark and Governor Cass. The natives agreed on spe-

---

[21] Simerwell, Journal, November 16, 1826, and May 1, 1827.

cific tribal boundaries. This agreement of boundaries would help maintain peace, they were told,[22] but it was intended primarily to facilitate land cessions and removal. With the boundaries set, government commissioners could begin at once to "persuade" the tribesmen to surrender their lands. In the fall of 1826, at Paradise Springs on the Wabash, McCoy was on hand to witness this gentle art of persuasion when three professionals, Governor Cass, General Tipton, and Governor James B. Ray of Indiana, opened negotiations with the Potawatomis and the Miamis.

The purpose of the negotiations as described to McCoy by Tipton was to "remoove the Indians out of the reach of British influence and American whiskey."[23] McCoy was aware of other motives, but had his own reasons for attending. He wanted some of the education funds that probably would be provided, and he wished to discuss specific colonization plans with the commissioners. The proceedings followed the usual stereotyped pattern, and began with a message from the "Great White Father" with pious exhortations to industry, temperance, and sobriety. To set the stage for the actual negotiations, the commissioners then asked the tribesmen what land they were prepared to surrender and if they would remove farther west. Governor Cass added a special appeal:

> I am authorized to state to you, that if you will sell your lands and remove, your friend, Mr. McCoy will go and select a suitable situation, will remove and settle with you . . . . Look around you. You will soon be left alone. The Delawares have gone, the Shawnese are going. *Be wise.*[24]

22 *Statutes at Large*, VII, 240–44, 272.
23 Tipton to McCoy, September 8, 1826, McCoy Correspondence.
24 "Record of the Proceedings of His Excellency, Lewis Cass, His Excellency, James B. Ray, Gen. John Tipton—Commissioners, appointed to treat with the Indians owning lands in the State of Indiana, in the year 1826," *Papers*, I, 577, 581.

The braves withdrew to consult among themselves, and then began four weeks of negotiating, feasting, and drinking, interrupted by Sabbath observances conducted by McCoy. It was only after vast quantities of food had been gorged, barrels of whisky consumed, and brilliantly colored cloth distributed, all supplied by the "Great White Father," that the natives weakened and indicated they might cede some land. They refused to discuss removal.

The commissioners did not only have to treat with the Indians, but with the traders as well. Instead of the Indian's furs, the traders now sought his annuities in payment for real and imaginary debts. They were at the treaty grounds in full force, plying the chiefs with drink and presents, fighting to have their claims allowed. Usually they demanded about three times the actual amount of credit they had extended to the Indians. To get the co-operation of the traders, commissioners would sometimes include in the treaties provisions authorizing the patenting of certain lands to chiefs, half-bloods, or other important members of the tribes. These Indians would then convey the reserves to traders in payment of debts or even to agents for special services. There was considerable opposition in Congress to the granting of individual reserves because they were often followed by the grossest frauds.

In the treaties concluded at Paradise Springs in October, 1826, the Miamis and the Potawatomis surrendered joint ownership of a large strip of land just north of the Wabash. The treaties also included many individual reserves.[25] Four days after the signing of the treaty, the Miami chief, Le Gros, stipulated that the four sections granted to him should go to Tipton. To assure that the individual reserves not be stricken during the ratification proceedings, the commissioners included a number of small grants

[25] *Statutes at Large*, VII, 295, 300.

for students at Carey and intimated that the school could expect to be the main beneficiary. Senator Johnson revealed their main purpose when the Miami and Potawatomi treaties came before Congress. He wrote to Tipton, "The popularity of these students & the missionary Station there saved the whole of the grants."[26] Had the student grants, in addition, placated McCoy, John Tipton, for one, would have thought them most useful.

When weighed in the balance, the friendship of a missionary was not as valuable as that of a member of the Senate Committee on Indian Affairs. Tipton persuaded the Potawatomis to designate that the entire education fund of $2,000 provided by the Paradise Springs treaties be given to Senator Johnson's Choctaw Academy.[27] Because he had a school operating in the Potawatomi country, McCoy naturally assumed that he would get the whole appropriation. He asked Johnson for at least part of the funds. The Senator confided to Tipton, "I am afraid our Worthy friend Mr. McCoy may be hurt," but indicated that he did not intend to part with any funds that had been rightly vested in Choctaw Academy.[28] The individual grants made to Carey students proved to be of little value to the school. They sold the reserves and spent the money for other things. Tipton, as an afterthought, attempted to persuade the Miamis to apply some of their education funds to Carey, but had little success.[29] Even then, Johnson's agents, who were everywhere, tried to get the Miamis to send their children to his school.[30]

McCoy was curiously restrained about his double-dealing friends. He reserved his ire for the "Board." Yet, while increasingly critical of the managers, and while becoming more and

[26] Johnson to Tipton, January 23, 1827, Tipton, *Papers*, I, 642–43.
[27] 26 Cong., 2 sess., *House Exec. Doc. 109*, Pt. 3, p. 37.
[28] Johnson to Tipton, February 26, 1827, Tipton, *Papers*, I, 665.
[29] Tipton to McCoy, December 20, 1826, McCoy Correspondence.
[30] Johnson to Tipton, September 22, 1827, Tipton, *Papers*, I, 785–86.

more concerned about Indian colonization in the West, McCoy, ambivalently, involved the board in new missions in the Old Northwest.

The Ottawa situation could no longer be put off. In November, 1826, McCoy packed up his family and, with oxen, cows, and plows, made his way to a site previously chosen at the rapids of the Grand River, forty miles from Lake Michigan, and there began a mission. He named it Thomas, in honor of John Thomas, a British medical missionary in India. The McCoys encountered the usual hardships of blizzards and supply problems in the first months. Even so, McCoy opened a school almost immediately and in the spring built fences and put some land under cultivation.[31] He started language study again, but relied on Gosa, a former student at Carey, as an interpreter and general good-will ambassador.

Tribal culture continued to fascinate McCoy. He took time to visit a sacred lake which emitted loud noises like the rolling of cannon. The Ottawas claimed it was the abode of spirits, who performed strange feats. McCoy concluded that surface waters seeping through air vents to the bottom of the lake caused the sound. He discovered a number of Indian mounds in the region of the mission, and he plowed up earthenware in nearby fields. He surmised that a "non-tribe" had once resided in the area in pre-Columbian times. Unlike those of a contemporary, Joseph Smith, the founder of the Latter-day Saints, McCoy's speculations went no farther. The origin of the American Indian was a popular topic, and the Baptist periodical, *Columbian Star*, which styled itself "A Journal of Religion and Science," in its "science" section frequently carried articles on the subject. One writer detected a great resemblance between the language of the Miamis and ancient Greek, but most commonly, other philolo-

[31] "Missionary Intelligence," 238–40.

gists sought to relate the Indian languages to Hebrew.[32] Another
of McCoy's contemporaries, John Heckewelder, a Moravian
missionary, was constantly searching for evidence to identify the
Indians with the ten lost tribes of Israel.[33] Indian mounds and
artifacts, such as earthenware, suggested to men like Heckewelder and Smith that a race of men had once existed more
capable and industrious than the modern native. McCoy ridiculed such conjecture. By calculating the amount of earth one
Indian could move in a day and considering the fact that wives
performed as much work as husbands, he concluded that any
mound he had seen could have been built by two hundred
Indians in less than one day. When he read that one philologist
had heard the Indians on festival occasions use the Hebrew word
"Hallelujah," McCoy stated that at such ceremonies he had
never detected anything more than "whooping," which a
"fruitful imagination" could associate with any language.[34]

While at Thomas, McCoy was instrumental in extending
Baptist missions to the Chippewas, a tribe closely related in
language and culture to the Ottawas and Potawatomis. Governor Cass invited McCoy to attend treaty negotiations at Green
Bay, Michigan Territory, and intimated that education annuities
would be discussed.[35] McCoy could not go and had no one to
send. As a result the commissioners offered the $1,000 annual
education fund provided in the Green Bay Treaty of 1827[36] to
the Episcopalians. Not all was lost, however. Abel Bingham, a
Baptist missionary who had worked with the New York tribes,

[32] *Columbian Star*, Vol. II (March 22, 1823), 46, 48; Vol. III (January 3, 1824), 115; Vol. III (July 10, 1824), 110.
[33] Heckewelder to Peter S. Du Ponceau (a French linguist), August 12, 1818, quoted in *Ethnohistory*, Vol. VI (Winter, 1959), 74.
[34] McCoy, *Baptist Missions*, 9–12, 26–27.
[35] Cass to McCoy, May 22, 1827, McCoy Correspondence.
[36] *Statutes at Large*, VII, 303.

wrote to McCoy and expressed a willingness to work at Carey. McCoy directed him instead to Sault Ste. Marie, and on one of his visits to Washington, McCoy persuaded the Bureau of Indian Affairs to allot the annuity to the Baptists. Bingham established a school in 1828, and also served as military chaplain to the United States soldiers garrisoned at Fort Brady.[37] The pressure on the Chippewas to remove to the West was never very great, and, as a result, the station at Sault Ste. Marie continued for some time as one of the most stable Baptist Indian missions.

With Thomas well underway, McCoy turned the mission over to Leonard Slater and Jotham Meeker, and returned to Carey. He was careful to secure the government appointment of teacher for Johnston Lykins, even though Lykins did not take up residence at Thomas. This precaution kept the salary in the "missionary family." After an absence of almost one year, McCoy soon realized that Carey had lost much of its isolation.

The pattern of drunkenness and murder, so familiar at Fort Wayne, began to repeat itself. McCoy's original instructions from Cass had indicated that he was to report all trade offenses to the nearest agent. He dutifully notified Tipton about all violators, and the General replied that he would take "grate [sic] pleasure at all times in bringing such men . . . to the punishment thier [sic] crime deserves."[38] The agents licensed traders to certain posts; a roving system of trade was frowned upon. McCoy complained at times about the "French," although it was never quite clear who they were. Joseph Bertrand had moved his post from St. Joseph to Parc aux Vaches, not far from Carey, but he was the only French and the only licensed trader in the vicinity.[39] The traders who caused McCoy the most grief were not

[37] *American Baptist Magazine*, Vol. IX (January, 1829), 32.
[38] Tipton to McCoy, April 11, 1825, Tipton, *Papers*, I, 454.
[39] Wolcott to Tipton, November 19, 1824, *ibid.*, I, 409–10.

the Bertrands, but the Squire Thompsons, who settled on public lands and sold whisky freely for cash or barter. They had no property and no reputation to lose, and it mattered little whether they were driven from place to place. McCoy described them as "crows around a carcass."[40] The agents could not control this type of trade. Tipton forwarded McCoy's complaints to Cass, but nothing further was done. Ramsey Potts brought charges against two men for selling liquor to the Potawatomis. The case came to trial in a United States district court in Indianapolis, where it was continued from session to session and finally dismissed.[41] Twenty-five natives lost their lives in the vicinity of Carey from causes directly attributable to liquor during the winter of 1827. Understandably, McCoy became very cynical about the government's attempts to control the liquor traffic with the Indians.

Other factors helped break the mission's isolation. Congress in 1825 authorized the survey of a road between Detroit and Chicago. Instead of following a direct route through heavy timber, the surveyors took the line of least resistance and followed a path known as the Great Sauk Trail, which went by the mission. The proposed road passed through small sections of land still held by the Potawatomis, and, in the summer of 1827, Governor Cass and his retinue arrived at Carey to negotiate for right-of-way privileges. The Potawatomis signed an agreement for a straight cash indemnity.[42] Whisky traders set up camp near the mission during the negotiations, and McCoy sardonically noted that the tribesmen were rid of the "burden of carrying the money" twenty-four hours after they received their payments.[43]

[40] McCoy to Tipton, March 23, 1825, McCoy Correspondence.
[41] Tipton to Potts, December 15, 1826, and February 3, 1827, Tipton, *Papers*, I, 627–28, 650.
[42] *Statutes at Large*, VII, 305.
[43] McCoy, *Baptist Missions*, 319.

The actual development of the Detroit-to-Chicago road did not begin until the 1830's, when it became a natural extension of the Erie Canal route to the Old Northwest; but before then, the Carey missionaries already referred to it as the "Chicago Express." There was a flurry of troop movements along the "Express" in 1827 during the Winnebago war, a minor frontier incident precipitated by the Winnebagos when they attempted to expel lead-miners who had invaded their lands south of the Wisconsin River. This disturbance created considerable anxiety at the mission. The main concern was that the Sacs, allies of the Winnebagos, might be in a belligerent mood on their return from a pilgrimage to Malden in Lower Canada, where they went annually to receive gifts from the British. The Sacs were familiar visitors at Carey, for they invariably stopped and suggested that American gifts, such as two or three head of cattle, would be equally acceptable. McCoy had always pacified them with smaller gifts and allowed them to repair their guns at the smithy, but their visits usually created uneasiness, heightened by tales the Potawatomis delighted in spreading that the Sacs practiced human sacrifice and cannibalism.[44] Actually, the transient Sacs were in a far greater predicament than the missionaries. The Sacs recognized the danger of falling in with soldiers or groups of hostile frontiersmen. When they stopped at Carey at the height of the Winnebago war, they showed an outdated certificate from the War Department certifying their "favorable character" and also letters from white settlers near Detroit stating that they had passed through peaceably.[45]

There was increasing activity on the "Chicago Express" of another sort. Detroit newspapers as early as 1825 described the excellent lands in the St. Joseph River Valley, without reference

[44] Simerwell, Journal, July 27, 28 and August 2, 1827.
[45] McCoy, *Baptist Missions*, 313.

93

to the Indians who occupied it.[46] By late 1827, the first settlers began trickling in. When McCoy founded Carey, the region was a trackless wilderness, inhabited only by Indians and a French trader, but in an incredibly short time all this isolation changed. He now committed himself completely to the colonization of all the Indians living east of the Mississippi, not merely scattered bands of civilized tribesmen. His views had finally crystallized, and he formulated them in a manuscript entitled, "Remarks on the Practicability of Indian Reform, Embracing Their Colonization."[47]

McCoy, in his treatise, attempted first of all to come to terms with the problem of the relative merits of culture. On the matter of the common practice of referring to the Indians as savages he wrote:

> The names we have given the Indians are merely, arbitrary, and are made to signify nothing more, than that their manner and customs differ from ours; and in our estimation are less desirable. Let us suppose invaders of our rights, setting up the same plea, and our question is answered.

And then to counter the prevalent argument that the Indians had degenerated to the state of nature, McCoy added:

> Surely the round of nature cannot furnish an argument to justify the taking away of a people's country, merely because the inhabitants have their peculiar modes of living; when too, these modes of life, which differ from those of other nations, are the result of their own free choice, and have never disturbed the peace of others.[48]

[46] Buley, *The Old Northwest*, II, 84.

[47] MS in the Kansas State Historical Society Library. Published in 1827, and republished in 1829 with appendix.

[48] Isaac McCoy, *Remarks on the Practicability of Indian Reform, Embracing Their Colonization*, 5.

The problem must be faced as it existed, however. The Indians, McCoy knew, had lost much of their land and forgotten most of their traditions. The fault did not lie with the Indians. "There is something among us, not among the Indians, radically wrong in this business; this wrong must be righted." The Indian, in short, had been deprived of his rights. However enlightened McCoy's views on Indian culture might seem, in the end the Indian's rights were "white" property and title rights. One factor, more than any other, McCoy claimed, had militated against the Indian's getting his rights—the doctrine of effective occupancy. Showing some familiarity with the writings of Montesquieu and Adam Smith and Supreme Court cases such as *Fletcher v. Peck*, McCoy believed that they all reflected the philosophy that the Indian could not actually claim title to the soil because he did not effectively occupy it. But the Indians had never been merely hunters, for from time immemorial they had also been cultivators of the soil and "were people at *home*." The red man's strong predilection for roaming had been grossly exaggerated. Just as the son of a blacksmith might become a blacksmith, so might the son of a hunter tend to become a hunter. "Men as they come into existence are pretty much of an equality. . . . it is not a question at all, whether the mental faculties of Indians generally, are equal to those of their fortunate neighbours." And as for the charge the Indian claimed too much territory for his numbers, McCoy asked, parenthetically, when in history had a nation's laws prescribed the quantity of land which must be cultivated by a given number of citizens? Given this argument, the Chinese should claim the entire North American continent.[49]

McCoy was realistic enough to know that appealing to the white man's sense of justice would not deter him from further invasion of Indian lands. Had the Indians not consented to Wil-

[49] *Ibid.*, 4–7, 10–12.

liam Penn's Quaker settlement on the Delaware, he would have proceeded anyway and used force, if necessary. McCoy's solution to "right the wrongs" was legislative action. He had amazingly little faith in missionary activity. Missionaries, he wrote, had never accomplished more than to "soften the pillows of the dying." He further observed that missionaries had "too recently been transplanted from the sterile plains of religious bigotry, to expand with liberal views of the character, and of the just rights of man." But no matter what had happened in the past, the federal government could still act to protect the Indian's rights and patrimony. Congress must create for the perishing tribes "a country of their own" where under the guardianship of the government they could "feel their importance, where they can hope to enjoy, unmolested, the fruits of their labours, and their national recovery need not be doubted."[50]

All Indians, to McCoy, had a single national identity. He did not distinguish between race and nation, nor between nation and tribe. He assumed that the Indians had intense national feelings that needed but an opportunity to be expressed. He did not explain how this Indian nationalism would be superimposed on the various tribes, nor how it would fit in with the larger American nationalism, for he never doubted that the Indian Country would be part of the United States. First it would become a colony and later a state, but it would always imbibe the "spirit" and admire the "enlightened age" of the American nation. Laws for the regulation of the Indian communities, at first few and simple, would be provided by the federal government. Constables, sheriffs, clerks, and judges would also be furnished until the Indians developed their own. This system would enable the federal government to dispense with the hiring of agents and subagents. There would, of course, be great consternation among

[50] *Ibid.*, 8–9, 11–17.

the agents and traders, but remove the Indians, McCoy exulted, "and the fountains fail." No tribesmen would be forced to move, nor would their consent be bought. "Naught but sound argument, strengthened by an exhibition of the facts."[51]

Where should the Indian colony be located? The shores of the Great Lakes, a region once suggested by Calhoun, would not be suitable. McCoy observed that this area would be too cold for the southern tribes, and it would soon be hemmed in by the white population. Furthermore, the non-slaveholding states would object. But along the Rocky Mountains nature had spread a desert from five hundred to six hundred miles in width. There was no way of knowing the extent of this desert west of the mountains, nor the exceptions to its barrenness. The few who had hastily crossed it had provided scant details, but McCoy did not doubt that some of the land would be reclaimable, and much of the rest would afford grazing opportunities. But even then he believed that this was no region to tempt the enterprise of the whites. Fortunately the absence of navigable streams would make it even less desirable. "Nature has marked the boundaries for us." Since the territory was so vast, collisions between the different tribes could be avoided. Because the Indians in the West had more latitude, McCoy assumed that their condition was far superior to that of the Indians in the crowded eastern reservations. Given more information about the region and precise knowledge about the part to which they should go, such tribes as the Potawatomis and the Miamis would soon overcome their reluctance to move. Conducted tours should be provided for representatives of the tribes, and they should be allowed a voice in choosing their new lands.[52]

An opportunity to help prospective emigrant tribes find loca-

[51] *Ibid.*, 17, 40–42.
[52] *Ibid.*, 32–36.

tions beyond the Mississippi presented itself unexpectedly. In late 1827, McCoy went to Boston with an ill-defined hope of forming a society to promote his views on Indian colonization. He abandoned this plan when the Board of Missions expressed surprising interest in his proposals and prepared a memorial to Congress favoring them. McCoy took the petition to Washington, where Wilson Lumpkin of Georgia placed it before the House of Representatives. Other members of Congress expressed their support. McCoy chose to believe that they did so "out of humanitarian reasons." He ignored the fact that they came from southern and western states with Indian problems. Some of these same men had come out in opposition to a recommendation by Secretary of War James Barbour (who had succeeded John C. Calhoun in 1825), that Indian removal be on an individual rather than a tribal basis. They would have nothing to do with the proposal unless the Indians they wanted removed from their states were specifically mentioned by tribe.[53]

The pressures to be rid of the Indians in Georgia, Alabama, and Mississippi were particularly acute. The Cherokees with their many schools, mills, and well-kept farms presented a special problem. Although a minority, the civilized Cherokees were highly influential in the tribe. Understandably, they could foresee few advantages in removal. The Chickasaws, Choctaws, and Creeks were more amenable. While McCoy was in Washington, Congress, by a narrow margin, appropriated $15,000 for the exploration of the territory west of the Mississippi by delegations of the three tribes, "with a view to the selection of a future home, should they be satisfied with the country."[54] For the Choctaws at least, the privilege of choice was all but lost, for in 1825 they had surrendered much of their valuable eastern forested lands for

[53] *Register of Debates in Congress*, Vol. II, P. 2, appendix, pp. 40–42.
[54] *Statutes at Large*, IV, 302.

a desolate western tract beyond the Arkansas Territory. McCoy was named a commissioner for the exploring tour. He immediately sought permission to take along representatives from the Potawatomi and Ottawa tribes. Also he asked that he be allowed to undertake a more extensive survey than might be necessary to meet the needs of just the southern tribes.

The arrangements for the exploration were on a very tenuous basis. The Chickasaws, Choctaws, and Creeks could not be compelled to send delegations, and neither the Potawatomis nor the Ottawas had committed themselves in any way. Nevertheless, McCoy, on his return to Carey, made all the necessary preparations for a tour, and persuaded three Potawatomis and three Ottawas to accompany him. Convinced that his future activity would be focused in the West, McCoy began to prepare the Baptist public for his withdrawal from Carey and Thomas. The latter mission had only been in operation for about a year, and until recently he had portrayed the work at both missions in glowing terms. He now informed the readers of the *American Baptist Magazine* that the missionaries were still diligent in their work, "but let it not be supposed that the Puttawatomie, Ottawa, Miamai, or any other tribe of Indians on our frontiers, or on small reservations, is in reality improving as a tribe or nation; on the contrary, we reiterate the cry, 'They are perishing.' "[55]

McCoy received his commission and instructions from the War Department's Bureau of Indian Affairs in June, 1828. Thomas L. McKenney, head of the bureau, informed him that he would be allowed to take three Potawatomis with him. McCoy would act as treasurer for the tour, and although Congress had appropriated $15,000, he was to try to limit the expenses to $10,000. McKenney's letter further directed McCoy to proceed to St. Louis, where he would confer with General William

[55] "Missionary Intelligence," 301–302.

Clark, the superintendent of Indian affairs, and meet with the southern Indian delegations and the other members appointed to the tour. From here the exploring party would go to the "Country west of the Mississippi."[56] In spite of the ambiguity of the term, government officials used it constantly to refer to the regions beyond the boundaries of the state of Missouri and Arkansas Territory, an area without a name and without actual government, except for the Superintendent of Indian Affairs and a few agents who had established themselves with the eastern-most tribes. For McCoy, it was an unknown country, but one which he already thought of as the Promised Land for the American Indian.

[56] McKenney to McCoy, June 10, 1828, McCoy Correspondence.

Chapter VI

Exploring the Land

The great prairies beyond the ninety-fifth meridian, for the most part undisturbed by the white man, were not so unknown as Isaac McCoy imagined. The Spaniards and the French had cast a passing shadow, and the Americans had sent out exploring parties to examine this part of the Louisiana Purchase. The indigenous tribes, the Kansa and the Osage, except for two large reserves, had already surrendered much of their claim to the territory to United States commissioners, but still roamed over it at will. Meanwhile, hunters and traders, many of them French, had become increasingly active. The Chouteaus, a family long connected with the fur trade, operated depots on the Kansas and Verdigris rivers,[1] and in 1821, François Chouteau built a trading post on the banks of the Missouri near the mouth of the Kansas. Several French families encamped nearby, to form the nucleus of the first settlement within the present site of Kansas City, Missouri.[2] While the French concentrated on the fur trade, enterprising Americans in the early 1820's developed the new and immensely profitable Santa Fe trade. Independence, fifteen

[1] George C. Sibley to William Clark, November 15, 1818, Clark Papers (the bulk of which pertains to the Superintendency of Indian Affairs, St. Louis), Vol. II, MSS in the Kansas State Historical Society Library.
[2] "Reminiscenses of Frederick Choteau: From Notes Taken by Franklin S. Adams, at Westport, Mo., April 24, 1880," *Kansas Historical Collections*, Vol. VIII (1903–1904), 423–24.

miles from the "Great Bend" of the Missouri, became the main outfitting point for the first important western trail. Increasing intercourse with the Plains Indians led to the establishment of military posts at Cantonment Gibson, near the "three forks" of the Grand, Verdigris, and Arkansas rivers, in 1824, and Cantonment Leavenworth, on the Missouri, in 1827. Protestant missionaries established missions on the Great Plains about the same time McCoy began his work in the Old Northwest. The American Board of Commissioners for Foreign Missions, supported by Congregationalists and Presbyterians, singled out the Osage Nation for special attention, and, by 1828, had three missions in operation; Union on the Grand River in what is now northeastern Oklahoma; Harmony on the Marais des Cygnes, just inside the Missouri state line; and a small station on the Neosho, the first Christian mission in the present state of Kansas.[3]

Emigrant tribesmen had already moved to McCoy's "Canaan" before his exploratory tour. Thomas Benton of Missouri, a member of the Senate Committee on Indian Affairs, and many of his constituents agreed that the Indians in their state should be the first to be moved to happier hunting grounds. After the Kansa and Osage cessions of 1825, Clark hastened to complete additional agreements with the Missouri Shawnees. According to the terms of a treaty signed in November, 1825, the Shawnees gave up their interests near Cape Girardeau for a twenty-five-mile-wide strip south of the Kansas River. The movement of these first immigrant Indians into present Kansas began late in 1825.[4]

Since almost every literate American believed the legend of a barren wasteland beyond the ninety-fifth meridian, it was under-

---

[3] *Missionary Herald*, Vol. XVIII (February, 1822), 30–31; XIX (July, 1823), 214; W. W. Graves, *The First Protestant Osage Missions, 1820–1837*, 41–45, 87–175, 182–96.

[4] *American State Papers: Indian Affairs*, II, 544.

standable, perhaps, that McCoy thought that he was about to enter a land of "irreclaimable sterility." The Indians who planned to accompany him had their own impressions. According to legends handed down to them, the land far to the West was hot and unhealthy, full of serpents and man-devouring monsters.[5]

McCoy had completed all arrangements for the expedition before he obtained any definite word that it would be undertaken. He left Carey with a party of six Indians two days after he received his commission.[6] Without authorization, he took along three members of the Ottawa tribe. The high purpose and the urgency of this undertaking demanded such liberties.

> We are going to look [for] a home for a homeless people who were once lords of all the Continent of America, and whose just claims have never been acknowledged by others, nor conveyed away by themselves .... We are limited to the regions west of Arkansas Territory, and Missouri State. Should the inhospitableness of that country deny them a place there, they will be left destitute.[7]

The overland trip to St. Louis took fifteen days. At Chicago, McCoy tried to convert the agent, Alexander Wolcott, to the colonization cause, but with little success.[8] Most agents opposed removal, if for no other reason than to safeguard their own positions. Often they allied themselves with the interests of the traders, who fought removal with even greater vigor. To them it meant the loss of the annuities and other stipends and gifts the government distributed to the Indians, but which they usually managed to acquire.

[5] McCoy, *Baptist Missions*, 334.
[6] McCoy to McKenney, July 1, 1828, McCoy Correspondence.
[7] McCoy, Journal, July 6, 1828.
[8] *Ibid.*, July 5, 1828.

When McCoy arrived at St. Louis, he found that Clark had appointed his brother-in-law, Captain George H. Kennerly, leader of the expedition. The southern Indians had not arrived. Clark dispatched a messenger to find the reason for the delay and discovered that the Chickasaws and Choctaws had received no communications from the War Department and knew nothing about the proposed tour. McCoy surmised that their agents had purposely neglected to inform them.[9] An indefinite delay was in prospect.

To use the time to best advantage, McCoy worked out a plan to give his amorphous Indian Canaan more definite shape. He attempted to visualize the problems and expenses involved in establishing an Indian state, and to amuse himself, he drew up elaborate salary schedules for the officers who would be needed. In the first stage, McCoy would have the War Department remove the Indian Country from the jurisdiction of the superintendent in St. Louis and appoint a superintendent, two agents, two subagents, and two physicians, who would proceed immediately to some central location in the territory and prepare for the introduction of civil government. Then, following the territorial pattern, the President would appoint a governor, secretary, district attorney, and two judges. These officers would reside at a central "metropolis," which would become the future capital. They would mark out county lines according to the location of the various tribes, and appoint the county officials, who would be Indian from the start. McCoy believed that Congress should continue to subsidize Indian education and encourage the establishment of Christian missions. Having planned for all possible exigencies, McCoy felt that his scheme was realistic and practical and that the federal government could be persuaded to base its removal policy on the guidelines he had

[9] *Ibid.*, August 17, 1828.

provided. After all, it had taken the first step in ordering the exploring expedition. "What weighty responsibility devolves upon those to whom the charge of this expedition is intrusted!"[10]

More immediately, McCoy faced a less abstract but equally difficult problem. He could not keep his six Indians out of the grog shops. His patience wearing thin, he asked Clark that he be allowed to proceed on the exploring tour with his party. Clark informed McCoy that such a venture would be contrary to his instructions from the Bureau of Indian Affairs,[11] and therefore he could not assume responsibility for it. Since the General did not explicitly veto his proposal, McCoy decided to go on alone. When Clark realized that McCoy was determined to proceed, he suggested that he explore the region to the south of lands recently allotted the Shawnees. Clark warned McCoy not to venture beyond this point for fear that he fall in with Pawnee war parties.[12]

McCoy, his six Indians, and two white packers set out in late August on an expedition that would last fifty days and take them 150 miles west of the Missouri state line. McCoy would not allow the party to travel on Sundays, and on these days he conducted two religious services for his captive audience.

On the first leg of the journey across central Missouri to Harmony Mission, McCoy endeavored to stay away from the settled areas where liquor might be available. The trip to the mission passed without incident except that McCoy had his horse stolen, presumably by a frontiersman and his wife, near whose "solitary and wretched hut" he camped for a night. Game was scarce, although one of the Indians managed to shoot a young

10 McCoy, "Thoughts Respecting the Indian Territory," MS in the Kansas State Historical Society Library.

11 For the War Department's instructions to Clark and his reply see, 20 Cong., 2 sess., *Sen. Doc. 31*, Vol. I.

12 Clark to McCoy, August 20, 1828, McCoy Correspondence.

bear, much to the dismay of the Ottawas in the party. The "bear family" and the Ottawas had always been friendly. Chief Noonday arranged a proper burial for the remains and delivered a funeral oration to placate the spirits of the offended family.[13]

Harmony Mission was a fairly large establishment, and at its peak employed as many as ten missionary couples. By the time of McCoy's arrival most of the missionaries had departed. The few Osages who remained in the vicinity had received orders to leave Missouri and join the main body of the tribe on the Neosho. One missionary, Benton Pixley, had already left to start a mission there.[14]

At Harmony, McCoy hired Noel Mograin, a half-blood Osage, to act as interpreter and guide. When the party was ready to leave, Mograin quixotically decided that he could not go without an Osage friend of his, whom McCoy judged to be between sixty and seventy years old. When McCoy pointed out that he had no extra horses, the old man agreed to walk.

> He had Deerskin Moccasins and leggings, and the usual cloth, but was destitute of shirt. . . . Even hair on his head was scarce. He carried an old gun. . . . His blanket, which was a mere rag, was thrown across his shoulder under his gun. A small bag . . . containing his smoking apparatus, was hitched under the belt of his cloth. Thus this almost naked old man . . . set out on a six week's tour.[15]

McCoy followed the "Miry Desein" [Marais des Cygnes] to the West, through territory the Osages had ceded in 1825. He was pleased with the rolling countryside and noted, to his surprise, that the soil was universally rich. He thought the streams too sluggish, although there was evidence of frequent inunda-

13 McCoy, Journal, August 24 and 29, 1828.
14 *Missionary Herald*, Vol. XXXII (January, 1836), 25.
15 McCoy, Journal, September 3 and 4, 1828.

Isaac McCoy. Courtesy Kansas State Historical Society, Topeka.

Kennekuk, the "Kickapoo Prophet," sketched by Catlin. Courtesy Kansas State Historical Society, Topeka.

"The Prophet" Shawnee, sketched by Catlin. Courtesy Kansas State Historical Society, Topeka.

Little White Bear, a Kanza Indian, sketched by Catlin. Courtesy Kansas State Historical Society, Topeka.

White Plume, Kanza chief. Courtesy Kansas State Historical Society, Topeka.

William Clark. Courtesy National Park Service.

Kansas Reservation

Smoky hill fork

Shaw[anoe]

Plat
of the Shawanoe lands
Westward of the 20 mile from the line of Mo.
Survey made in Sept & Oct 1833.
Under instructions of Genl. Wm Clark Supt Ind. Affs.
Shawanoe Mo.   (signed) Isaac McCoy
Jan. 30. 1833.   Surveyor.
Attest
(signed) Jno. C. McCoy
Ass.t Surveyor.

Note
The foregoing is a corrected plat of returns of the survey herein stated as made by Isaac McCoy
recorded on a scale reduced one half.
Scale on the original map not laid down.

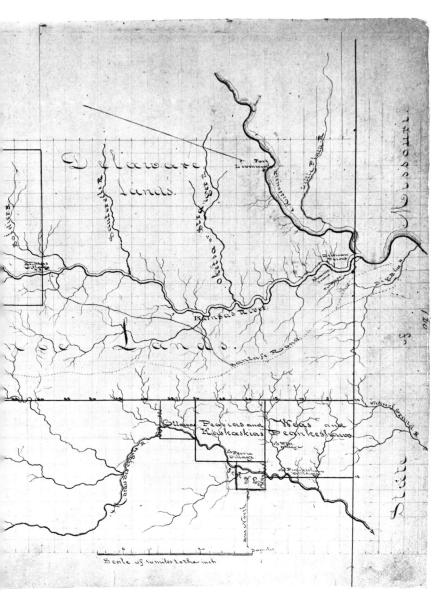

McCoy's plat of the Shawnee lands, 1833.

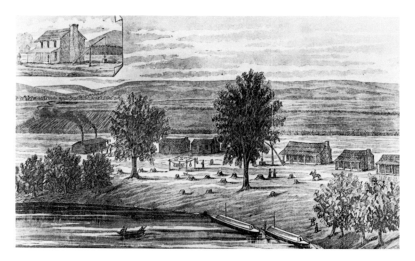

Residence of Daniel Morgan Boone, northwest of Lawrence.
Courtesy Kansas State Historical Society, Topeka.

Shawnee Baptist Mission. From Joseph Tracy (ed.), *History of American Missions to the Heathen*, 1840.

John C. McCoy. Courtesy Kansas State Historical Society, Topeka.

Mrs. Isaac McCoy. Courtesy Kansas State Historical Society, Topeka.

Johnston Lykins. Courtesy Kansas State Historical Society, Topeka.

Jotham Meeker. Courtesy Kansas State Historical Society, Topeka.

Robert Simerwell. Courtesy Kansas State Historical Society, Topeka.

tions. Game such as deer, geese, and elk was plentiful. The vaunted skill of the Indian seemed singularly lacking in McCoy's group, however. The Indians spent considerable time in hunting, but the party seldom had fresh meat. On one occasion the Indians surprised a gang of twenty elk and managed to bag one, but during the night wolves came to the camp and ate a large part of the meat. Mograin's dog lay quietly by the fire, a few feet from the carcass, but was either "too lazy or too liberal" to give the alarm.[16]

While in St. Louis, McCoy thought his Indian companions troublesome and even murderous when intoxicated. Chandonois, a Potawatomi, had buried his tomahawk in the skull of one of McCoy's horses in a drunken rage. Out on the prairies, with the whisky supplies cut off, McCoy found them quite agreeable. McCoy observed that, contrary to the popular image of the Indians as taciturn and phlegmatic, they were loquacious and cheerful. Even after a hard day of riding, they would sit and tell each other humorous anecdotes, which they enjoyed "exquisitely," far into the night. The stories were partly true, partly fictitious, but told with great "art." On the other hand, McCoy considered the two hired white men "poor sticks," and scarcely a day passed out in the wilderness when he did not threaten to discharge them.[17]

The expedition followed the Marais des Cygnes to a point where it crossed the Santa Fe Trail. McCoy had heard of raids on traders by hostile Indians, and with exaggerated care the party covered up its trail. When he reached the upper branches of the Neosho, McCoy was no longer sure of his location. He had already discovered that Mograin was of little use as a guide, and the maps prepared in St. Louis were inadequate. Always eager to

[16] *Ibid.*, September 6 and 13, 1828.
[17] *Ibid.*, September 11, 1828.

prove that the Indian had no great inherited ability for life in the wilds, McCoy now felt that he could dispose of another shibboleth. The Indians he knew possessed no uncanny skill to steer a course through the trackless wilderness. The party returned to the Santa Fe Trail and, after crossing and recrossing it, found a creek which flowed north. This led them to the Kansas River and the Kansa Indian country. They sighted three Indian villages and stopped to visit one. Here in a large bark lodge, amid a "scene of crowding, of men women & children, talking, scolding, crying of children, a few good mothers singing to quiet them, dogs fighting & the conquered begging aloud for quarters," McCoy and his group smoked with the "naked Kansaus" and engaged in small talk.[18]

McCoy intended to cross the Kansas River and return to Missouri on the north side, but found that the Kansa Indians owned no canoes or river boats. Rather than take time to build rafts, the party continued eastward along the divide between the Kansas and the Marais des Cygnes to the Shawnee Reservation. Here he met a number of Ohio Shawnees who had arrived the previous spring to join the Missouri Shawnees who had come earlier. One of the recent immigrants was Tenskwatawa, the Shawnee "Prophet." He called on McCoy's visiting delegation.[19]

Outwardly, the Ohio Shawnees seemed content, and McCoy was willing to accept this impression as proof of the merit of his colonization plans. Either the tribesmen did not tell him, or he chose to ignore, the story of mismanagement and suffering they had experienced in getting to the western reservation. The tribe had not yet given up its Wapakoneta and Lewiston reserves in Ohio, but, desiring to escape the pressure of white population and to heed the urgings of the War Department and John

18 *Ibid.*, September 10, 15, 16, 17, and 18, 1828.
19 *Ibid.*, September 22, 24, and 26, 1828.

Johnston, their agent, a large group, estimated at about 500, departed for the West in 1826. Many of Johnston's promises failed to materialize, and the Shawnees had only reached Kaskaskia, Illinois, when winter set in. Starved and destitute, they subsisted on emergency rations provided by Pierre Menard, the subagent for Indian affairs at Kaskaskia.[20] The following winter they were camped on the Osage River in central Missouri, living in whatever shelter they could find. In the spring of 1828, some 250 of the original company finally reached the reservation granted to the Missouri Shawnees in 1825.[21] The whole affair illustrated a haphazard and careless removal policy, one which set a pattern for the coming years. The Department of War permitted commissioners to make extravagant promises, but it was unable or unwilling to back them up.

McCoy spent many hours working on plans for his Indian Canaan, but he never dwelled long on the problems of removal or the upheaval naturally involved in resettlement. The important thing was that the Indians get a country of their own; and the territory that he had examined, 80 miles in length and 150 miles from east to west, was much better suited than he had expected. Here was a good place to begin. The region contained more wood and water than reported, and by "judicious arrangement" could support a large population. Each Indian family, he calculated, should be allowed about fifty acres of woodland, and as much prairie as it could use. Like the Hebrew patriarchs of old after they had viewed the "Promised Land," McCoy, before he crossed the border into Missouri, pronounced his benediction on the country he had just seen.

And now, O thou father of the fatherless & friend of the

[20] Menard to Clark, October 8, 1830, Clark Papers.
[21] Louise Barry (ed.), "William Clark's Diary," *Kansas Historical Quarterly*, Vol. XVI (Spring, 1948), 32–33.

poor. Grant that in these deserts, where, with a few, I have
been allowed the privilege of bowing the knee, and lisping a
song, prayers & praises may arise from the thousands of a
people *Saved by Thee!*[22]

McCoy was anxious to elicit a favorable response from the
Indians in his party, but they were much less effusive in their
praise of the new land. They lamented the scarcity of wood and
the total absence of sugar trees. Chandonois perceptively questioned why the Indians would not also be driven from this region
by an influx of white population.[23]

When McCoy returned to St. Louis, he learned that the southern Indian delegations had recently arrived. He now prepared to
make the excursion the War Department intended. He sent the
Potawatomi and Ottawa tribesmen back to Michigan, escorting
them past the temptations of St. Louis, which apparently was not
far enough, for Robert Simerwell reported that the three Potawatomis returned with nothing but the shirts on their backs.
They had traded everything else, including the horses that McCoy had provided, for liquor.[24]

The second expedition started in late October. It included,
besides McCoy and Kennerly, two topographers, one surgeon,
twelve Chickasaws, six Choctaws, three Creeks, the subagents of
the tribes, interpreters, hired hands, and slaves—a company of
forty-two in all.[25] The Indians had reluctantly consented to participate in the tour, and their agents had to be bribed before they
would co-operate. McCoy acted as treasurer for the expedition,
and the subagent for the Chickasaws presented a letter in the

22 McCoy, Journal, September 24, 1828.
23 *Ibid.*, October 7, 1828, including a "Copy of my Report to Genl. Clark,
St. Louis, Mo., Oct. 7, 1828."
24 Robert Simerwell, Journal, October 26, 1828.
25 Clark to McCoy, "Letter of Instructions," October 17, 1825, McCoy
Correspondence.

name of his delegation demanding $1,000. McCoy knew it to be a fraud, but to his chagrin, General Clark told him to pay it.[26] There were other problems. Before the company was halfway through Missouri, the Choctaws decided to break off and go down to Arkansas to visit kinsmen who had just migrated there. They stayed with the tour only after Kennerly promised that it would be considerably shortened. McCoy did what he could to win the confidence of the Indians, and Levi Colbert, the chief of the Chickasaws, usually rode with him in his dearborn. Throughout the trip the Indians, despite McCoy's constant prodding, refused to comment on the country they had come to inspect, and they would not discuss removal.[27]

The Department of War had instructed Kennerly and Mc-Coy to explore certain regions north of Missouri, as well as those to the west, but they gave up all thought of this because of the lateness of the season and the promises to the Choctaws. They headed directly toward Cantonment Leavenworth. Major John Dougherty, Indian agent for the Upper Missouri temporarily residing at the cantonment, warned that a fifteen-hundred-man Pawnee war party was active along the Santa Fe Trail. Survivors from several trading companies had straggled back to the Missouri settlements on foot. From Leavenworth the Kennerly-McCoy expedition headed southwest toward the Osage villages on the Neosho which were only about fifty miles west of the Missouri boundary. There was little danger here of falling in with the Pawnees. McCoy had traversed some of this region in his first tour when the high, rolling prairies were "clothed with grass of Autumnal gray, spotted, and streaked with woodlands in cheerful green, describing the course of every stream." But the winter scene was hardly one to impress the visiting delega-

[26] McCoy, Journal, October 14 and 15, 1828.
[27] *Ibid.*, November 2, 1828.

tions of southern Indians. The grass on the prairies was burnt or burning. The atmosphere was smoky and the visibility limited, and the whole situation was aggravated by winds which blew incessantly. McCoy attempted to convince the Indians that the land should not be judged by superficial appearances, and periodically he scooped up some earth to show them that it was rich and fertile. They were not impressed. McCoy observed, "Liability to mistake in this respect becomes the greater where one whose possessions have been found in a timbered country, is required to judge of what may be termed a prairie country."[28]

The exploring party camped near the village of White Hair, principal chief of the Osages, for a few days, and this rest period afforded an opportunity for the southern Indians and the Osages to reciprocate expressions of friendship. Early in the 1820's, Choctaw and other southern immigrants in western Arkansas frequently intruded on Osage hunting grounds, and this intrusion resulted in a number of bloody skirmishes. With the establishment of a military installation at Cantonment Gibson, the situation quieted down. McCoy and Kennerly hoped that the meeting of the southern delegations and the Osages would help smooth over old animosities and encourage better relations in the future.[29] The Osage chiefs invited the visiting company to a council. An Osage crier announced the arrival of each participant, and this formality so amused the Chickasaws, Choctaws, and Creeks that they gave their names over and over again for the sake of hearing them bawled aloud. Ceremonies of smoking and speech-making ensued. McCoy observed that the Osages were great orators, and that in comparison, the civilized Indians appeared awkward. At the conclusion of the council, the Osages

[28] McCoy to Porter, January 29, 1829, McCoy Correspondence.
[29] Kennerly to Porter, February 4, 1829, 20 Cong., 2 sess., *House Report 87*, 24–48.

presented a Pawnee scalp to the southern chiefs, signifying that if they became neighbors, they would also be allied in war against the Pawnees, traditional and mortal enemies of the Osages, a rather unwelcome implication for the visitors.[30]

The stay in the Osage villages gave McCoy an opportunity to comment on the customs, manners, and general appearance of the tribe. He watched the women prepare buffalo meat, taking it off in thin, unbroken fleeces and rolling it like a blanket to dry. When dried hard, it was one-quarter of an inch thick. McCoy found that he had to employ considerable "industry" to eat it. Sometimes the women cooked this meat with rancid tallow. "To the olfactories of a novice in buffalo eating, it is far from pleasant." As usual, McCoy made notes on burial habits. The Osages, he discovered, deposited their dead in shallow holes, over which they heaped stones. They planted a pole nearby, on which to suspend the scalps of the enemy. Thus the spirit of the dead foe became a slave to the deceased Osage, "the best service that can be performed for a deceased relative."[31] The Osages did not limit slavery to the afterlife. They used Pawnee prisoners in this capacity and kept them in a state of utter degradation. The Osages, McCoy observed, had developed a popular reputation as an "uncommonly fierce, courageous, warlike nation." This image was perpetuated by such writers as Washington Irving, who described the Osages as "stately fellows, stern and simple in garb and aspect . . . fine Roman countenances . . . the finest looking Indians I have ever seen in the West."[32] Another contemporary referred to them as the "tallest and best proportioned

---

[30] McCoy to Lykins, November 18, 1828, McCoy Correspondence; McCoy, *Baptist Missions*, 354–58.

[31] McCoy, *Baptist Missions*, 359–60.

[32] Washington Irving, *A Tour on the Prairies* (ed. by John Francis McDermott), 21.

Indians in America, few being less than six feet."[33] Stories about happy, virtuous people in the state of nature failed to impress McCoy. To him the Osages were "barefooted, bareheaded, naked, miserable," and no taller or shorter than any other tribesmen. He had never seen Indians so obedient to their chiefs, so subservient to traders, and so easily managed by Indian agents.[34]

While in the Osage country, McCoy visited the Neosho mission of the American Board, and found the lone missionary, Benton Pixley, involved in a bitter dispute with the Osage agent, Major John F. Hamtramck. Pixley, in letters to the War Department, had dared to criticize the agent for not residing with the Indians to whom he was appointed. Hamtramck lived in St. Louis and visited the Osages infrequently.[35] McCoy did not know that this was the cause of the misunderstanding, but noted that the agent had persuaded the Osage chiefs to sign a petition to the War Department asking for the missionary's release. Charles van Quickenborne, a Jesuit priest, had visited the Osages on the Neosho in 1827 intending to establish a Roman Catholic mission, but found so many obstacles that he postponed the plan indefinitely. Of Hamtramck and the subagents he wrote, "Once offended, they have it in their power to make the situation of the missionary so cruel that he could not stand it. The Protestant missionary [Pixley] who lives at the Indian village gets nearly every week a good flogging."[36] The mission closed shortly after McCoy's visit.

[33] Quoted by Phil E. Chappell in "A History of the Missouri River," *Kansas Historical Collections*, Vol. IX (1905–1906), 246. Many of the romantic notions about the Osages are perpetuated in the most recent history of this tribe, John Joseph Mathews, *The Osages*.

[34] McCoy, *Baptist Missions*, 346, 358–60.

[35] *Report of the American Board of Commissioners for Foreign Missions for 1829*, 79–80.

[36] Quoted in Garraghan, *Jesuits*, I, 192.

From the Osage villages, the exploring expedition made its way to Cantonment Gibson. Fifteen hundred Creeks, known as the McIntosh faction, were encamped nearby. A struggle had developed among the Georgia Creeks when Chief William McIntosh signed a dubious document at Indian Springs in 1825 which ceded all Creek lands in the state in exchange for an "equivalent" tract in the West. The treaty was so objectionable to the majority of Creeks that they executed McIntosh. The national government renegotiated the treaty the following year. Somewhat embarrassed by the inconvenience this caused the former friends and supporters of McIntosh, federal commissioners arranged their early removal. The delegation accompanying Kennerly and McCoy were anti-McIntosh Creeks. Kennerly and McCoy expected the worst, but fortunately old animosities were forgotten in the new environment, and no unpleasant incidents occurred. They hoped that their visit marked the beginning of friendlier relations, for the future peace seemed threatened if the whole tribe would be forced to live on one western reserve.[37]

The exploration terminated just inside the Choctaw Reservation, south of the Canadian River. The party disbanded, and the Indian delegations made their way back to their homes in the southern states, while the others returned directly to St. Louis. According to McCoy's calculations the tour cost the government $22,000,[38] a heavy expenditure for what little was accomplished. Ostensibly, the purpose of the exploration was to afford the Choctaws and the Creeks an opportunity to inspect their western territories and to locate a reservation for the Chickasaws, who as yet owned no lands beyond the Mississippi. These

[37] Kennerly to Porter, February 4, 1829, 20 Cong., 2 sess., *House Report 87*, 24–28.

[38] McCoy, *Baptist Missions*, 350.

objectives could hardly be achieved within fifty miles of the borders of Missouri and Arkansas Territory.

Kennerly's brief report to the Secretary of War reflected the sparse achievements.[39] The topographers submitted their notes, but they contained little information that was not already known.[40] Realizing that these men would say little about the suitability of the country for an Indian state, McCoy prepared a statement in which he commented and offered recommendations on every conceivable aspect of Indian removal and reform. To make sure that his report got out of the Bureau of Indian Affairs, McCoy asked Congressman William McLean, chairman of the Committee on Indian Affairs in the House of Representatives, to make a call for the document.

Although McCoy's two explorations had not ventured very far into what he already called the Indian Country, he had clearly in mind what the extent of its boundaries should be. Congress had discussed general removal since 1825, but the most that anyone had suggested was that the Indians should be located far enough west of the Mississippi that they would never be disturbed again. McCoy now recommended a specific area. In his report with accompanying maps, he maintained that the permanent Indian territory should be bounded by the Red River in the south, the Puncah River on the north, the Rocky Mountains to the west, and the State of Missouri and Arkansas Territory on the east. McCoy estimated the distance from north to south at about six hundred miles and thought that an average of two hundred miles from east to west would be inhabitable. He recognized that this area no longer seemed so spacious as he once thought, for almost half of the region had already been assigned

[39] Kennerly to Porter, February 4, 1829, 20 Cong., 2 sess., *House Report 87*, 24–48.
[40] Washington Hood and John Bell to Porter, January 13, 1829, *ibid.*

and the work of removal was scarcely begun. But, by careful distribution, there would be room for all. He believed grants made to the Choctaws and the Cherokees were much too large and recommended that some of this land be bought back. The Western Cherokees had received seven million acres below the Arkansas in 1828. What was even more disturbing was that they had been given a permanent outlet to the buffalo country to the west. This would encourage roaming habits and detract from the over-all goal of an organized agricultural life.[41]

Besides defining the boundaries of his proposed Indian Country, McCoy, in his report to the War Department, recommended that the whole region beyond the ninety-fifth meridian be taken out of the hands of the Superintendent of Indian Affairs at St. Louis and that civil government be introduced as quickly as possible. Suggestions such as these were not ones likely to excite the Secretary of War, but for McCoy all the pieces had to fit. He went on to remind the Secretary that the future of the Indian Country depended on peaceful relations between immigrant and indigenous tribes. On his tours, he had found the Shawnees huddled in villages on the Missouri border because they feared the Pawnees and Comanches farther west. McCoy now proposed the erection of trading posts in the interior to divert the attention of these tribes to trapping in the mountains. These posts in turn should relieve the trading caravans on the Santa Fe Trail, along which the Pawnees and Comanches had discovered excellent opportunities for thievery.[42]

Never given to half-measures, McCoy decided not to return to Carey after the completion of the explorations, but to go directly to Washington to make his reports and to lobby for an

[41] McCoy to Porter, January 29, 1829, McCoy Correspondence; also printed in 20 Cong., 2 sess., *House Report 87*.
[42] *Ibid.*

Indian Country until such time when he and his family could move to the West. The letters that he received from the mission during his tour seemed further to justify this decision.[43]

When McCoy left Carey, he placed Johnston Lykins, loyal follower and now his son-in-law, in charge. One of Lykins' first assignments was to complete arrangements for treaty negotiations to be held at the mission between the Potawatomis and two United States commissioners, Lewis Cass and Pierre Menard. In September, 1828, the tribe gave up all of its land between the St. Joseph River and the Indiana boundary except for Notawatsepe's reserve, about ten miles square, and a seven-mile-square tract which encompassed Carey and Topenebee's and Pokegan's villages. The treaty said nothing about Indian removal, although it did specify that the government would reimburse the Carey missionaries for the value of the buildings and improvements if they decided to move. Some of the treaty provisions in fact suggested that the St. Joseph Potawatomis might remain on the two small reservations indefinitely. They received $7,500 for clearing and fencing the land and a $1,000 annuity for education.[44] Lykins described the treaty as one made with traders, not Indians. They gathered like locusts to present their claims. The "wretched" Indians stood around wanting help, but the commissioners, instead of listening to their entreaties, "admitted the unjust claims of traders and other vagabonds to the amount of almost Eleven Thousand Dollars!!!" Lykins observed that this amount might well go higher because parts of the document which the Indians signed were blank, particularly those places where the amounts to be paid to the traders should have appeared.[45] Simerwell, also a witness of the negotiations, wondered

[43] McCoy, Journal, October 1, 1828.
[44] *Statutes at Large*, VII, 117.
[45] Johnston Lykins, Journal, February 26, 1829.

why payments to the Indians were made in silver currency, when it could so conveniently be exchanged for liquor.[46] As well as annuities and other provisions, the treaty stipulated that the Potawatomis receive immediately gifts worth $30,000. Simerwell witnessed one transaction where an Indian traded fifty shirts for two quarts of whisky.[47]

When Mrs. McCoy heard of her husband's decision not to return to Carey, she immediately packed up her family and moved to Lexington, Kentucky. Lykins accompanied her. This left Simerwell, the "blacksmith," solely in charge. Slater and Meeker were at Thomas, but McCoy had administered and financed that mission from Carey. Two missions and two boarding schools, with farms and blacksmith shops, were still in operation, with heavy financial obligations. Added to this plight, Detroit merchants pressed for payment of past debts. Overwhelmed, Simerwell wrote a plaintive letter to the Board of Commissioners. "I should say the missionaries at Carey had sufficient to do at home if they will attend to it. . . . Why should we grasp at more than is our portion."[48]

Neither McCoy nor Lykins informed the board of their departure from Carey. McCoy later wrote:

> We did not believe, that they [Board members] would grant us permission at that time, to go west, and we therefore did not ask for it; for it would have been more painful to go *contrary* to direct orders, than to go *without* orders.[49]

When Lucius Bolles, through Simerwell's letter, heard that the two missionaries had abandoned Carey, he severely reprimanded

[46] Simerwell to J. H. Kennard, November 21, 1829, Simerwell Correspondence.
[47] Simerwell to D. Clark, February 28, 1829, *ibid.*
[48] Simerwell to Bolles, December 16, 1828, *ibid.*
[49] McCoy, *Baptist Missions*, 371.

Lykins, but said nothing to McCoy. Mrs. McCoy, in the absence of her husband, took it upon herself to defend her son-in-law. In the end she blamed Simerwell, already the most injured of all parties. Mrs. McCoy, in one of her infrequent letters, sent a curt, ungrammatical note to Simerwell, part of which read:

> I was astonish to day at receiving a letter from Dr. Bolles to Mr. Lykins in which he says he was told by you that there was a debt at Detroit which ought to be payed and intimated we had gone and take all the money. a few days ago we got a letter from you abusing us for no send you glass sheet iron a part of which was your business to have got at detroit . . . we left the extbleshment in good repair and money coming to support it & cannot feel gilty.[50]

The departure of McCoy and Lykins gave Bolles an ideal opportunity to take control of Carey and Thomas. He did not think the conditions so hopeless as McCoy had portrayed and firmly believed that both should be kept in operation. He separated the two missions and appointed Simerwell superintendent of Carey, and Slater and Meeker joint superintendents of Thomas.[51] Bolles then attempted to administer the stations through letters. He issued lengthy directives which indicated that the corresponding secretary, sitting in his Boston office, still did not understand how the missions operated. The missionaries could not possibly fulfill all that Bolles directed them to do.

Meanwhile, it never occurred to McCoy that he had abandoned the Michigan missions. He heard about Bolles's actions when he arrived in Washington and thought them incredible. By commission of the federal government, Lykins had charge of the United States property at Thomas, and he held a similar com-

[50] Mrs. Christiana McCoy to Simerwell, January 28, 1829, Simerwell Correspondence.
[51] Bolles to Simerwell, January 15, 1829, *ibid.*

mission for Carey, with the general superintendency of both. "The Board with no less precipitancy set about now modelling affairs of which they knew little more than they did of the geography of the moon."[52]

Simerwell, caught between the board's determination to carry on the work in Michigan and his loyalty to McCoy, who wanted to sell the buildings out from under him as soon as possible, carried on as best he could. He tried to keep up an extensive correspondence with all the people who had become interested in Carey and Thomas, discreetly explaining McCoy's absence. Women's and junior missionary societies from different parts of the nation kept sending boxes of clothing of little value and small donations. These gifts had to be acknowledged. Simerwell even attempted the role of peacemaker between McCoy and the board. McCoy did not appreciate this effort. "You mention in your letter the want of harmony between the Board and myself, as though I might be equally blameable with the Board. . . . I do not admit that I am blameable at all."[53] On Sundays, Simerwell preached to the Indians; and on weekdays he taught at the mission school, where he at times had difficulty keeping the interest of the students. For diversion they invented a game where two grabbed each other by the "windpipe" and squeezed until one dropped. "James had become most expert in this art and choked R. C. till the blood sprang from his nose and then commenced his skill on Kewatnance."[54]

Compressed into their small reservations and increasingly surrounded by white settlers, the St. Joseph Potawatomis deteriorated rapidly. The first large wave of pioneers came to the valley in 1829, and platted the town of Niles, a few miles from Carey.[55]

---

52 McCoy, Journal, March 8, 1829.
53 McCoy to Simerwell, May 13, 1830, Simerwell Correspondence.
54 Simerwell to Lykins, November 8, 1829, *ibid.*
55 Simerwell to Bolles, December 29, 1829, *ibid.*

Although they had deprived the Indians of almost all their lands, the whites nevertheless now resented the presence of the few who remained and called them intruders. They ridiculed the missionaries who tried to do something for the natives. A newspaper in nearby Wayne County, Indiana, derided the "Holy managers" and the "Blacksmith superintendent," who received iron from the United States government to repair Indian guns.[56]

To McCoy, Simerwell's vivid description of the demoralizing conditions at Carey merely proved the wisdom of his policy. Simerwell had the uneasy feeling that the Michigan missionaries should redouble their efforts where they were, but in every letter McCoy urged them to devote their efforts to the promotion of removal. Petitions from the Potawatomis and the Ottawas requesting reservations in the West, he intimated, would greatly bolster his cause in Washington.

[56] Simerwell to R. W. Cheeseman, May 14, 1829, *ibid.*

Chapter VII

Politics of Removal

Isaac McCoy was in Washington during the transitional days between the Adams and Jackson administrations. McCoy counted himself on the Adams side of the "political effervescence,"[1] until Peter B. Porter presented his last annual Department of War report. The outgoing Secretary of War clearly recognized the inconsistency of previous federal policy and advised withdrawing all national support from Indian civilization projects because it defeated the goal of removal.[2] McCoy interpreted the report as a sweeping indictment of all missionary activity, even though it was frankly pro-removal.

For more than a decade the President had decided that the annual appropriations for the civilization of the Indians should be "applied in cooperation with the exertions of benevolent associations." With the exception of Senator Richard M. Johnson's private organization, which bestowed its benevolence on Johnson, these associations were religious in character. More lucrative than the appropriations from the civilization fund was the portion of Indian annuities which the government paid to the societies for education purposes as provided in a number of treaties after 1820. Of the several denominational organizations, the American Board of Commissioners for Foreign Missions,

[1] Isaac McCoy, Journal, March 8, 1829.
[2] *Register of Debates in Congress*, V, Appendix, 7–10.

now primarily Congregationalist, received the largest appropriations from either source.[3] As co-sponsors with the government of Indian missions the societies actually had much in common. One goal they all professed was the preservation of the Indians. Early-nineteenth-century Americans who claimed some concern for the Indians could not conceive a *laissez faire* attitude. They started with the basic premise that the Indians faced extinction if left to their own devices. In Washington, McCoy met frequently with Jeremiah Evarts, corresponding secretary of the American Board. They agreed on many things about missions in general, but vigorously disagreed on how best to "preserve" the Indians.[4]

The American Board concentrated its work in the South, and by 1829 was operating twenty-one of the twenty-eight mission schools in that region. For various reasons, some segments of the southern tribes showed a ready adaptability to white civilization. Many of the missionaries of the American Board were optimistic about the ability of the Indians to become civilized and absorbed into American life. On the other hand, McCoy's experiences with the Indians of the Old Northwest completely colored his outlook. He did not believe that the red man could be civilized within the confines of white habitation. There were only two alternatives, "remove or perish." McCoy realized that the topic of removal had been widely debated in the past. The problem, he wrote, was as old as discovery, for the white man had always moved the Indian at will and would continue to do so in the future, unless the red man received a territory permanently safeguarded for him. McCoy objected to the constant harping on

[3] For a table of government appropriations for missions, see George Dewey Harmon, *Sixty Years of Indian Affairs: Political, Economic, and Diplomatic, 1789–1850*, 354–60.

[4] McCoy, Journal, March 31, 1829.

removal itself, for he believed that it should be discussed only in connection with the purpose of finding the Indian a "permanent home." He believed that he alone had this concern. "I feel myself acting not only for myself & my immediate associates, but also for missionaries of other denominations. I feel a great weight of responsibility to them, to the Indians, and to my God."[5]

Before the tribesmen could be provided with "a home" they had to be removed, and to this extent McCoy acknowledged that his objectives coincided with those of some political leaders. But most members of government agencies and congressional committees on Indian affairs, he observed, "content themselves usually in cold Speculations, and attend to the duties of their office in relation to the Indians merely as politicians." This situation did not preclude people with religious and benevolent motives from concerning themselves with politics nor that friendships with politicians should be used to good advantage. "Many suppose that preachers should not meddle in such things. . . . But we must either look on and see the Indian perish, or else we must take an active part in matters approximating a political character." McCoy firmly believed in "building fires" under politicians and observed, "When members of Congress discover that matters relating to the Indians become a popular theme, then, and not till then will many of them bestow attention to it."[6]

To "stimulate the voices" of the people and to rouse Congress into action, McCoy mounted his own publicity campaign. He had his report to the Secretary of War printed and distributed in every direction, and he also circulated a communication from "a few Ottawas" and "some Putawatomis" indicating their desire to emigrate. Lykins had gone back to Carey and Thomas to or-

[5] *Ibid.*, March 8, 1829.
[6] *Ibid.*, February 27, 1829.

ganize an emigration movement among the natives, but for the most part, they had firmly rebuffed his efforts.[7] Duff Green, editor of the *United States Telegraph*, became interested in Mc-Coy's colonization plans, and published six articles written by McCoy under the pseudonym of "Candon." Finally, McCoy revised his pamphlet, "Remarks on the Practicability of Indian Reform, Embracing Their Colonization," and in a private interview, got President Jackson to endorse it.[8]

McCoy faced more immediate and mundane problems in Washington. He could not get his accounts for the recent explorations in the West settled with the War Department. While waiting, he attended the sixth triennial Baptist General Convention. The General Convention of the Baptist Denomination in the United States for Foreign Missions, and Other Important Objects Relating to the Redeemer's Kingdom had reduced its name to a more manageable title. According to McCoy, the delegates discussed many topics, including "the stale and sickening subject of Columbian College," but said little about the American Indians. Some of the leading men of the Convention, including the editor of the *Columbian Star*, in private conversations frankly admitted to McCoy that there were so many problems connected with Indian missions that they believed a resolution should be introduced in the Convention to the effect "that their [the Indians'] reformation was impracticable." For the first time, McCoy felt an undercurrent of criticism toward Baptist missions which accepted government subsidies. He still had some influence in the Convention, however, for it passed a resolution to permit him to work in the West, thus softening the sting of the board's rebuke for leaving Carey. The Convention

---

[7] Johnston Lykins, Journal, January 28, 1829.
[8] McCoy, Journal, March 31 and May 11, 1829.

also dutifully prepared another petition to the President of the United States in favor of McCoy's colonization plan.[9]

The staff of the Bureau of Indian Affairs in the War Department consisted of Thomas L. McKenney and three clerks, but McCoy found bureaucracy already deeply entrenched. It took the agency four months to settle his accounts. According to McCoy's calculations the War Department had not spent all of its original appropriation, and so he asked that it sponsor another tour to enable him to lay before the next Congress a more accurate description of the Indian Country. The proposal was ignored.[10]

Upon completion of his Washington affairs, McCoy made a quick trip to Carey to stir up enthusiasm for removal. He asked the Potawatomi chiefs to call a council. An ingenious trader, anxious to frustrate McCoy's designs, sent over a gift of several barrels of cider, which McCoy innocently accepted and distributed. The beverage was heavily laced with whisky. McCoy had great difficulty in getting the attention of his hearers.[11]

The brief visit to Carey forcibly revealed to McCoy that he had left Simerwell in a very unenviable position. That Simerwell survived all of the difficulties and still had a school in operation qualified him, in McCoy's estimation, as one of the few who could properly be judged a missionary. The other missionaries, McCoy claimed, could hardly manage three or four of their own children. Furthermore, they felt "preaching" their only appropriate business. But the Simerwells, with a large family of their own, could take the trouble of feeding, clothing, lodging, and teaching, thirty-seven Indian children. At Thomas, where

[9] *Ibid.*, May 5 and 10, 1829.
[10] *Ibid.*, March 31 and April 3, 1829.
[11] Robert Simerwell, Journal, June 30, 1829.

Slater was now the sole superintendent, McCoy found little to commend. He felt that the mission had come to a complete standstill.[12]

Both McCoy and Lykins still held their government appointments as teachers for Carey and Thomas. Although it would mean the end of their salaries, McCoy hoped to get the missions closed as soon as possible. Peter B. Porter had regarded missions as a major obstruction to removal. The new Secretary of War, John Eaton, agreed, but he adopted the expedient of offering missions the prospect of liberal remuneration if they would close and move to the West. Before he left Washington, McCoy, at the Secretary's request, had named a commissioner to make an evaluation of the property at Carey and Thomas. Four years later, Simerwell was still at Carey waiting for it to be sold. Slater, through persistent effort and despite McCoy's protestations to Cass, managed to get the appointment of teacher to the Ottawas, and he stayed another twenty years. McCoy, however, after his short visit, never again returned to his Michigan missions.

In June, 1829, McCoy moved his family to Fayette, Missouri, an outpost on the Missouri frontier. His two eldest sons, Rice and Josephus, who had just graduated with medical degrees from Transylvania University in Lexington, Kentucky, accompanied the family and set up practices in Fayette.[13] Their father, with whom the establishment of an Indian Country took precedence over everything else, frequently conscripted them for surveying duties.

In the fall of 1829, McCoy and Josephus arrived at the Kansa Agency, about fifty miles down the Kansas River Valley, to undertake an exploration at McCoy's own expense. General Marston G. Clark, the first resident subagent, had arrived in the

[12] McCoy, *Baptist Missions*, 387–91.
[13] *Western Monitor* (Fayette, Missouri), January 16, 1830.

Kansa country in the spring of that year, although prior to that time Daniel Morgan Boone, son of the famous pathfinder, had come to live with the tribe as a government-appointed "agriculturist."[14] Clark and White Plume, the principal chief, joined McCoy on his tour. McCoy made no comment about the specific purpose or the direction of the exploration, but, clearly, he wanted to find a suitable reservation for the Potawatomis and the Ottawas. Immediately upon his return to Fayette, he dispatched Josephus to Michigan Territory to arrange for a delegation from these tribes to go to Washington to urge the government to assist in their removal to the West.[15] McCoy returned to Washington in November, 1829, for a seven-month stay. During this time he witnessed and participated in a historic debate on Indian removal.

Not many months of the new administration had passed before Andrew Jackson made it clear that he intended to take a forceful stand on Indian policy. The Georgia legislature had passed resolutions that all state laws applied to Indians and that a red man could not be a witness or a party in a legal suit where a white man was involved. In personal addresses to the Cherokees and the Creeks, Jackson and his Secretary of War, John Eaton, told the tribes that the federal government would not interfere with the authority of a state within its own limits.[16] They disavowed coercive measures, but the alternatives were not inviting. The Indians could choose between submission to state laws or emigration. In the southern region, state action was tantamount to forced removal. The Secretary of War used the threat of state control of Indian affairs as an effective instrument to urge the tribesmen to emigrate to a territory in which the federal gov-

14 William Clark Papers, Vol. XXIX, 4, 31.
15 McCoy, *Baptist Missions*, 393–95.
16 *Niles' Weekly Register*, Vol. XXXVI (June 13, 1829), 257; Annie H. Abel, *The History of Events Resulting in Indian Consolidation West of the Mississippi*, 370–71.

ernment would have authority to protect them. To Jeremiah Evarts, the policy of Jackson and Eaton amounted to an unconstitutional renunciation by the federal government of its duty to protect the Indians. He believed it made a mockery of rights guaranteed to the tribes by treaty. Evarts began a vigorous campaign to defend the right of the Indians to stay unmolested on their lands.[17]

When the Twenty-first Congress met in December, 1829, it received its first annual message from Andrew Jackson, which advised Indian emigration mainly to protect state rights.[18] In keeping with the President's recommendations, both the Senate and House committees on Indian affairs reported bills for removal and exchange of lands. The two bills aroused factional and sectional feeling, for in spite of Jackson's assurances that force would not be used, removal under Georgians could mean nothing more or less than compulsory. Meanwhile, Jeremiah Evart's crusade gained momentum, particularly in the Northeast, a region already alive with religious and humanitarian ferment. There the reformers placed the demand for recognition of Indian rights alongside such causes as temperance and the abolition of Negro slavery. Religious and benevolent societies, colleges and communities, presented innumerable petitions to Congress praying for the protection of the Indians. One western newspaper with ill-concealed sarcasm reported, "Indeed there has not been so much zeal in favor of the dear Indians since the days of those philanthropists Arbuthnot and Ambrister."[19]

At the nation's capital, the ubiquitous corresponding secretary of the American Board urged McCoy to join him in the move-

[17] J. Orin Oliphant (ed.), *Through the South and West with Jeremiah Evarts, in 1826,* 50–53.

[18] James D. Richardson (ed.), *Messages and Papers of the Presidents,* II, 456–59.

[19] *St. Louis Beacon* (May 27, 1830).

ment "to save the Indians." McCoy would admit that in the past easterners such as Evarts had contributed much more to the missionary and benevolent movement than westerners or southerners, but on the matter of Indian reform they "deserved more credit for the piety of their hearts than the information of their heads." He maintained that although it might be cruel to uproot the Indians from their ancestral homes, it was better than allowing them to remain and then be driven out at the point of a gun. The trust of the native could never be regained as long as he remained in a region where he would constantly be subjected to new instances of insincerity.[20]

The thousands of petitions that flooded Congress did not accurately portray the position of organized religion in the United States. The Baptists presented the only counter-petitions to come from a church body, but Baptists were far from unanimous in their support of the administration's Indian policy. McCoy was particularly unhappy with the memorial the board prepared, which merely asked the government to "undertake" for the Indians in the event of removal. McCoy suspected that the members of the Baptist Board, residing in or near Boston as they did, "drank deeply of the spirit of opposition evidenced by the American Board, also in Boston."[21] To counteract this influence, McCoy wrote to friends in diverse places requesting them to solicit signatures for petitions favorable to the removal bills. Thus Evarts and McCoy appeared before the American religious public as leaders of opposing views.

If the Baptists did not solidly favor removal, it was also true that other denominations did not unitedly oppose it. An association of clergymen organized "The Indian Board, for the Emigration, Preservation, and Improvement of the Aborigines of

[20] McCoy, *Baptist Missions*, 380, 397–99.
[21] *Ibid.*, 378–79.

America" to counteract the influence of the American Board. The short-lived society did not excite many churchmen, and the fact that Thomas L. McKenney, of the Bureau of Indian Affairs, was one of its chief sponsors made it somewhat suspect;[22] but about thirty ministers of Dutch Reformed, Episcopal, and Presbyterian churches in the New York area did lend it their support, proving that there was proremoval sentiment in these denominations. Methodists also divided on the issue. Nathan Bangs, a missionary to the southern tribes and a contemporary Methodist chronicler, wrote, "The Indians can neither prosper in the vicinity of the white population, while they remain in an insulated state, governed by their own laws, and usages, nor so amalgamate with the whites as to become identified with them."[23] The Congregational denomination itself did not unanimously oppose removal. At the height of the removal controversy, missionaries from the American Board's western missions at Harmony, Union, and Dwight met and drafted a resolution in favor of Indian consolidation west of the Mississippi. They received a severe reprimand from Evarts and were told to remain silent or forfeit the patronage of the American Board.[24] The Roman Catholic church issued no official statements on Indian policy, but Father Charles van Quickenborne, the Jesuit missionary, wrote to Secretary of War Eaton in October, 1829, arguing that the Indians should be segregated from white population. Earlier, van Quickenborne had enthusiastically approved Calhoun's removal proposals.[25] It may well have been, as McCoy

[22] Francis Paul Prucha, "Thomas L. McKenney and the New York Indian Board," *Mississippi Valley Historical Review*, Vol. XLVIII (March, 1962), 635–55.

[23] Quoted in Wade Crawford Barclay, *Early American Methodism, 1769–1844*, II, 189.

[24] McCoy, Journal, November 12, 1831.

[25] Garraghan, *Jesuits*, I, 173–74.

intimated, that the advocates of the government policy "didn't manage their side of the question, in debate or in public prints, as well as the subject admitted,"[26] and that more churchmen shared McCoy's views on peaceful removal than is commonly recognized.

Congressional leaders consulted both Evarts and McCoy during the debates on the removal bills. Theodore Frelinghuysen of New Jersey, leader of the opposition forces in the Senate, found Evarts' arguments "entirely conclusive."[27] McCoy appeared before the House Committee on Indian Affairs and met frequently with its chairman, John Bell of Tennessee, and another member of the committee, Wilson Lumpkin. The proponents of emigration in Congress could also rely on the testimony of a number of men, like William Clark and George Kennerly, experienced in treaty negotiations, who honestly believed that removal was in the best interest of the Indians. Like McCoy, they had seen only the impoverished Indian who suffered from scarcity of game and the ravages of the whisky trade. Unlike McCoy, they believed the values of a Christian civilization offered meager solace. Clark and Kennerly had little sympathy for missions, yet believed that the Indian should be sheltered from the intruder.[28] Since removal seemed so obviously to the Indian's interest, supporters of the administration's policy conveniently concluded that it was also his wish.

McCoy realized that it was difficult to see the emigration problem in proper perspective in the heat of controversy. He wrote, "What passed for sound argument at that time will be viewed

[26] McCoy, *Baptist Missions*, 399.

[27] For a collection of the principal House and Senate speeches on removal, see Jeremiah Evarts (ed.), *Speeches on the Passage of the Bill for the Removal of the Indians, Delivered in the Congress of the United States, April and May, 1830.*

[28] McCoy, Journal, March 8, 1829.

very differently by the historian who may narrate the whole affair."[29] Despite such insight, McCoy's own position provided one of the better examples of unsound argument. He could trust the federal government in the role of protector of the Indians, but had little faith in the states themselves. He could accept Jackson's contention that state sovereignty was at stake, but he did not want the states to have any part in the actual control of the Indians.

The debate in Congress on the removal bills finally concluded in May, 1830. Congress passed by a narrow margin an "Indian Removal Bill." The act implied no new departure from a policy that had been pursued for years, except that individual communities need no longer apply for extinguishment of Indian titles. The President, by executive order, could now set aside western lands, which would be guaranteed to the Indians forever, in exchange for tribal lands in the states and organized territories. To complement the enabling act, Congress appropriated $500,000 for the negotiation of removal treaties.[30]

Because of its spirited opposition to Jackson's policy, the American Board felt the heavy hand of reprisal. It was obstructed, for example, in collecting its former allotments from the Civilization Fund, and, significantly, the Baptists were the largest recipients by 1834.[31] There were, however, immediate rewards for McCoy. Jackson asked him to administer the entire Civilization Fund for the purpose of developing schools in the West. The Secretary of War offered McCoy an appointment as teacher to the Choctaws. This proposal appealed to him, for it would afford him "a quiet home in the Indian country." But McCoy refused both offers because "the first and most im-

[29] McCoy, *Baptist Missions*, 400.
[30] *Statutes at Large*, IV, 411–12.
[31] 23 Cong., 1 sess., *House Report 474*, 69–70.

portant of all matters in relation to Indian reform appeared to be the judicious location and permanent settlement of all the tribes, where they could 'sit under their own vine and fig tree without fear.' "[32] The Removal Bill was vague about the location of tribes, and it said nothing about the apportionment of lands. He resolved to become better acquainted with the Indian territory so that he could recommend the exact boundaries of the reservations.

Throughout the first Jackson administration, McCoy received a number of commissions directly from the Department of War to make surveys, to adjust boundaries, and to undertake general explorations in the Indian Country. This work provided enough remuneration to support Lykins' family as well as his own, and he magnanimously offered to share his income with Simerwell and Meeker until they could get established beyond the Mississippi. There was another side to his character, however. These years marked the height of his influence in Washington. When he returned there periodically to make his reports, he sometimes met with the President and the Secretary of War. "I am informed that the government relies on me for information on many . . . important points." McCoy developed an exaggerated sense of his own importance. On one of his sojourns at the capital, the board expressed a desire to meet with him before he returned to the West, but he declined because

> I have an aversion for polite nonsensical company. My business leads me among Politicians, where I come in sight of much intrigue and abuse of right things. On all occasions I receive all the kind of *polite attention* that I could desire.[33]

And Jackson and Eaton held before him the prospect of larger

[32] McCoy, Journal, May 6, 1831.
[33] *Ibid.*, February 16 and May 6, 1831.

things. That this "polite attention" might be transitory escaped McCoy. There were warnings. Thomas L. McKenney had been indefatigable in his efforts to rally church support for the government's Indian policy. Shortly after the passage of the Removal Bill, he became one of the first victims of Jackson's "spoils system." But for the present, McCoy was still useful to the administration.

The removal controversy was far from settled. In a talk to a group of Chickasaw chiefs in the fall of 1830, Jackson reiterated that the federal government had no intention of forcing Indians from "the soil which covered the bones of their ancestors." But in a strange analogy he told them, "Our forefathers had the same feeling when a long time ago, to obtain happiness, they left their lands beyond the great waters."[34] Such reassurances did little to allay the fears of those who had opposed Jackson's state rights Indian policy. As a last resort, they hoped that the Supreme Court would declare illegal the laws by which Georgia and other states had extended their jurisdiction over the Indians. Meanwhile, Evarts continued his literary efforts in defense of Indian rights, and Samuel A. Worcester, an American Board missionary in Georgia, and the "real and ostensible editor" of a tribal paper called the *Cherokee Phoenix*, bitterly attacked the state government for abolishing a national constitution that the Cherokees had drawn up for themselves. These editorials, thought McCoy, were calculated to provoke Americans to extremities. "Lamentations are raised relative to the persecution—as they term it—of their missionaries." And if the Supreme Court upheld Cherokee sovereignty, then the "vast territory along the Potomac, including Washington & Baltimore" belonged to the Delawares.[35]

[34] From Jackson's speech as reported in the *Western Monitor*, September 29, 1830.
[35] McCoy, Journal, November 12, 1831; McCoy, *Baptist Missions*, 444.

Georgia officials arrested and imprisoned Worcester and other American Board missionaries for refusing to recognize state authority, but their plight aroused little sympathy in McCoy. Had they attended to their missionary business, no one would have interfered with them, strange reasoning for one so deeply involved in the politics of removal. The specter of religious persecution haunted some Americans, however, and emotions ran high. The delegates to the seventh triennial meeting of the Baptist General Convention in 1832 agitatedly discussed the issues, and Francis Wayland, the influential Baptist minister of Boston, organized a movement to oppose the adoption of any further resolutions favoring removal. Because of an upcoming general election in the nation, the Convention decided to take no action that could be construed as political. Since it had officially endorsed removal for nine years, this was a reversal of policy. McCoy blamed his "Massachusetts friends," and resolved again to sever his connections with the board.[36]

President Jackson may well have snubbed the Supreme Court when it decided that Georgia authorities had illegally arrested the missionaries, for federal and not state law ran in the Cherokee country, but he and his advisers were not oblivious to the political consequences of the controversy. Pro-Jackson periodicals denied that the President was antimissionary, as suggested by spurious letters published under his signature and designed to put him in a bad light.[37] At the request of Lewis Cass, Eaton's successor as secretary of war, McCoy called on Senators Frelinghuysen and Peleg Sprague, of Maine, two champions of the Cherokee cause in Congress. "I plead that they let the merits of particular questions be what they might, the Indians had better

36 McCoy, Journal, May 9, 1832.
37 Bernard C. Steiner, "Jackson and the Missionaries," *American Historical Review*, Vol. XXIX (July, 1924), 722–23.

remove. That where they are, difficulties would continue to accumulate upon them." Administration supporters in the House of Representatives also solicited McCoy's aid and asked him to encourage visiting Cherokee delegations in Washington to seek removal.[38]

The rewards for McCoy's lobbying during the Cherokee crisis were less apparent than on previous occasions. As Governor of Michigan Territory and ex officio superintendent of Indian affairs, Cass had actively supported McCoy's missionary enterprises. Although he conferred "pretty freely" with Cass, the secretary of war, McCoy had been on better terms with John Eaton. Before he left the cabinet, Eaton had authorized the reservation of a portion of the Indian Country as a common ground for the seat of government, and where with the "smiles of Providence" an Indian college might one day be constructed. To McCoy, this had been an example of the administration's earnest intention to follow his plan for an organized Indian state. When he first heard that Cass had replaced Eaton, McCoy was thoroughly disappointed, for he believed that it would mean a return to the "old agency policy."[39]

Actually Cass, more than his predecessor, realized the need for working out a definite program of Indian consolidation. In his first annual report, Cass outlined seven fundamental principles: (1) a solemn declaration that the country assigned to the Indians should be theirs as long as they or their descendants occupied it; (2) a determination to exclude all ardent spirits from their new territory; (3) the employment of an adequate force in their immediate vicinity, and a fixed determination to suppress the slightest attempt at hostilities among themselves; (4) encouragement of the severalty of property; (5) assistance in beginning

[38] McCoy, Journal, March 28 and April 15, 1832.
[39] *Ibid.*, September 4, 1831, and January 17, 1832.

138

farms; (6) allowing the Indians their own institutions; and (7) the eventual employment of persons competent to instruct them, as far and as fast as their progress might require, and in such a way as might be most useful to them.[40]

McCoy had ardently advocated most of these points in the past, and, in fact, thought himself the originator of some of them. The intimation that the Indians should be left to themselves, with the prospect of schools and missionaries somewhere in the dim future, disturbed McCoy, however. To him this proved that Cass had adopted the antimissionary "agency policy." Now that he had defined basic principles to guide a program of consolidation, Cass thought that the next step should be to gather all possible information about the country west of the Mississippi and the Indians inhabiting it. He suggested the appointment of three commissioners who would make fact-finding tours and who would also temporarily manage the affairs of the Indian territory. McCoy had long realized that government officials in Washington had only vague notions about the territory, and he had done his best to familiarize himself and others with it. But he believed that Cass's plan for administering the Indian Country much "too lean."[41] However, when the Secretary of War led him to believe that he would be appointed one of the commissioners, McCoy overcame some of his reservations.

An act of Congress passed in July, 1832, authorized the appointment of three commissioners for a two-year period, and although McCoy's friends in the capital worked diligently to get him named to the commission, the final appointees were Montford Stokes, governor of North Carolina; Henry L. Ellsworth, a former Connecticut congressman and a speculator in Indian

[40] 22 Cong., 1 sess., *House Doc. 2*, 30. See also, 22 Cong., 2 sess., *House Doc. 2.*
[41] McCoy, Journal, January 17 and March 28, 1832.

lands; and the Reverend John F. Schermerhorn, a Presbyterian minister from Utica, New York, who had once been briefly engaged by the American Board to visit various Indian tribes to locate sites for prospective missions. Not being named was a severe blow, but Schermerhorn's appointment was a crowning insult. McCoy had met him in Washington and "found him full of zeal without much knowledge and still less discretion." He further described him as one of those officious characters in the "City" who "affect to know all about what is going on here, and would have me believe that they are the chief instruments in bringing about things."[42]

His usefulness to the administration apparently ended, McCoy now also found that the Secretary of War no longer had so many special assignments for him. Throughout much of the 1830's, McCoy continued to make surveys and adjust boundaries in the Indian territory, but after 1832 he was subject to the authority of the superintendent of Indian affairs at St. Louis. "Previously, I had no superior in this country, and I made my reports directly to the Secretary of War . . . and also there are Indian Commissioners in this country whose duty it is to speak of things of which I could formerly speak."[43]

[42] *Ibid.*, April 15, 1832.
[43] *Ibid.*, July 16, 1833.

Chapter VIII

Dividing the Land

The decade of the 1830's marked the height of the hegira of emigrant tribesmen to the region now commonly called Indian Territory. After the passage of the Removal Bill in 1830, the federal government turned to the monumental task of concluding treaties with tribes still residing east of the Mississippi, of supervising their removal, and of caring for their needs en route and after they had settled. Some of the migrations resembled the pioneering experiences of white frontiersmen, but the overall story of removal is a sordid and depressing phase of American history. Sickness decimated the ranks of the Indians, and unscrupulous traders and drummers relieved them of most of their possessions even before they reached their destination. Isaac McCoy was not directly involved in removal, but he participated in the location of almost every emigrant reserve. He was aware of the abuse and fraud connected with the migrations, but he did not consider this a prohibitive price to pay for the larger good, a land secured to the Indian in perpetuity, or at least as long "as the grass grew."

The concentration of the emigrant tribes in a relatively small area provided a more ideal situation for missionary effort than most societies had known. McCoy felt that because of his exploratory work and his unique influence with the government, the Baptists had an excellent opportunity to dominate missionary and civilization projects in the territory. In the course of the 1830's, it was clear that he would be satisfied with nothing less than a Baptist mission with every tribe, indigenous and emigrant; and at one juncture he was negotiating with agents, superintendents, and the Commissioner of Indian Affairs for missions with the Otoes, Omahas, Pawnees, Kickapoos, Delawares, Weas, Peorias, Piankashaws, and Choctaws.[1] The Baptist Board of Managers decided in 1830 that there should be little enlargement of missionary activity until the dust had settled on the removal controversy.[2] While McCoy railed against the "criminal negligence" of the board, other denominations entered fields where he had already secured permission to establish stations. At times the various missionary agencies literally overwhelmed some tribes with offers of schools and missions. The tendency of the tribesmen to accept the proposal of the last one to solicit their consent added to the confusion.

The Shawnees formed the emigrant vanguard in Indian Territory. The mission societies singled them out for special consideration, although McCoy, while on his exploring tours, had been the first to approach them in their new homes. Since they had just arrived, he had not pressed them to arrange for a station immediately. McCoy's appointment to survey a western reserve for the Delawares gave him an opportunity not only to broach the subject of missions with that tribe, but to contact the Shawnees again.

The Delawares, now concentrated in Missouri on the White River, consented to leave the state in a treaty signed in September, 1829. Federal negotiators allotted them a new reservation which McCoy was commissioned to survey in 1830. The lines

---

[1] McCoy, Journal, July 28, 1833.
[2] "Report of the Annual Meeting of the Baptist Board of Foreign Missions," *American Baptist Magazine*, Vol. X (June, 1830), 162.

were to extend from the confluence of the Missouri and Kansas rivers to the eastern border of the Kansa Indian reserve. This allotment placed the Delawares directly north of their friends, the Shawnees. Delaware lands would also extend up the Missouri to Cantonment Leavenworth and westward. The treaty further provided an "outlet" to the western hunting ground via a ten-mile strip extending along the northern boundary of the Kansa country.[3]

McCoy gathered and outfitted his surveying crew at Fayette. It included two sons, Rice and John Calvin, two chainmen, and three hired hands. With what now must have seemed remarkable foresight, both boys had studied surveying at Transylvania University.[4] It was a respected profession, although few were as fortunate as George Washington in their fees. Rice McCoy left a "thriving medical practice" in Fayette to become an assistant surveyor at three dollars a day. Surveyors lived a hard and primitive life. Unlike scouts, hunters, and trappers, they could not avoid swamps, sand, and hills. McCoy's crew had to pack equipment and supplies for four months of wilderness living, as well as paraphernalia such as chains, instruments, compasses, maps, and notebooks.

The party entered Indian Territory at the Shawnee Agency, and there met John Quick, second chief of the Delawares. At the main Shawnee village, appropriately called Prophet Town, McCoy met in council with twenty Shawnee chiefs and proposed the establishment of a mission. Tenskwatawa, "The Prophet," responded in behalf of the rest, and although he expressed approval, McCoy concluded that not many of the other chiefs really favored the proposal. While on the Shawnee Reser-

[3] *Statutes at Large*, VII, 327.
[4] John C. McCoy, "Survey of Kansas Indian Lands," *Kansas Historical Collections*, IV (1886–90), 300.

vation, McCoy participated in a council between that tribe and the Kansa Indians, one of the first meetings to be held between indigenous and immigrant tribesmen in Indian Territory. Here he had an opportunity to discuss the Delaware grant with the Kansas, who had ceded the territory in 1825. McCoy discovered that the chiefs were no longer aware that they had given up the land.[5]

The Secretary of War had ordered that a "Corporal's guard" accompany the survey team to protect it from wandering war parties. He also advised General William Clark to ask the agents of the Pawnee, Osage, and Kansa nations to explain the purpose of the surveying expedition.[6] At Cantonment Leavenworth, McCoy discovered that the commandant, Major William Davenport, had received no orders and that the agents had not been informed of his coming. McCoy blamed the "crooked stick" in St. Louis. He gave no clue about the nature of his difficulty with General Clark, but it was obvious that he had not endeared himself to the Superintendent of Indian Affairs. McCoy had anticipated difficulties of this sort and had with him a copy of the Secretary of War's order to Clark. Davenport was unimpressed but, after some cajoling, provided a nine-man escort. The surveyors could now begin to run the western line of the Delaware general reserve. When they reached Kansa country and Daniel Boone's residence, they were told that they might well need military protection. As a buffer tribe between the Pawnees and the Osages, the Kansa Indians normally had peaceful relations with both, but because of a serious transportation problem, Kansa parties were out "hunting" horses. There was danger of falling in with hostile Pawnees tracking down the thieves or of a dis-

---

[5] McCoy, Journal, August 23, 24 and October 27, 1830.

[6] For the War Department's instructions to Clark, see McKenney to Clark, June 5, 1830, 23 Cong., 1 sess., *Sen. Doc. 512*, Pt. 2, p. 8.

appointed Kansa raiding party's venting its frustration on the surveyors.[7]

After setting the western boundary, McCoy returned to Cantonment Leavenworth to run the northern line of the general reservation and the outlet. At the point of origination, McCoy realized that the cantonment was on the Delaware grant, and that no provision had been made to reserve a site for the use of the United States government. On his own initiative, McCoy laid out a tract for the use of the garrison[8] and got Chief John Quick to agree to it. While surveying near the cantonment, McCoy discovered a number of Indian mounds. McCoy took time to excavate one, and unearthed a stone-lined kiln with skeletons in it. Since fires had scorched the bones but had not reduced them to ashes, McCoy speculated that a pre-European tribe had used the kiln for human sacrifices.[9]

The most difficult part of McCoy's assignment was the survey of the outlet. Chief Quick decided not to accompany McCoy any further. Satisfied with what he had seen, he returned to Missouri to bring in his people before the winter. Although the outlet survey would take McCoy and his party "half way to the mountains," the post commander still insisted they needed no military escort.[10] John Dougherty, agent for the Upper Missouri, was not so sanguine, and took it upon himself to call the Pawnee Republic Indians into council at the cantonment. About one hundred Pawnees attended, including their head chief, Capote Bleu, who assured McCoy that there would be no interference with his survey.[11]

[7] McCoy, Journal, August 30, September 3 and 4, 1830.
[8] Isaac McCoy, "Field Notes of the Survey of the Western Boundary of the Delaware Lands North of the Kansas River," William Clark Papers, Vol. I.
[9] McCoy, Journal, October 4, 1830.
[10] *Ibid.*, September 28 and October 5, 1830.
[11] Dougherty to Cass, March 9, 1832, Dougherty Collection (typewritten

Beginning in mid-October, the surveyors ran a 210-mile line for the northern boundary of the general reservation and the outlet. They found much of the prairie burned. High winds blowing the ashes, together with dust and sand, made traveling conditions very uncomfortable. On several occasions, prairie fires came on them so quickly that they barely had time to set their own fires in self-defense. McCoy wrote,

> The fires around us were sublime—the long lines and the flame ascending ten, fifteen, and sometimes 20 feet high. On seeing these prairies on fire in such a dry time as this we cease to wonder that the wood does not increase faster—we only wonder that a vestige of wood is left.[12]

The survey of the north boundary terminated at the Solomon River. McCoy and his weary party with its worn-out horses moved eastward as quickly as possible, although they did go out of their way to see "a great natural curiosity," a large salt spring with a high mound the waters had formed. The spring was known to the Pawnees and Kansas as *Nee-woh-kon-da-ga* (Waconda) or "Spirit water," and the tribesmen believed that it had miraculous healing powers. They drank from it and bathed in it, or when passing they would throw in some small article of value as a "conjuring charm." From the spring, the surveying company moved on to the Kansa Agency, where McCoy discovered that two Methodist missionaries, William Johnson and Alexander McAlister, had just arrived to discuss the opening of a mission. McCoy had already applied for permission to begin a work with the Kansas, but was willing to defer to the Methodists because he believed the condition of the tribe all but hopeless. Even if something could be done, he doubted that the

copies of original Dougherty papers lent to the Kansas State Historical Society by O'Fallon Dougherty, of Liberty, Mo., in 1906).

[12] McCoy, Journal, October 18 and 21, 1830.

Methodists were the people to do it. "Their [Kansa Indians] circumstances are such as to require the exercise of faith and patient perseverance, in labourious, and often discouraging operations, rather beyond what we can expect from that denomination." The Methodists also seemed determined to begin a mission with the Shawnees, and this intention conflicted with a more vital interest. McCoy protested that the Baptists had a prior claim and the tribe was not large enough for two missions.[13]

After leaving the Kansa Agency, McCoy and his party ran the southern boundary of the Delaware reserve. They found Delawares already moving in. So anxious had they been to leave Missouri they decided not to wait for spring or for government assistance as specified in their late treaty.[14] McCoy happily reflected on the consternation this would create among superintendents, agents, and contractors, who usually profited handsomely in the business of removal. Chief William Anderson told McCoy that he was gratified that he had lived to see his people settled in their own country again. The old chief had written to the scattered remnants of the tribe in Ohio, Canada, and Spanish territory, asking them to settle on the new reservation.[15] Anderson would not discuss the matter of a mission with McCoy, however. And yet when the Mormons sent missionaries to the Delawares a few months later, Anderson was obviously impressed, and promised to build a school for them. When the news reached the frontier settlements in Missouri, the outcry was so great that the Delaware agent ordered the Mormons off the reservation.[16]

13 *Ibid.*, November 7, and November 20, 1930.

14 Clark Papers, Vol. VI, 65–66.

15 McCoy to Cass, April, 1831, 23 Cong., 1 sess., *Sen. Doc. 512*, Pt. 2, pp. 439, 599. For Anderson's effort to get the Canadian Delawares to migrate, see Menard to Clark, November 2, 1830, Clark Papers, Vol. VI, 65.

16 Grant Foreman, "Missionaries of the Latter Day Saints in the Indian Territory," *Chronicles of Oklahoma*, Vol. XIII (June, 1935), 196.

Before returning to Fayette after the completion of the Delaware survey, McCoy stopped at the Shawnee Reservation. The chiefs confirmed their previous consent to the establishment of a Baptist mission,[17] but a few weeks after McCoy's departure they granted Thomas Johnson permission to begin a Methodist work on a site near a Chouteau trading post on the Kansas River, six miles west of the Missouri border.[18] About the same time, William Johnson opened a school for the Kansa Indians.[19]

In the spring of 1831, McCoy received a commission from the Secretary of War to survey the boundaries of the Cherokee Reservation and to explore the Osage lands to try to determine whether the Chickasaws might be located there. The War Department contemplated moving the Osages farther north and apparently feared that the tribesmen might get an inkling of this plan, for it ordered that McCoy be provided with a military escort from Cantonment Gibson. The Secretary of War appointed John Donelson, President Jackson's nephew, and Rice McCoy assistant surveyors. McCoy decided to take along his entire family and domicile them at the Osage Agency while he undertook his work. When he left Missouri behind, he wrote in his journal, "I am happy and thankful that I have at length seen my family within the *Indian Territory*."[20]

McCoy and his entourage made its way to the Osage Agency and found that the only people in residence were a French trader and a clerk, and they seemed but "a few degrees removed from the rudeness of the Osages."[21] McCoy decided that he

17 McCoy, Journal, November 22, 1830.
18 R. W. Cummins to Clark, January 13, 1831, Clark Papers, Vol. VI, 96.
19 William Johnson to the Corresponding Secretary of the Missionary Society of the Methodist Episcopal Church, June 26, 1831, "Letters from the Indian Missions in Kansas," *Kansas Historical Collections*, Vol. XVI (1923–25), 227–28.
20 McCoy, Journal, June 17, 1831.
21 *Ibid.*, June 20, 1831.

could not leave his family there. He continued on to Union Mission, a large station operated by the American Board on the Grand River, close to Fort Gibson. Established in 1820, Union was the first mission to the Osages and at one time employed about twenty missionaries and assistants. The Osages had left the region, and the missionaries attempted to adapt their work to the immigrant Cherokees and Creeks, with limited success.[22] In his usual patronizing manner, McCoy commented that it was evident that the mission needed a superintendent "qualified to manage men and matters under difficult circumstances. All pious persons are not qualified for missionaries."[23] Fortunately the "pious missionaries" were also hospitable, and provided accommodations for McCoy and his family.

At Union, McCoy found a full-blooded Creek busily proselytizing for the Baptist faith among his own people. John Davis, a convert of a short-lived Creek Baptist mission in Alabama, came to the West in 1829. To McCoy's horror, Davis cooperated with the Presbyterian missionaries at Union, and communed with them "at the Lord's table." "What a shame it is—if not a sin—that the fields should thus whiten for harvest, that the people should wait and look for Baptist missionaries, and finding none, be obliged to unite themselves with other denominations!"[24]

McCoy split his party into three groups to make the actual surveys. Donelson ran a traverse line to Fort Smith, marking the boundary between Cherokee lands and the Territory of Arkansas. Rice McCoy moved northward, surveying the line between the Cherokee reserve and the state of Missouri. Indian Territory was only about one year old, but young McCoy discovered

22 *Missionary Herald*, Vol. XXXIX (December, 1833), 466.
23 McCoy, *Baptist Missions*, 368.
24 McCoy, Journal, July 3, 1831.

"half-wild" white families already living on the Indian side of the lines.[25] Isaac McCoy refused to recognize this as an omen of future difficulties.

While his assistants did the surveying, McCoy, with a military escort from Cantonment Gibson and an Osage interpreter with the impressive name of Stephen van Rensselaer, explored the region north of the Cherokee reserve to attempt to find a suitable location for the Chickasaws. McCoy found military men to be poor traveling companions, for their only object in life seemed to be "to spend time without incurring censure." Whatever their personal defects, their presence proved of some value. The excursion took the party deep into the Osage country, and on one occasion a band of two hundred Osage warriors, armed for battle, rushed their encampment. When the warriors came over the rise and saw the handful of soldiers, their war cries changed to "hallooings." They seemed relieved that they had an opportunity for shaking hands instead of taking scalps.[26]

The incident substantiated McCoy's belief that the Indians had no inherent warlike tendencies, and the plains tribesmen, supposedly the fiercest warriors on the continent, were no exception. This opinion was further corroborated, according to McCoy, by stories told him by traders returning from Santa Fe of how comparatively small caravans would be rushed by bands of Indians "exhibiting an appearance as frightful as possible . . . but on discovering that the assailed are not to be driven from their places by their impetuous onset, they wheel and retreat." McCoy continued, "We have been too long deluded and amused with false theories and romantic stories . . . served up to the taste of the novelist."[27] At least one contemporary student of Indian

[25] *Ibid.*, July 18, 1831.
[26] *Ibid.*, July 9 and 28, 1831.
[27] McCoy, *Baptist Missions*, 22–23.

life would have disagreed with him. Rudolph Friedrich Kurz, Swiss artist and amateur ethnologist, visited a number of plains tribes in the late 1840's and observed that when the missionary advised the Indian to renounce war he asked him to give up his chief purpose in life, for without war "an Indian is no longer an Indian."[28] Neither man seemed interested to learn why the Indian should fight at all. If the Indian braves did not often attack the white man, intertribal warfare could be vicious, and mute evidence of this was a Delaware woman McCoy found wandering alone on the prairies. She was the sole survivor of a hunting party waylaid by the Pawnees.[29] This incident might well have caused McCoy to reflect on the wisdom of sending eastern tribesmen to Indian Territory.

McCoy, after his exploration of the Osage tract north of the Cherokee reserve, concluded that the Chickasaws should not be located there. He recommended instead that the Choctaws be made to share part of their reserve south of the Canadian River.[30] McCoy also took the liberty of running the northern boundary of the Cherokee reserve farther south than originally intended. He prided himself in saving a large part of Indian Territory for other uses.

While McCoy was busy with his southern survey, Johnston Lykins attempted to get a Shawnee mission underway. He had received an appointment from the Baptist Board, but it made no provision for building funds.[31] To McCoy and Lykins this again revealed the obstructionism of the board, for they knew that a federal commission had finally evaluated the property at Carey, and they assumed that the government had already reimbursed

28 *Journal of Rudolph Friederich Kurz* (trans. by Myrtis Jarrell, ed. by J. N. B. Hewitt), Bureau of American Ethnology *Bulletin No. 115*, 295.
29 McCoy, Journal, October 22, 1831.
30 23 Cong., 1 sess., *Sen. Doc. 512*, Pt. 2, 418–21.
31 Johnston Lykins, Journal, July 18, 1831.

the board. This was not the case, however.[32] Lykins bought a
small tract of land, just inside the Missouri border and across
from the Shawnee Reservation, and commenced putting up
buildings with private means. McCoy deposited his family here
when he went to Washington to report on his southern surveys
and explorations.

Lykins accomplished little mission work during the first
months because of a smallpox epidemic. Thomas Johnson, of the
Methodist Shawnee Mission, wrote that "everything was in a
state of confusion . . . and Indians flying in different directions."[33] With the help of the Shawnee subagent, Lykins began
a vaccination program. Lykins had no formal training in medicine, but through reading and practice had already achieved
somewhat of a reputation as a physician. Since comparatively
few practitioners in any part of the nation were medical school
graduates or had ever "attended lectures," it is difficult to determine whether Lykins qualified as a "regular" or as a "quack."

The smallpox epidemic on the Shawnee and Delaware reservations was not serious and subsided by 1832, but it continued
unabated among the Plains Indians. After a visit to four Pawnee
villages, John Dougherty reported, "I am fully persuaded that
one half the whole number of souls of each village have and will
be carried off by this cruel and frightful distemper."[34] He estimated that four thousand Pawnees, Otoes, Poncas, and Omahas
had died of the disease. Grant Foreman, a modern historian of
the American Indian, in his *The Last Trek of the Indians*, de-
scribes how McCoy in the Pawnee villages in the spring of 1832
shuddered at the sight of "more than 3,000 human carcasses cast
upon the open field in the space of a few days."[35] This account

[32] Bolles to Simerwell, August 4, 1831, Simerwell Correspondence.
[33] "Letters from the Indian Missions," 236–37.
[34] 22 Cong., 1 sess., *House Exec. Doc. 190*, 1–3.
[35] Foreman, *The Last Trek of the Indians*, 237.

is spurious, for McCoy's surveys had kept him in the opposite end of Indian Territory; and, in fact, he was in the East during the first half of the year, although judging from Dougherty's accounts, the situation was grim enough. Part of the problem of controlling the epidemic, according to McCoy, was that white men encouraged its spread. McCoy, in great anger, related as an accepted fact that the men of the Santa Fe caravans and the Rocky Mountain trappers deliberately spread the disease to remote Pawnees and Comanches through infected tobacco and clothing.[36]

While still in the West, McCoy wrote to Lewis Cass entreating him to start a vaccination program, and when McCoy arrived in Washington in February, 1832, he learned that an Indian vaccination bill was before the Senate. Told that Senator Alexander Buckner of Missouri had blocked the bill, McCoy called on him. With utter callousness, the Senator informed McCoy that he had no right to save the Indians. "If they were all dead it would be a blessing to our country. We ought not to endeavour to save them because they had murdered our people, and would so again." In the face of such cynicism it was remarkable that McCoy could continue to believe that the eastern tribesmen could be consolidated just west of the borders of Missouri and there be safeguarded in perpetuity. The Senate passed a whittled-down bill which allowed for a small appropriation. Instead of concentrating these limited funds in the areas of critical need, the Secretary of War decided to divide them among all tribes so that no feelings would be hurt. McCoy persuaded Senator William Hendricks of Indiana to move for a reconsideration of the whole vaccination problem, but nothing came of it.[37]

Anxious to find other ways to promote the welfare of the

[36] McCoy, *Baptist Missions*, 442–43.
[37] McCoy, Journal, March 28 and April 22, 1832.

Indians, McCoy conceived the idea of publishing a periodical which would place the Indians' "past and present condition fairly before the public." To finance the project, he attempted, while in Washington, to secure a $1,000 printing-press fund that had been set aside for the Cherokees in the treaty of 1828. The commissioners had intended that the money be used to further the type of pioneering work in native orthography carried on by Sequoyah, a half-blood Cherokee. McCoy planned to use it to establish a printing plant somewhere in the West and there publish material to educate English-speaking people on Indian problems. He hoped to use Jotham Meeker's talents as a printer, but Meeker had little enthusiasm for the plan.[38]

The young missionaries whom McCoy had trained at Carey and Thomas were no longer amenable to his wishes, and had developed ideas of their own about missions and reform. Slater had differed with McCoy from the start. He believed the enormous amounts of money spent on boarding schools was wasted, and favored instead small village day schools. Although he finally wrested the appointment of teacher to the Ottawas from Lykins, he professed to believe that reliance on government support injured the cause of missions. Missionaries should receive their support "from praying people." And while McCoy and Lykins wrote to their former Ottawa students urging them to work for removal among their fellow tribesmen, Slater advocated that they stay.[39] Discouraged with the work at Thomas, Meeker had left and returned to his home in Ohio. Despite McCoy's repeated urgings to "jump into a dearbourne" and head west, Meeker decided to join Abel Bingham's mission at Sault Ste. Marie instead. Here he spent his time "studying Indian and preparing firewood." The Chippewa dialect was similar to that of the

[38] McCoy, *Baptist Missions*, 428–29.
[39] Slater to Simerwell, April 17, 1831, Simerwell Correspondence.

Ottawas, and he was soon involved in devising an orthography which could be written or printed with the characters of the English alphabet.[40]

After a long struggle to keep the Carey boarding school open and many unhappy experiences with the maladjusted young men that McCoy had sent to eastern colleges and who had returned to their villages, Simerwell also became a convert to the village school. He concluded that the missionaries should live with the Indians in their communities and become acquainted with their customs and languages. The children should live at home, and at the schools instruction should be in the native dialects. Simerwell diligently continued his study of Potawatomi and attempted to work out a grammar. This was no simple undertaking for the erstwhile blacksmith. He could discover "no article, the pronoun admits of no declension, [I] discovered no infinite mood and but the present, past and future tenses." He isolated 1,300 inflections for one verb, and there were more.[41]

In most of the major missionary organizations, the whole concept of Indian education underwent a change after the removal controversies of the early 1830's. The views expressed by the young Baptist missionaries in Michigan Territory reflected more and more the policy of the Baptist Board. The Prudential Committee of the American Board recommended in 1832 that in the future there be no Indian boarding schools and no English-language instruction. With considerable insight, the committee observed that because of the Removal Bill of 1830, no mission could ever be secure in any locality.[42] Roman Catholic missionaries had long shown a concern to adapt education to Indian needs. Father Samuel Mazzuchelli, a missionary to the Indians in

[40] Jotham Meeker, Journal, September 10 and November 27, 1832.
[41] Simerwell to S. H. Cone, December 20, 1830, Simerwell Correspondence.
[42] *Report of the American Board of Commissioners for Foreign Missions for 1837*, 115–16.

the Green Bay region, was an ardent advocate of the instruction of both children and adults in their native languages. He informed the War Department that children trained in English and in subjects taken by all other American children were of little use to their tribe.[43] The War Department now tended to favor manual-labor schools, which taught in English but provided practical training. The Methodists became increasingly interested in this type of institution. McCoy remained a firm believer in the boarding school. He thought that if the Indian children stayed at home, their parents would not make an effort to send them to school regularly. In a boarding school the students could be given constant supervision in a proper environment.[44]

In 1832, however, differences in approach to Indian education were not a main issue for McCoy. He wanted to get Baptist missions started in Indian Territory, no matter what missionaries' individual views might be. Lykins had developed a working relationship with the Shawnees, and an opening with the Creeks presented itself through John Davis. The removal of the St. Joseph Potawatomis seemed imminent, and McCoy intended to insure that Baptist missionaries continued to maintain a dominant position with them. This position could no longer be taken for granted. After many years the Jesuits decided to revive their work with the Potawatomis. Father Stephen Badin attempted to secure the Carey property from the government. The subagent who resided at Carey firmly vetoed this proposal, and so Badin built a small mission in Pokegan's village.[45] According to Simerwell, Badin and his successors, with the aid of the trader, Joseph Bertrand, actively opposed relocation of the Potawatomis in the

[43] 22 Cong., 2 sess., *House Exec. Doc. 2*, 171.
[44] McCoy, *Baptist Missions*, 490–92.
[45] Garraghan, *Jesuits*, II, 176–79.

West. Since the principal chief Topenebee, who had come to believe that the tribe's survival was at stake, favored removal, the issue caused considerable agitation and ill will.[46]

On his return from Washington, McCoy followed the example of Lykins and settled on a small tract just inside the Missouri border but close to Indian Territory. A short time later, John Calvin McCoy opened a store nearby where he hoped to tap the Santa Fe trade as well as to deal with the Indians from the neighboring reservations. His father had first call on his services, however, and in the summer and fall of 1832, he and John Donelson assisted the elder McCoy in locating lands for the Ohio tribes.

The initial step in executing the Removal Act outside of the South was the appointment of Colonel James B. Gardiner as a special agent to negotiate with the Ohio Indians. He concluded four treaties in quick order.[47] As a result of these treaties, McCoy surveyed a tract for the Senecas of the Sandusky, and another for a mixed band of Senecas and Shawnees living at Lewistown, Ohio, in territory that he lopped off the Cherokee grant. Farther north, he surveyed a smaller reserve bisected by the Marais Des Cygnes for a band of Ottawas from Blanchard's Fork, Ohio. This seemed to be a very pleasant region, and so McCoy took time out to complete a project for which he had received previous authorization. He laid out a six-mile-square section just below the Ottawa reserve where the seat of government for all the tribes of the new Indian Territory would be located. Here there would be a great council-house with ample grazing grounds adjacent for the ponies of the delegates in attendance at the annual and called meetings of the body politic.[48]

The Ohio Indians began arriving in the summer of 1832, and

---

[46] Simerwell to E. B. Smith, December 20, 1830, Simerwell Correspondence.
[47] *Statutes at Large*, VII, 348, 351, 355, 359.
[48] McCoy, Journal, July 30 and August 2, 1832.

McCoy helped direct them to their reserves. These removals
followed a pattern of mismanagement and hardship already established. It was in fact incredible that so many arrived at all, but
McCoy did not dwell on this sad truth. Groups set out in winter
when it had been planned that they start in spring. Agents could
not agree on routes. The emigrating agent for the Senecas of
Sandusky thought that his responsibility ended once the Indians
were out of Ohio, and so he abandoned them when they crossed
into Indiana.⁴⁹ Left to themselves, the Indians were at the point
of starvation. It took several months for word of their plight to
filter through to Washington and then to General Clark in St.
Louis. When the Senecas finally arrived at their destination, the
sight of the land that McCoy had chosen for them further depressed them. Henry C. Brish, a subagent who accompanied the
Senecas, reported that there was not more than one hundred
acres of good land in the whole tract. "Mr. McCoy's report to
the contrary notwithstanding . . . God help the poor Senecas;
they expect to become agriculturists at their new home."⁵⁰

Preoccupied with his surveying work, McCoy did not become
involved in the settlement of emigrant tribes, although he did
find time to continue his drive to establish Baptist missions. On
one tour he went on to the Creek Reservation, and in a grove
near the Verdigris River constituted the "Muscogee Baptist
Church." Its first members included John Davis and his wife and
three slaves, Quash, Bob, and Ned, who had been brought to
Indian Territory by their Creek masters. Compared to the
Methodists, who had just completed a rousing camp meeting and
gained about eighty Creek converts, it seemed an insignificant
beginning, but McCoy prided himself in the quality of his mem-

---

⁴⁹ 23 Cong., 1 sess., *Sen. Doc. 512*, Pt. 2, pp. 691–724.
⁵⁰ Quoted in David Eaton, "Echoes of Indian Emigration," *Missouri Historical Quarterly*, Vol. VIII (April, 1914), 150.

bers. He had little faith in the Methodist "revivals of religion," where Indians became enthusiastic converts at services conducted in a language they did not understand.[51]

McCoy next turned his attention to the Shawnees. The board had at last provided funds for a building. McCoy and Lykins chose a site about three miles south of the Methodist Shawnee Mission. On Lykins' recommendation, the board commissioned Alexander Evans of Indiana to assist him as missionary to the Shawnees. Despite past rebuffs, McCoy was still determined to have a Baptist Delaware mission. Captain Anderson had died and could no longer obstruct his efforts. The Delaware chiefs now indicated that they would accept a school, but they would not tolerate proselytizing. While at the Delaware reserve, McCoy and Lykins, to their great surprise, came upon a young Baptist by the name of Ira Blanchard, who for more than a year had lived with the tribe to learn their language which he had "pretty thoroughly acquired."[52] Blanchard had worked at the Thomas mission for a time until the board discovered that he had a prison record. It advised Simerwell to discharge him immediately.[53] McCoy and Lykins, ignoring Blanchard's past, baptized him and hired him as a teacher.

By 1833, the Baptist Board decided that it should expand its operations in Indian Territory rather than to waste "life, labour and money, on Indians unsettled." Jotham Meeker and Moses Merrill, a fellow missionary at Sault Ste Marie, had planned to open another Chippewa mission at the northwestern extremity of Lake Superior, but the board advised instead that they go West. McCoy had often urged the board to set up a printing office in Indian Territory where a monthly or perhaps a weekly could be

[51] McCoy, *Journal*, September 9, 1932.
[52] *Ibid.*, February 12 and April 3, 1833.
[53] Herman Lincoln (treasurer of the Board of Managers) to Simerwell, June 28, 1831, Simerwell Correspondence.

published. "I feel inclined to take charge of the editorial department myself."[54] The board finally accepted the idea and authorized Meeker to purchase a printing press and take it with him.

Merrill and Meeker arrived at the Shawnee Mission in the fall of 1833. Meeker decided to wait for an opening with the Ottawas, while McCoy arranged with John Dougherty for Merrill to begin a mission with the Otoes. Merrill moved into an abandoned trading post at the mouth of the Platte River. Subsequently, McCoy secured for him a government appointment as teacher.[55]

The increasing consolidation of Indians and missionaries in Indian Territory seemed at least a partial fulfillment of McCoy's dream of an Indian Canaan. The broad lines had been set. Much of the land had been divided. Missionary societies, unable to cooperate, had staked out their separate claims. But the problems and difficulties involved in organizing the territory into some semblance of a whole, caused the vision, once so clearly seen, to become hazy even in McCoy's mind.

[54] McCoy, Journal, April 3, 1833.

[55] *Ibid.*, June 5 and October 25, 1833; "Extracts from the Diary of Rev. Moses Merrill, a Missionary to the Otoe Indians from 1832–1840," *Transactions and Reports of the Nebraska State Historical Society*, Vol. IV, (1892), 158.

Chapter IX

Trials on Every Side

Isolation had been a constant theme in Isaac McCoy's missionary career. In isolation, the Indian, with the help of missionaries, preferably Baptist, would reorganize his society so as to cope better with life in a white nation. But when McCoy, in 1832, erected his residence in the "woods" on the west edge of Jackson County, white settlers had already moved into the western tier of Missouri counties. Many of them could hardly be considered desirable neighbors to the Indians in Indian Territory. Henry L. Ellsworth, member of the special Indian commission appointed in 1832, after a visit to Clay County wrote, "the mob govern every thing they [*sic*] got together and said they would knock down any man that bid upon certain sections of land but themselves and they bought the whole at a shocking low price."[1] And yet McCoy believed that through sound legislation and good administration these people could be kept out of the Indian reserves.

If McCoy intended to enjoy a measure of isolation himself, his own son soon shattered the illusion. John Calvin, who operated a store nearby, laid out a townsite and filed a plat for "West Port." To shorten the haul of his merchandise, he broke a rough wagon track through to a natural rock levee on the Missouri River a few miles from his store. Santa Fe shippers realized the

[1] Quoted in John Treat Irving, Jr., *Indian Sketches* (ed. by John Francis McDermott), xxii.

advantage of bringing their freight to the new landing, and before long Westport rivaled Independence as the principal eastern terminus of the Santa Fe Trail.[2]

Although McCoy was absorbed in the Indian Territory which began one mile to the west, he could not remain entirely aloof from the struggles of the nearby white settlements. Beginning in 1831, Jackson County attracted a number of Mormon immigrants. Joseph Smith, founder of the movement, visited Independence that year. Irritations soon arose between "saints" and non-Mormons. Difficulties accumulated and reached crisis proportions by the fall of 1833, when a mob destroyed the press and offices of a Mormon newspaper in Independence. Ellsworth described the Mormons as "perfectly inoffensive people having their religion to themselves."[3] Wild rumors circulated that the Mormons were armed for a life-or-death battle and that the Indians might take their side. A fight broke out in November, 1833, in "real warlike style" leaving several killed and wounded on both sides.[4] On that day, McCoy went to Independence and attempted to ease the situation. "Two guns were at one time cocked for the purpose of shooting a Mormon, when I rushed forward and prevent it. I had to use similar efforts afterwards to prevent one from being beaten with a stick, and another with a gun." A week later, at a meeting of the town's "influential citizens," McCoy presented a resolution that the Mormons be allowed to provide for their own safety.[5]

For McCoy, however, the affairs of Independence or Westport were secondary to those of Shawnee Mission. The mission, about twelve miles from where he lived, became the headquarters

2 Nellie McCoy Harris, "Memoirs of Old Westport," *Missouri Valley Historical Society Publications*, Vol. IV, (October, 1924), 465.
3 Quoted in Washington Irving, *Indian Sketches*, xxii.
4 Meeker, Journal, November 5, 1833.
5 McCoy, Journal, November 4 and November 11, 1833.

for Baptist missionary projects in Indian Territory. McCoy initiated every program, but ironically he had no official connection with any particular one. He and his family worshiped at the mission, and the other missionaries acknowledged him as the elder statesman by allowing him to "preside at the communion," but they did not recognize him as their superintendent. To clarify his position, McCoy asked them to submit written statements on what they thought his status should be. Almost unanimously, they advised him to "settle among, and preach to, some Indian tribe."[6] This was not the answer he wanted, for in his own mind he considered everything that he did, writing, surveying, or preaching, to be missionary work. The crowning insult came when the annual reports of the Board of Managers no longer listed him as a missionary.

In spite of the views of his colleagues, McCoy had no intention of abdicating control over the missions he had inspired. Rumblings of discontent soon resulted, especially among the new men. Charles E. Wilson came to the West and decided "with himself" to work with the Delawares. McCoy felt that he should go to the Osages, but he refused. In disgust, McCoy noted, "We have so very often been scalded with these very wise—smart—zealous,—confident . . . missionaries." Evans, at the Shawnee Mission, chafed under McCoy's domination, and in less than a year asked to go to the Choctaws. McCoy wrote, "Our principal objection is . . . We fear that bro. Evans would not be useful in any tribe of Indians."[7] Experienced missionaries like Meeker came to believe that McCoy drove the new missionaries away,[8] but subsequent events bore out most of McCoy's caustic appraisals. The board soon dismissed Evans, because he drank too much. Wilson

6 Meeker, Journal, December 19, 1834.
7 McCoy, Journal, June 8 and October 3, 1832.
8 Meeker to S. L. Lynd, September 26, 1842, Meeker Papers.

left the Delawares after he began to have doubts about his own faith.[9] McCoy had questioned the ability of David Lewis when the board sent him to the Creeks. Before long the board asked McCoy to go to the mission to investigate its heavy expenditures. Lewis gave up his missionary career and returned to the East, where he bilked a man, who had "accommodated" the board and its missionaries, out of $1,000 and fled to a Latin-American country.[10]

One of McCoy's great ambitions was to publish a journal which would inform the American public about Indian Territory and publicize its needs. He gave up the idea of a monthly, let alone a weekly, and decided it would be more practical to start with *"An Annual Register of Indian Affairs within the Indian Territory."* As soon as Meeker arrived, McCoy urged him to set up the press. When he began to operate it, Meeker became so engrossed in printing material in Indian languages that he had little time or inclination to do McCoy's work.

McCoy was an enthusiastic supporter of Meeker's work in native languages, and did not object to his preoccupation with it. Actually, McCoy was the only missionary to leave an adequate description of Meeker's orthography. He not only described it, but philosophized at great length on the whole problem of languages. "We are slaves of habit. We have acquired a knowledge of the art of printing our thoughts on paper . . . by the tedious process of spelling." Meeker's system, on the other hand, enabled the learner "to paint his thoughts on paper . . . as soon as he acquired a knowledge of a number of characters about equal to the English alphabet."[11]

Meeker was familiar with the work of Sequoyah, who dis-

[9] McCoy, Journal, October 25, 1833.
[10] McCoy, *Baptist Missions*, 486.
[11] *Ibid.*, 472.

covered that Cherokee could be written with about eighty syllabic characters. This system involved the introduction of many arbitrary characters, and the method was impractical when tried on other languages. It occurred to Meeker to use the letters of the English alphabet, not to "spell" syllables, but to represent certain positions of the organs of speech. The assignments of the English letters to different phonetic duties was arbitrary, although the system seemed to work; for the missionaries could actually read to the Indians, even if they did not succeed in teaching very many Indians to read for themselves. The method had obvious defects as a general system for use with all Indian languages. But McCoy, with his typical enthusiasm, claimed that any "English scholar" could be taught the system with a twenty-line "key." To the uninstructed eye, Meeker's Indian imprints present a jumble of utterly unpronounceable combinations, but McCoy claimed that a missionary could accompany a band of Indians on a buffalo hunt for two or three months and teach the tribesmen to read as they occasionally rested in their encampments. McCoy believed that the system was so superior that all missionaries would want to adopt it immediately. He invited Presbyterians and Methodists to a meeting to discuss the new system, but they voiced some skepticism. McCoy attributed this to jealousy and to the fact that it did not "emanate from a *college of celebrity*."[12] The Baptist Board also failed to find the method a panacea for all of its missions, and so McCoy asked the faculty at the Hamilton Library and Theological Institute to communicate news of the "notable" discovery to Baptist missionaries in foreign lands.[13]

For a brief period there was a great flurry of activity in the crudely built printing office, where Meeker used part of his

[12] *Ibid.*, 474–76.
[13] McCoy, Journal, June, n.d., 1837.

scarce paper supply to paste over cracks to keep out the wind. The first book to come off his press based on the new orthography was Ira Blanchard's, *Linapi 'e Lrkvekun, Apiwivuli Kavuni Vawini Wato*, or the *Delaware Primer and First Book*.[14] It was followed in quick succession by "first books" in Shawnee, Potawatomi, Oto, Creek, and Choctaw for other Baptist missionaries. The Methodists and Presbyterians overcame their initial reservation and asked Meeker to publish books in Shawnee, Wea, and Iowa.[15] The best-known product of Meeker's press was the *Siwinowe Kesibwi* (*Shawnee Sun*), a diminutive newspaper edited by Lykins and published entirely in the Indian language.[16]

The interest in the Indian language publications seriously hampered McCoy's journalistic ambitions. He had a manuscript ready for the first issue of "*An Annual Register of Indian Affairs within the Indian Territory*," but Meeker claimed that the board had refused to authorize its publication. McCoy accepted this explanation. "Brother Meeker cannot be blamed for doing as he understands that the Board has directed, still were the case reversed, and I were the printer, and another missionary the publisher, I should not have obeyed the Board."[17] Meeker's correspondence with the board clearly revealed that it was he who had objected to printing the journal because he did not think it relevant to missionary affairs.[18] Meeker criticized McCoy in other letters to the board, but McCoy never suspected the underlying antagonism. Lucius Bolles, the corresponding secretary, directed Meeker to publish McCoy's magazine at cost. Mc-

[14] Meeker, Journal, March 1, 24, April 17, and August 28, 1834, May 26, 27, and June 13, 1835.

[15] For a bibliography of extant literature in Indian languages based on this system, see Douglas C. McMurtrie and Albert H. Allen, *Jotham Meeker, Pioneer Printer of Kansas*.

[16] Meeker, Journal, February 24, 1835.

[17] McCoy, Journal, January 25, 1835.

[18] Meeker to Bolles, January 14, 1834, Meeker Papers.

Coy did not object too strenuously, although he noted that "this is a missionary matter, as much so as the books printed by the other brethern . . . it seems not a little singular that they should charge me."[19] With the help of his family, McCoy bound one thousand copies of the first fifty-two page edition. They ironed each sheet with a common iron, trimmed and stitched every copy by hand, and corrected numerous misprints with a pen. McCoy sent a copy to each member of Congress, and gave away many of the rest. The magazine, with its description of the tribes in Indian Territory, its vignettes of various Indian chiefs, and its information about the missions, created considerable interest. McCoy received inquiries from various members of Congress. The board was also impressed, and offered to bear the printing costs of future issues.[20] Not all the readers reacted favorably, however. "I was sorry to find a letter to me from Rev. Thos. Johnson, Superintendent of Methodist Indian missions, and another from Rev. J. C. Berryman, missionary to the Kickapoos, in which they indulge in low, vulgar, ungenerous abuse."[21] The Methodists, probably with good reason, believed that their work had not been fairly represented.

The rivalries of the missionaries seriously hampered the efforts of the emigrant tribes to reintegrate their societal life in a new environment. One faction of Delawares, for example, had allowed Ira Blanchard to open a Baptist school. Another faction had permitted Edward T. Peery, a Methodist, to begin a mission. The two missionaries connived and schemed to supplant each other. As a result, a vigorous young chief by the name of Shawanock led a delegation to Washington to ask for the removal of all whites from the Delaware country. McCoy claimed

19 McCoy, Journal, January 25, 1835.
20 Bolles to Meeker, August 11, 1835, Meeker Papers.
21 McCoy, Journal, April 11, 1837.

that Major Alexander Morgan, sutler, postmaster, and trader at
Fort Leavenworth, together with "Wicked Catholics...craving
& broken down men at St. Louis" instigated the trip.[22] A somewhat similar situation arose among the Shawnees. With two
missions and the prospect of another,[23] some of the chiefs decided
they would be better off without any.

The missionaries finally realized the need of better inter-
denominational relations and instituted an annual conference.
Presbyterians, Methodists, and Baptists met for the first such
meeting at the Shawnee Baptist Mission in the summer of 1834.
Amity quickly ended when someone offered a resolution "relating to the manner members should be received from one mission
church to another of a different denomination."[24]

As "Father of the Indian Territory" McCoy was in a unique
position to dominate events in that region, but he was denied the
official status that could have made this possible. With the influx
of Indians and missionaries, he could at best merely attempt to
influence decisions affecting the territory. There were those in
state and church who did seek his advice. Ellsworth, member of
the special Indian commission responsible for administering the
territory, consulted McCoy on many occasions.[25] Secretary of
War Cass, in his annual report to Congress in 1833, commended
a plan of Indian land cessions that McCoy had long advocated.
McCoy had argued that instead of taking Indian lands and allowing annuities, the government should have the lands surveyed
and sold to the highest bidder. After the costs of the survey and

[22] *Ibid.*, April 11 and May 20, 1837.

[23] The Society of Friends had decided to move its mission from Wapakoneta, Ohio, to Indian Territory. See Wilson Hobbs, "The Friends' Establishment in Kansas Territory, Personal Recollections of Wilson Hobbs, M.D.,
Among the Shawnee Indians from November, 1850, to November, 1852,"
Kansas Historical Collections, Vol. VIII (1903–1904), 261–62.

[24] Meeker, Journal, July 25, 1834.

[25] McCoy, Journal, September 27, 1832, August 30 and November 22, 1833;

the sale of the land were paid, the net proceeds should go to the Indians. Except for their immediate wants, this money should be invested for them in productive stocks. Commissioners treating with the Chickasaws in the spring of 1834 adopted this procedure for the first time.[26] Although the board no longer listed McCoy as a missionary, it frequently sought his advice. Unfortunately, McCoy's advisory services provided no remuneration, and in addition, his surveying appointments had dwindled away. Early in 1833 he wrote, "My spirits have been greatly depressed for some time. My family is pretty large, and we daily have . . . company to increase our expenses of living. I am earning nothing."[27] An "influential friend" called on the President in his behalf, and this visit led to a brief spate of surveying commissions. They included tracts for two tribes who held special interest for Mc-Coy, the Weas and the Kickapoos.

The Weas, the Indians with whom McCoy had begun his missionary career, drifted into lands just north of the Marais des Cygnes long before treaties legalized their presence. Here they eked out a precarious existence, next door to the Kansas. Their chiefs complained to William Clark that the Kansas "infest us constantly; they beg every thing from us, and what we do not give them, they steal."[28] The Weas asked McCoy to resume his mission, but he was satisfied to survey a reserve for them on the lands they occupied.[29] Of much greater significance to McCoy, because of a previous acquaintanceship with Chief Kennekuk, was a commission to survey a reserve for the Kickapoos.

When still at Carey, McCoy had received a request for a school from a Kickapoo chief called "The Prophet," then resid-

Washington Irving, *Indian Sketches*, xxii.
[26] McCoy, *Baptist Missions*, 459; Kappler, *Indian Affairs*, II, 418–23.
[27] McCoy, Journal, February 12, 1833.
[28] 23 Cong., 1 sess., *Sen. Doc. 512*, Pt. 2, 115–17.
[29] McCoy, Journal, July 16 and August 16, 1833.

ing on the Vermilion River in Illinois. Kennekuk had formed a religious party with the object of "reforming" the lives of the Indians, and one of its basic tenets was abstention from liquor. McCoy had not been able to fulfill the request.[30] Simerwell later wrote that Kennekuk's influence had spread to the Potawatomis. His teachings had become more rigorous in the meantime, for he now had drunken followers publicly whipped.[31] The Kickapoos gave up all of their land in the Old Northwest in 1819, but Kennekuk and his people stayed in Illinois. One segment of the Kickapoo tribe lived in southwestern Missouri, and in 1832 the Missouri Kickapoos agreed to trade their lands for a large reservation in the northeast corner of Indian Territory.[32] Kennekuk and his intertribal following joined the main band of Kickapoos and migrated to the new tract early in 1833.[33]

John Treat Irving, nephew of the writer, Washington Irving, accompanied Ellsworth to the West, and visited Kennekuk shortly after his arrival. He described him as a "tall bony Indian, with a keen black eye, and a face beaming with intelligence."[34] The Kickapoo Prophet had other callers—Baptists, Methodists, Presbyterians, and Roman Catholics—all seeking special privileges for their missionary societies. The Methodists had an important advantage, however, for through some inexplicable stratagem, Kennekuk, while still in Illinois, had secured a Methodist license to preach. Jerome C. Berryman, the Methodist missionary in Indian Territory who had written to McCoy expressing an unfavorable opinion of his "Register," now hired Kennekuk as a helper; and within a short time they baptized about four hundred tribesmen.[35] The Baptists sent Daniel

---

[30] *Ibid.*, May 23, 1833.
[31] Simerwell to S. H. Cones, April 11, 1833, Simerwell Correspondence.
[32] Kappler, *Indian Affairs*, II, 365–67.
[33] 23 Cong., 1 sess., *Sen. Doc. 512*, Pt. 3, pp. 511–18.
[34] Washington Irving, *Indian Sketches*, 43.

French, a young man who had served his apprenticeship at Carey under McCoy, to the Kickapoos, but he could make no impression on the tribe.[36] The Baptist missionaries stood critically by as the Methodists added large numbers of Indians to their church rolls. It soon became apparent, however, that Kennekuk was not a reliable Methodist. One of the provisions of the treaty of 1832 had stipulated that a church be built for Kennekuk. Once it was completed, he would not allow any missionaries to officiate in it, but developed his own form of worship and theology.[37]

McCoy began to survey the Kickapoo reserve in the fall of 1833. He visited Kennekuk's church and observed some of the practices, but with little of the appreciation he had once felt for the religious exercises of Menominee. McCoy described Kennekuk's religion as "less Christian than ideas inherent in the religion of common wild Indians."[38] The main part of the service, McCoy noted, was Kennekuk's speech, which lasted three hours. The congregation responded in "a kind of prayer, expressed in broken sentences, often repeated, in a monotonous sing-song tone." To preserve harmony in the chant, the participants held small boards engraved with five figures which they followed with their fingers until the last character "admonished" them that they had completed the prayer. During the service, certain persons with whips circulated among the congregation to keep order. McCoy observed that flagellation performed other functions in Kennekuk's system. An offender, whose sins were known only to himself, might go to one of five appointed whippers, state the offense that he had committed, and ask for the

35 Jerome C. Berryman, "A Circuit Rider's Frontier Experiences," *Kansas Historical Collections*, Vol. XVI (1923–25), 216.
36 *American Baptist Magazine*, Vol. XV (January, 1835), 36; Meeker to Bolles, January 13, 1835, Meeker Papers.
37 Berryman, "Circuit Experiences," 216.
38 McCoy, Journal, August 16, 1835.

commensurate punishment. The penitent, after the flagellation, would shake hands with the "Executioner," express his thanks for the favor done him, and declare that he felt relieved of a heavy burden.[39]

As the Indian's knowledge of the white man's religion increased, his own traditional beliefs often came into clearer focus. Sometimes he concluded that the "Great Spirit" had ordained two roads to the "Happy Hunting Grounds." Kennekuk ultimately adopted the theory of the two ways. Berryman reported that Kennekuk began to assert that he was the "Son of God" sent to the red people, just as Jesus had been sent to the white people.[40] Grant Foreman gives a vivid description of Kennekuk's death in 1854. Many of Kennekuk's infatuated followers supposedly stayed with his body because they "were desirous of witnessing his last prophecy, that 'in three days he would rise again.' "[41]

McCoy interrupted the Kickapoo survey to go to Washington early in 1834. The special commission appointed in 1832 was about to make its report to Congress and he wanted to be there. Before presenting his recommendations, Ellsworth told McCoy that he would advocate diminution of the number of Indian agencies if not their entire abolition, that a seat of government be located for the Indian Territory, that a governor or general superintendent be appointed, and that civil tribunals be fixed in different parts of the territory.[42] This announcement was gratifying to McCoy, for he had recommended these measures. The commissioners submitted a report to Congress in the spring of

[39] McCoy, *Baptist Missions*, 456–68.
[40] Berryman, "Circuit Experiences," 215–17.
[41] *Last Trek of the Indians*, 215. Unfortunately, Foreman's source for the story, McCoy's *Baptist Missions*, is hardly unimpeachable. The only edition was published in 1840.
[42] McCoy, Journal, November 22, 1833.

1834, and the House Committee on Indian Affairs drafted a legislative program based largely on their recommendations.

Edward Everett, chairman of the House committee, introduced three bills. Two bills passed[43] and became an important part of the fabric of Indian law. The Indian Trade and Intercourse Act redefined the Indian country and enabled the government to deal better with intruders by providing for the control of traders through regulated licenses and heavy penalties for trade violations. The Indian Reorganization Act made more efficient the administration of Indian affairs, and supplemented an earlier act which created the office of Commissioner of Indian Affairs. Superintendencies and agencies were consolidated and, in some cases, eliminated. Three agencies had served the Kansas, Osages, and emigrant tribes from the Old Northwest, but now there was to be only one.[44] McCoy was thoroughly disappointed that the third bill, which would have provided for the organization of the Indian Territory, did not pass. He felt that the failure of this bill to pass left the basic issue, Indian self-government, unsettled. He doubted that either Cass or Everett really favored the measure.

McCoy returned to his home without the prospect of any further government work. These were hard years financially. "Much of my time . . . has been employed in the business of Bookkeeping for a neighbouring store for wages!! We are also boarding several men for the same reasons—namely to earn something for a living!!!" He was too proud to seek help from his denomination. "I suppose if I were to apply, the Board would give me a living, but in that case my labours would become cir-

[43] *Register of Debates in Congress*, Vol. X, Pt. 4, p. 4200. The report of the special commission was appended to the report of the House Committee on Indian Affairs.

[44] For the reorganization of this agency, see Records of the Office of Indian Affairs, "Letters Sent," XIII, 91–94, 105, 111–13, 131, 180.

cumscribed to a little neighbourhood of Indians." "Influential friends" again called on the Secretary of War in his behalf, but Cass informed them that there was no provision for any further surveying projects. McCoy noted, "This is strange! Treaties provide for much surveying."[45]

In spite of the provisions of 1834, McCoy professed to find "miserable management" in almost all matters relating to Indian affairs. Government officials never had given much consideration to the problems of peaceful relations between the intruder and the intruded in Indian Territory. A long series of skirmishes resulted. Delaware hunting parties were often waylaid by the Pawnees. Shawanock finally gathered a small contingent of Delaware warriors and attempted to retaliate, but when they reached the Platte they had the good fortune to find a deserted Pawnee village, and so they satisfied themselves by setting fire to it.[46] Shawanock's "initiative" caught the imagination of some of the white men at Fort Leavenworth, and to McCoy's disgust they "petted & humored and flattered" the young chief.[47]

A more explosive situation arose when Comanche and Kiowa bands raided emigrant villages in the southern part of the territory. The Secretary of War appointed three negotiators early in 1835 and called the Comanches and Kiowas into council. The Indians assembled at the treaty grounds. After waiting two months for the commissioners to arrive, the Comanches dispersed for their spring buffalo hunt. Perhaps there was some justification for McCoy's evaluation of two of the commissioners.

> Col. Arbuckle is a good commander of a military post, and there his qualifications end. He is just about equal to *nobody*

[45] McCoy, Journal, March 10, May 3, and June 22, 1835.
[46] 23 Cong., 1 sess., *Sen. Doc. 512*, Pt. 1, p. 523; Pt. 3, pp. 238, 306; Pt. 4, pp. 523, 654.
[47] McCoy, Journal, July 7, 1833.

in a business of important negotiations. Gov. Stokes is an ignorant, profane old man in his dotage, a mere sot in drunkeness, and a card-player. He is therefore ten degrees worse than a *nobody*.[48]

McCoy reserved even harsher expletives for those who granted the Potawatomis a reserve outside of what he considered to be Indian Territory.

After making provision for the extinguishment of Indian titles in Ohio, Congress turned its attention to the Potawatomis in Illinois, Indiana, and Michigan Territory. A number of minor cessions followed. The tribe surrendered the small reservation surrounding Carey; and in Indiana the erstwhile "Prophet," Menominee, now a respectable chief and a practicing Roman Catholic,[49] gave up all but twenty sections of his reserve. President Jackson was unhappy with the minor and partial cessions; consequently, the commissioners who treated with the major segments of the Potawatomi tribe at Chicago in the fall of 1833 acted with much more vigor. The Prairie Potawatomis surrendered all claim to land in Illinois in exchange for a five-million-acre reserve northeast of the Missouri River in what is now western Iowa.[50] The Reverend John F. Schermerhorn attended the negotiations as a special commissioner, and McCoy blamed him for this arrangement. "It would have been just as easy to have given them a residence on the Osage River as where they did. . . . But the Old Simpleton knew too little."[51] The St. Joseph Potawatomis in Michigan Territory ceded their last small reservations in the Chicago treaty, despite violent opposition within the bands. To pacify these and other unhappy Pota-

[48] *Ibid.*, August 16, 1835.
[49] Father Louis Deseille, a Flemish priest, visited Menominee's band about three times a year. Garraghan, *Jesuits*, II, 179–80.
[50] Kappler, *Indian Affairs*, II, 367–70, 372–75, 402–15.
[51] McCoy, Journal, December 14, 1835.

watomis, the War Department agreed to allow them to remain on their tracts for three more years before moving to the West.

An opportunity to organize the first expedition of Potawatomis came unexpectedly. A band of destitute followers of Kennekuk requested that arrangements be made for them to join "The Prophet" on the Kickapoo reserve. Colonel Abel C. Pepper, the Potawatomi agent, asked Simerwell to recruit other emigrants among the St. Joseph Potawatomis.[52] Apprehensive about their future in their old homes, some consented to go, but when the time came few could muster the courage to leave. Simerwell decided it would be pointless to stay at Carey any longer, and so he secured permission to move with Pepper's contingent at public expense. He described a familiar story. About three hundred Indians assembled in June, but found that arrangements had not been completed for their departure. The agents issued clothing and other equipment for the trip, but there was little provision for food while the natives waited. They sold their equipment to "unfeeling whites, who would give the value of 6 pense or a shilling . . . for clothing to the value of five or six dollars," and then scattered in all directions. About sixty of the original group returned in late summer to begin the trip to the West.[53]

The removal controversy left the Potawatomi tribe rife with factionalism. The teachings of the Kickapoo Prophet further contributed to the fragmentation. About five hundred Potawatomi converts ultimately gathered on the Kickapoo reserve. Without any legitimate claim to land of their own, living with Indians with whom they had no kinship, the Potawatomis attempted to live by "the chase," wandering from spot to spot and

[52] Pepper to Simerwell, April 11, 1833, Simerwell Correspondence.
[53] Simerwell, Journal, June 22 to November 13, 1833, MS in the Kansas State Historical Society Library.

sleeping on the ground or in small smoky huts built from flag mats. Anthony L. Davis, an emigrating agent for the tribe, and Simerwell explored a triangle of land east of the Missouri River, but not yet part of the state of Missouri, for a possible home for the destitute Indians.[54] Davis, without authority, allowed some of them to settle there. Meanwhile, the Prairie Potawatomis sent out an expedition to view the large tract northeast of the Missouri River. The delegates found it more remotely situated than they had supposed and uncomfortably close to the bellicose tribes of the Upper Missouri. Because of the unfavorable report, the first large emigration of Prairie Potawatomis, which got underway in the fall of 1835, moved to the area where the Kennekuk Potawatomis had settled.[55] McCoy knew that they could not stay here permanently, for Missourians intended to annex this region to "round out" the borders of their state. Furthermore, McCoy believed that it was not properly in Indian Territory.[56] He decided to go to Washington to arrange a permanent location for the Potawatomis within the Indian country and also to attempt to bring about a general improvement in the management of the affairs of the territory.

McCoy arrived at the capital in January, 1836, and took up residence with John Tipton, now a senator from Indiana, for what became a stay of one and one-half years. Tipton left no indelible impression on the upper house during his tenure, but he was well informed on Indian matters. Formerly identified with the trader element which lived by exploitation of the Indians, he now professed a great humanitarian interest in the red man. Some of his associates in the Senate questioned his efforts to guard

[54] Simerwell to Bolles, February 18 and May 1, 1835, Simerwell Correspondence.

[55] A. L. Davis to McCoy, January 1, 1836, McCoy Correspondence.

[56] *The Annual Register of Indian Affairs Within the Indian (or Western) Territory* (January, 1836), 20.

against the practices that he had participated in and profited from when he was an agent. Apparently, he sincerely believed Mc-Coy's plan for a system of self-government among the Indians to be workable and the only satisfactory solution for the problem of Indian administration. With McCoy back in Washington, Tipton decided that the time had come to take up the matter of the organization of Indian Territory again.

On March 4, 1836, Tipton introduced a bill into the Senate for the confederation of twenty-eight tribes in the Indian country. Lands were to be secured by patents. A superintendent of Indian affairs was to be appointed for a four-year term by the President with the consent of the Senate. One of the Superintendent's main duties would be to organize a general council to which each tribe would send delegates. The council would enact laws and regulations for the general welfare of the Indians and appoint a representative to Congress. The laws could be vetoed by the Superintendent, but the council would have the right to appeal to the President.[57]

McCoy and Tipton collaborated closely during the debate on the bill. McCoy prepared detailed calculations and carefully measured maps for Tipton to substantiate his claim that there was room for all Indians in the territory. A Cherokee treaty pending in the Senate that would give the tribe another large section of land between Missouri and the Osage country in lieu of money owed them by the government complicated the task. McCoy believed that the Cherokees had too much land even without this proposed addition. Tipton became seriously ill during the debate, and with a note of desperation, McCoy wrote, "O Lord take care of thine own cause." McCoy spent many hours reading to the Senator while he recuperated so that he would be better prepared to sustain the bill. When Tipton re-

[57] From a copy of the bill in the McCoy Correspondence.

covered, McCoy helped him write his formal address to the Senate.[58]

Other Indian matters before Congress militated against the territorial bill. Opposition to removal among the Seminoles had developed into open hostility by 1836, and for seven years the United States strove to crush the sporadic resistance of a few hundred warriors hidden among the Everglades. In the same year several bands of Creeks reacted against intolerable conditions in the South and the "Creek War" was under way. McCoy, in a gross oversimplification, attributed "not a little of the distresses of these wars" to the missionaries of the American Board because they had encouraged the Indians to hope they could remain within the states, only "to be butchered." Another great distraction in Congress was the question of whether a fraudulent treaty signed with a small faction of Cherokees at New Echota in 1835 should be ratified. It provided for the cession of all Cherokee lands east of the Mississippi. The majority party under John Ross led a vigorous movement to stop ratification, and Jesse Bushyhead, a native Baptist missionary, asked McCoy to support the effort. McCoy was in a dilemma, complicated by the fact that the Reverend John Schermerhorn, had negotiated the "infamous" treaty, and was in Washington lending his support to its passage. McCoy did not think that the treaty should be ratified, but he believed that the Cherokees should emigrate. He advised John Ross and Bushyhead to work for a better removal agreement, although he expressed doubt that the Ross party would ever voluntarily go to Indian Territory.[59]

Secretary Cass officially favored the territorial organization bill, but McCoy felt that the War Department covertly worked to block it. "In almost every step that we take in the matter of

[58] McCoy, Journal, April 28, May 16, 22, 1836, and February 1, 1837.
[59] *Ibid.*, May 3, 17, 19, and 22, 1836.

securing to the Indians a permanent home, and laws, &c. we have
to contend with the injudicious counter measure of Gov. Cass."
McCoy suspected that Cass and Henry R. Schoolcraft, head of
the Michigan superintendency, intended to send the remaining
Indians in the Old Northwest to the upper regions of the Great
Lakes. "I want them if they sell any to sell all their land and go
to our Ind. Ter. and there let the govt. settle them on farms &c.
If this should not be done, from this time their decline must be
rapid and their destruction certain." Through the "blessing of
providence" McCoy hoped to be able to defeat "this mischievous
design."[60]

To McCoy it seemed foolish for Indians to remain in any part
of Michigan Territory, and the lone Baptist missionary at
Thomas now compounded this "foolishness." Because of the
great pressure on the Ottawas to sell their lands north of the
Grand River, Leonard Slater decided to accompany a delegation
of tribesmen to Washington to notify government authorities
that there would be no further cessions. He also advised the
Ottawas not to send chiefs but members of the tribe who had no
legal authority to treat. Schoolcraft cynically concluded a treaty
with the very delegation that came to Washington to prevent it.
In what McCoy called the most "rascally treaty" ever negotiated, the Ottawas ceded an area comprising a large part of the
present state of Michigan.[61] Ordinarily McCoy would have
looked upon such an agreement philosophically as the inevitable
result of "bad policy," which merely pointed up the need of
securing a permanent home for the Indians. But now, because of
the machinations of Schoolcraft, McCoy could not be sure that
the Ottawas would ever go to Indian Territory. And Slater again
complicated the problem, for he convinced a number of Ottawas

[60] *Ibid.*, March, n.d., April 29 and May 19, 1836.
[61] *Statutes at Large*, VII, 491.

to use their annuity funds to buy back some of their former lands.[62] He continued his ministrations to a small community of Indians totally encompassed by white settlements. McCoy was certain that the experiment would fail, for "200 years experience" had shown that the Indians could not prosper when surrounded by people of "other colour."[63]

The arduous demands of "disinterested benevolence" sometimes became confused with "benevolent self-interest" in the lives of early-nineteenth-century reformers, and never far from McCoy's mind in his zealous promotion of the organization of Indian Territory was the hope that he would obtain the superintendency. The position would compensate for all the trouble he had experienced during the first years of the Indian Canaan, and it would yet give him the opportunity to steer its development in its proper course. It would be a fitting climax to his career. The salary would be large enough to support his family comfortably for the first time and to pay the expenses of his own "printing concern." He talked to the President about the appointment, and Jackson assured him that he would get it if the territorial bill became law.[64] The measure died with the Twenty-fourth Congress.

[62] Slater to Meeker, July 28, 1836, Meeker Papers.
[63] McCoy, *Baptist Missions*, 496.
[64] McCoy, Journal, February 14 and May 16, 1836.

Chapter **X**

The End of a Venture

In all, Isaac McCoy made twelve or thirteen trips to Washington to lobby for his various projects. He traveled in a variety of conveyances—leaky lake schooners, keelboats converted to steam, open road wagons without seats, and stages. The last seemed the most dangerous, particularly on the treacherous roads through the Appalachians. On one occasion the stage had upset, killing some of the occupants, and leaving McCoy with permanent disabilities. But stages frequently provided the opportunity to travel with junketing politicians. On his return to the West in 1837, McCoy had as one of his fellow passengers for part of the way the "Indian educator" Richard M. Johnson, now also the vice-president of the United States. McCoy broached the subject of the organization of Indian Territory, and the Vice-President responded by "asking many questions relating to my relations to others . . . with a view of ascertaining the extent of influence which favors to me might have, or what influence which in the country I could exert." On another portion of the same trip, McCoy traveled with Henry Clay. McCoy gathered that he could expect no support from the Senator because of his hostility to the administration.[1]

There was little cause for optimism, but McCoy was confident that in the next Congress, Indian self-government would become

[1] McCoy, Journal, March 16, 1837.

a reality. In the meantime, he proposed to persuade the tribes to petition for enactment of a territorial bill. On his return to the Indian country, McCoy presented the substance of his territorial plan to the Delaware, Shawnee, Kickapoo, Sac, Iowa, Wea, Piankashaw, Peoria, Kaskaskia, Potawatomi, Ottawa, and Kansa tribes. All but the Kansas attached some importance to the discussions. Each tribe signed a petition. Liberal gifts of tobacco, freely distributed, and a few well-placed presents of bacon, paid for by McCoy, helped the situation immeasurably.

McCoy sometimes intimated that he envisioned an Indian country without tribal distinctions. He came to realize that its immediate destiny depended on unified tribal life. The problem of factionalism was acute, particularly among the Potawatomis. McCoy wanted all elements of the tribe consolidated within the borders of the region he defined as Indian Territory. While in Washington, McCoy, with the help of John Tipton, had brought about a treaty with the Potawatomis which gave them a reserve below the Marais des Cygnes.[2] Upon completion of his tour to the hustings, McCoy surveyed a large tract below the Ottawa lands and located a site for an agency on a tributary of the Marais des Cygnes which he called "Putawatomie Creek."[3] He secured the appointment of subagent for Anthony Davis, "a friend of missions"; but to McCoy's dismay the War Department created another subagency for the Potawatomis at Council Bluffs and named Dr. Edwin James to that post. James told Mc-Coy that his idea of an organized Indian Territory was utopian, and that the Potawatomis might as well keep their reservation on the Upper Missouri, for there really was no place from which they would not be forced by white men. In James's opinion the extinction of the Indians was inevitable, and all that could be

[2] Kappler, *Indian Affairs*, II, 488–89.
[3] *Annual Register of Indian Affairs* (1836), 58.

done was to alleviate the suffering of the dying tribes as much as possible and to erect "tombstones, or monuments to their memory." McCoy wrote, "From such friends, and they have become very numerous, we may well pray the Episcopalian prayer, 'God deliver me.' "[4] McCoy believed that, had it not been for James, the Potawatomis who had already moved to the Council Bluffs area would have been persuaded to come to Indian Territory. As it was, a bitter contest for immigrants developed between the two agencies that ultimately split the tribe.

The removals to Indian Territory in the first half of the decade of the 1830's, in spite of fraud, bribery, and threats, were largely voluntary. The tribesmen suffered many inconveniences, common to travel conditions of the day but complicated by inept government agents and corrupt contractors. In the latter part of the decade, it became clear that many Indians simply could not be persuaded to move West, and so removal agents resorted to force. What followed for the Cherokees was the traumatic journey over the "Trail of Tears." A less publicized northern counterpart took place in the same year, and it involved familiar names in the McCoy story—Potawatomis, Chief Menominee, John Tipton, and William Polke.

United States commissioners had granted the Potawatomis in northern Indiana, along with their kinsmen in Illinois and Michigan Territory, the privilege of remaining on their reserves for three years after they had ceded them. This period had expired. Squatters, in anticipation of pre-emption laws, had already moved on some of the lands. In the face of government impatience and threats, some bands showed no intention of moving; and Menominee, still in possession of a small reserve, adamantly refused to sell.

Governor David Wallace of Indiana asked Senator Tipton,

[4] McCoy, Journal, June 25, 1837.

because of his former influence with the Potawatomis, to persuade them to vacate the state. Tipton was unable to break down their resistance, and when it seemed that the settlers might take matters in their own hands, Wallace authorized Tipton to use the militia. While Colonel Pepper, the agent, pretended to council with the Indians at the village church, Tipton, by prearrangement, swiftly descended upon them, assembled them together, and before they had an opportunity to make preparations for departure, started them on the long trek to the Indian country. Some, like Menominee, had to be bound hand and foot. With the militiamen at their heels, between seven and eight hundred Indians marched off in double-quick time. There were insufficient wagons for the aged, the infirm, and the sick. Old women, pregnant women, and children went on foot. Sickness soon struck the ill-prepared expedition, and before it reached its destination, one-fifth of the original number had died.[5] Judge William Polke, McCoy's brother-in-law, conducted the expedition beyond the borders of Indiana. He regretted the haste and lack of preparation, but he believed that prompt action prevented a frontier war. Some of his actions belied his professed sympathy, however. With typical disregard for the privacy of the Indians, Polke marched them into the town square at Jacksonville, Illinois, because of the "very great curiosity manifested by the citizens."[6] Polke and the emigrants arrived at the Marais des Cygnes reserve in the late fall of 1838. No houses or cultivated lands awaited them. McCoy, oblivious as usual to the hardships entailed in removal, merely recorded Polke's arrival. With no further Potawatomi claims to worry about, the state of Indiana

[5] McKee, *Trail of Death*, 19–114.

[6] Dwight L. Smith, "A Continuation of the Journal of an Emigrating Party of Potawatomi Indians, 1838, and Ten William Polke Manuscripts," *Indiana Magazine of History*, Vol. XLIV (December, 1948), 396–408.

erected a statue of Menominee at the site of the Indian chapel where he was betrayed.

Their lands gone and the graves of their dead plowed up, a few St. Joseph Potawatomi bands remained to wander around in the region which once was a native habitat and the scene of McCoy's major missionary effort. Lykins, under appointment of the government, attempted to gather them up and take them west, but they refused to go or preferred to go to Canada.[7]

McCoy helped Robert Simerwell to get a Potawatomi mission established in the southern reserve, but Simerwell could make little impression on the tribesmen. The removal experience, the most drastic in a long series of upheavals, destroyed much of whatever cultural cohesion remained. According to Simerwell, the majority, after their arrival, were determined to remain in a state of permanent inebriation.[8] Anthony Davis reported that drunkenness prevailed among all tribes in Indian Territory, but most so among the Potawatomis.[9] Simerwell opened a day school but soon suspended it. Many of the tribesmen on the tract gravitated toward settlements on Sugar Creek. There they came under the influence of Roman Catholic missionaries,[10] and so the Baptists lost whatever influence they had with the tribe.

The fragmented condition of the Ottawa tribe also caused McCoy considerable concern. He extended the boundaries of the Ottawa reserve in the Indian country, but members of that tribe never came to the West in great numbers. They retained some relatively large tracts in Northern Michigan and many made their way to Manitoulin and Walpole Islands in Canada.[11]

[7] McCoy, *Baptist Missions*, 546.

[8] Letter from Simerwell dated November 28, 1838, *Baptist Missionary Magazine*, Vol. XIX (April, 1839), 91.

[9] *Annual Report of the Commissioner of Indian Affairs for 1839*, 505.

[10] Garraghan, *Jesuits*, II, 175–235.

[11] Robert F. Bauman, "Kansas, Canada, or Starvation," *Michigan History*, Vol. XXXVI (September, 1952), 296–98.

There was little escape for the Ottawas on the Maumee River in Ohio, however. They had ceded the last of their land in 1833, and yet they hung on, facing the threat of starvation and destruction. John McElvain, who received an appointment to superintend their migration, claimed that the greatest obstacle was the interference of creditors who presented exorbitant claims for debts and threatened to detain the Indians by force or imprisonment unless they were paid. He finally dispatched about two hundred by boat in 1837. Dresden W. H. Howard conducted the remaining Ottawas of the Maumee to the West in 1839 and left an interesting account of the drama and pathos of removal.

> The confusion, packing of equipage, goods and clothing commenced amid cries of children, barking of dogs, yelling of the young Indian boys wild with excitement and adventure of the journey to new hunting grounds. The women as was the Indian custom, did all the work of packing. . . . the men sat in the shade smoking their pipes of tobacco. . . . many insisted and were permitted to visit their English Father at Malden and receive their annual presents for the last time.[12]

The arrival of the Ohio Ottawas brought the number of that tribe in Indian Territory to 350,[13] a weak remnant, but enough to begin a mission, Meeker decided. In June, 1837, Meeker unloaded his wagons and moved into a small, rough cabin that he had previously constructed on the north bank of the Marais des Cygnes.[14]

After choosing a site for the Potawatomis and enlarging the Ottawa tract, McCoy received commissions for similar projects. His relations with the War Department had improved tempo-

---

[12] Robert F. Bauman (ed.), "The Removal of the Indians from the Maumee Valley: A Selection from the Dresden W. H. Howard Papers," *Northwest Ohio Quarterly*, Vol. XXX (Winter, 1957–58), 15–16.

[13] *Annual Report of the Commissioner of Indian Affairs for 1839*, 505.

[14] Meeker to Bolles, July 25, 1837, Meeker Papers.

rarily with the inauguration of Martin van Buren's administration. McCoy superintended the survey of what became known as the "Cherokee Strip."[15] He laid out a rectangular reserve for the Sacs and Foxes of Missouri north of the Kickapoo lands. Subsequently, William Clark decided to send the Iowas to the upper part of this reserve. The subagent for the Indians soon sent an urgent appeal to McCoy to mark out a division line between the tribes because fighting had broken out.[16] Friction continued, even after McCoy had divided the reservation. The Sacs and Foxes claimed that the Iowas subsisted on their livestock. McCoy selected a tract west and south of the Ottawa lands for scattered groups of Chippewas, but only one small band came to Indian Territory. In the fall of 1837, McCoy surveyed a large rectangular reserve of 1,824,000 acres north of the Osage country for the so-called New York Indians living in Wisconsin and New York. To the great dissatisfaction of the Potawatomis, McCoy reserved a choice section of country east of their tract for the Miamis. The Miamis were the only major tribe still in the Old Northwest. The rising tide of settlers soon hemmed them in and threatened to overflow their reserves, but the combined talents of Tipton, Pepper, Schermerhorn, and Ellsworth could not shake them loose from lands on the Wabash. An additional obstacle was the opposition of the traders to any treaty which did not take care of their interests.[17] As a result, the Miamis were among the last emigrants to reach Indian Territory.

With a new Congress already in session, McCoy returned to Washington early in 1838 to take up again the matter of the organization of Indian Territory. Tipton had already introduced

[15] McCoy to C. A. Harris, commissioner of Indian affairs, September 20, 1837, McCoy and Lykins Letters, from typewritten copies of original manuscripts in the Indiana State Library, Kansas State Historical Society Library.
[16] Andrew L. Hughes to McCoy, July 8, 1837, McCoy Correspondence.
[17] McCoy, Journal, May 31 and June 16, 1837.

a bill into the Senate which was essentially the same as the one of 1836. He had added, at McCoy's suggestion, a safeguard against alienation of lands. As a result of his recent visits to the tribes in Indian Territory, McCoy had come to believe that lands should be patented to individual families. This system would prevent a chief from selling, because of bribes, fraud, or force, property his tribe held in common. Further, land once deeded to a family, could never be sold to a white man. McCoy had also suggested changes for the proposed general council of Indians. The original organization bill provided for representation based on population, but this would give the Weas one representative and the Cherokees ninety-seven. In the new bill, each tribe would have not less than two nor more than five representatives, depending on an agreed ratio.[18]

While waiting for the bill to come before the Senate, McCoy called on members of Congress, including former President John Quincy Adams, to ask for support. He busied himself with other things, freely dispensing advice to those who asked for it and those who did not. He prepared and handed the draft of a bill to Secretary of War Joel Poinsett which would allow the Potawatomis to hold their lands in severalty. McCoy also appeared before the House Committee on Military Affairs and pleaded that military posts not be erected in Indian Territory. He had for some time contemplated writing a history of the aborigines of North America. He now spent many hours searching for material in Washington bookstores and libraries. He thought a series of lectures presented by George Catlin might be useful. McCoy saw the exhibits of materials collected and the paintings made by Catlin in a seven-year tour among the Indian tribes, but he claimed that he learned nothing of any value from this

[18] From a printed copy of the bill in the McCoy Correspondence. See also, McCoy to Harris, October 2, 1837, McCoy and Lykins Letters.

"romantic nonsense." He expressed contempt for Catlin's pa-tronizing expression of pity for the red man because he was "doomed to extinction."[19]

The organization bill came up before the Senate in April, 1838, and McCoy, sitting in the gallery, could scarcely contain his "passion."

> How could I feel otherwise? Here they were discussing a measure which I had labored fifteen years to promote—a bill which the Indian Department and the Committee of Ind. Affairs had reported according to my recommendation, the original of which I drafted myself, and some of the speakers apparently influenced in some measure by ideas that had been described by my pen."[20]

Impressed with what he believed to be his handiwork, McCoy had speeches by Tipton and Wilson Lumpkin in favor of the bill reprinted and circulated in all directions.

Few members of the Senate showed much enthusiasm for the territorial bill, but because there was little indication that such a measure would get by southern and western representatives in the House, it was relatively safe to support it, since it did seem to be the right thing to do for the Indian. Even then, William King of Alabama could not forgo the opportunity to raise the sectional issue. He offered an amendment to enlarge the proposed terri-tory by adding all of the country west of the Mississippi and north of the state of Missouri. Ambrose Sevier of Arkansas favored the resolution and charged that the original bill was a plan to get more states in the northwest. Although a southerner, Lumpkin attacked the amendment. He pointed out that at least two-thirds of Indian Territory was north of the Missouri Com-promise line, and therefore the South had no just cause for

19 McCoy, Journal, February 16, March 28, April 12 and 15, 1838.
20 *Ibid.*, April 27, 1838.

complaint. The Senate passed Tipton's bill without change by a vote of thirty-nine to six.[21] John C. Calhoun, one of the first to recommend an Indian country west of the Mississippi, opposed the bill.

The passage of the Senate bill was an empty victory. The House of Representatives showed no intention of calling for it. McCoy decided to return to Indian Territory and attempt to organize a general meeting of representatives of all the tribes to endorse territorial organization, with the hope that this endorsement might impress the members of the lower house. Furthermore, a general council could lead to a measure of Indian self-government through means other than congressional action.

While McCoy was making his preparations to return to the West, Congressman Richard Fletcher of Massachusetts enlisted his aid in writing "certain papers on the mismanagement of the Florida war." Fletcher obviously intended to use this material to embarrass the administration. McCoy had expressed his opinions openly, particularly on the policy of hiring Shawnee, Delaware, and Choctaw mercenaries with promises the army never intended to keep. He had no reluctance now to incorporate these views in the notes he sent to Fletcher. McCoy went on to advocate the complete withdrawal of the military forces, for there was not one officer in the whole army with "the right temperment to carry on negotiations." He recommended that civilian envoys be sent to the Seminole villages to assure the Indians that if they surrendered they would be treated humanely. "Presents of clothing should be made to them—not because they should be induced, but because they are needy."[22]

On his return to Indian Territory, McCoy began a tour of the tribes to urge the formation of a general council. The Delawares,

[21] *Congressional Globe*, 345–48.
[22] McCoy, Journal, May 19 through 24, 1838.

Shawnees, and Ottawas assumed that it was "a mischievous design" of the Cherokees. He arrived at the Choctaw reserve in time to sit in on a council of their own, which was conducted with all of the decorum and dispatch of a well-ordered meeting in Congress. The delegates voted to hear McCoy, but decided not to have anything to do with the measures he proposed. He was not too disturbed, for what he had seen had been a revelation to him of the "capacity of the natives to think and act for themselves." Upon further investigation he discovered that the Choctaws had abolished hereditary chieftaincies and had drawn up a written constitution. The tribesmen had divided their reserve into districts, and each district elected a chief for four years. Every district had an inferior and superior court and ten "lighthorsemen," who performed police and militia duties. Mc-Coy also attended a council of the Cherokee tribe, but found the proceedings more primitive. The Cherokees did not oppose the idea of a council of all Indians, but McCoy surmised that they would co-operate in a joint venture only if they could take the lead.[23]

As a result of this tour, McCoy concluded that, from an overall perspective, removal had been a success. He estimated that 73,200 immigrants had come to the Indian country. He claimed to find the large majority living by their industry "at home, and having among them scarcely a greater proportion of individuals who neglect the field or the shop for the chase, than are found among the whites in the frontier settlements." This fact, he thought, should silence the romantics who wrote that the Indian was born to hunt and make war and the prophets of doom who predicted the demise of the red man. He suggested that these people go to the "Hall of Legislation" of the Choctaws and hear

[23] *Ibid.*, August 8 and October 1 through 16, 1838; McCoy to Harris, November 9, 1838, McCoy and Lykins Letters.

men eloquently "pleading and establishing the cause of civil liberty."[24]

McCoy, however, could find few encouraging signs of progress among the 26,660 indigenous tribesmen in Indian Territory, although he expressed confidence that they would soon be "imbibing the spirit of improvement" from the immigrants. Actually, he portrayed an unusually gloomy picture of the plight of the Osages, "5000 friendless human beings . . . on every side they are repulsed, none, either red or white, being willing to have them nearer." Because there was not enough game on their own reserve, some Osages made a habit of returning to old hunting grounds in the sparsely settled regions of Missouri. The frontiersmen raised a clamor and claimed that the red men aimed to murder them in their beds. In the fall of 1837 the governor ordered 500 militiamen to the area. They rounded up about eighty Osages, men, women, and children, severely flogged some of them, and drove them out of the state. McCoy wrote, "I was deeply affected with the sight of some fifteen or twenty of these wretched people, who were peaceably hovering about some settlements of white people, begging for something to keep the soul and body together."[25] He blamed the traders, particularly "Old Chouteau . . . a gourd head . . . about 90,000 Dollars worse than nothing," for much of the Osages' plight. They kept them constantly in debt.[26] To remedy this disastrous condition, McCoy advised Commissioner Carey A. Harris of the Bureau of Indian Affairs to make Osage annuity payments in food instead of money and to hire men to plow fields for them. McCoy noted that the immigrant Indians all looked down on the indigenous tribesmen, and never asked them to their councils. Yet they com-

[24] From remarks prepared by McCoy for Tipton to deliver in Congress, dated January 30, 1839, McCoy Correspondence; McCoy, *Baptist Missions*, 579.
[25] *Ibid.*, 538.
[26] McCoy to Tipton, November 13, 1838, McCoy and Lykins Letters.

plained bitterly about depredations and thievery. He suggested
to the Cherokees that their difficulties with the Osages might be
eased if they invited them to their deliberations.[27] McCoy said
nothing about the Kansa Indians, but judging from the accounts
of the Methodist missionaries, their plight was equally serious.
Thomas Johnson met "4 or 500 of the Kanzas Indians going to
the white settlements to beg provisions, for they had nothing to
eat at home; and those that had not gone to the white settlements
to beg were nearly all scattered over the prairies digging wild
potatoes."[28]

The Twenty-fifth Congress adjourned without the House's
taking up the Senate's territorial bill. To add to McCoy's disappointment, Tipton indicated that he hoped soon to retire from
the Senate. The chief congressional advocate of Indian self-
government would be lost to the cause. "You cannot—you must
not be separated from Indian business at this important juncture."[29] In succeeding months McCoy tried to keep the issue
alive. He opened correspondence with a new generation of
politicians, men like Caleb Cushing and John Bell, and urged
them to work for the passage of an organization bill. Somewhat
wearily, he returned to Washington in January, 1841, because
the new Whig administration would be "ignorant of Indian
Territory affairs." Portents of future difficulties for the territory
began to haunt McCoy. Senator William Allen of Ohio declared
that he would oppose every measure designed to give the Indians
"eternity of residence," and Senator Thomas H. Benton of Missouri made similar statements. Almost in despair, McCoy wrote,

27 McCoy to Harris, October 26, 1837, *ibid.*; McCoy, Journal, August 13,
1838.
28 Johnson's letter to the *Christian Advocate and Journal* (September 8,
1837) is quoted in J. J. Lutz, "The Methodist Missions among the Indian Tribes
in Kansas," *Kansas Historical Collections*, Vol. IX (1905–1906), 199.
29 McCoy to Tipton, November 8, 1838, McCoy and Lykins Letters.

"Where are the friends of the Indians . . . are they never to find a permanent home in America?"[30]

Convinced that the organization of Indian Territory would not soon come about, McCoy redoubled his efforts to promote a movement for self-government within. The first step was to get the Indians to form better tribal governments. He urged that they adopt land laws that would permit patented family holdings and regulations that would enable them to enforce temperance. To McCoy's great satisfaction, the Delawares asked his help to frame a code of laws for the tribe.[31] In all of his contact with the Indians he encouraged intertribal co-operation. The thieving habits of the indigenous natives were a constant source of irritation to the immigrants, but McCoy advised them to "bury their tomahawks" because trouble among them would give the whites an excuse to interfere.[32] Despite McCoy's efforts, the problems of intertribal relations and liquor soon threatened to destroy the small measure of stability the Indians had achieved.

When John Bell arrived in Washington as a young congressman from Tennessee, McCoy had helped him prepare papers on Indian affairs. Installed as secretary of war in 1841, Bell appointed McCoy a "special agent" to settle disputes between various tribes and to promote temperance. McCoy conferred with the Delawares and the Potawatomis regarding a quarrel with the Otoes. The Pawnees had been stealing horses from the Kansas. In retaliation, the Kansas massacred fifty-five defenseless Pawnee women and children. McCoy held full councils with both tribes. The Potawatomis were attempting to promote a common confederacy against the Sioux, but the whole scheme depended upon the course the Delawares would take because the

30 McCoy, Journal, January 19 and March 3, 1841.
31 McCoy, *Baptist Missions*, 552.
32 McCoy, Journal, August 15, 1838.

immigrant Indians looked upon them as the "grandfather" of all their tribes. McCoy endeavored to dissuade the Delaware chiefs from participating. Everywhere he went, McCoy saw traders openly flouting the liquor laws of 1834. St. Louis suppliers sent large quantities of liquor up the Missouri by boat to Bellevue, the "whisky capital" of Indian Territory. McCoy wrote, "8000 gals. of common whiskey passed our door . . . in one single company."[33] In councils with the different tribes, McCoy urged the Indians to adopt self-regulatory measures, but to most it was pious talk, the kind they had come to expect from government agents. Had the government conscientiously enforced the law, as McCoy repeatedly urged, and controlled the liquor flow into the territory, there was no way the Indians could be kept from crossing into Missouri. The subagent for the Osages reported that the places along the western boundary of the state where whisky could be secured were so numerous and scattered that it would require all the dragoons in the United States Army to patrol the line.[34]

McCoy's struggle with the liquor problem and the presence of white settlers on the edge of the Indian country suggested earlier scenes at Fort Wayne and Carey. Yet McCoy professed to be optimistic about the future of Indian Territory. He claimed to see a difference between past and present conditions. With strange logic, which revealed more anxiety than optimism, McCoy argued that for the first time the Indian's position was undergirded by the white man's law. The very existence of the United States government was predicated upon the supposition that the Indians had no right to land east of the Mississippi. A European sovereign, wrongly perhaps, had conveyed this region

[33] McCoy to John C. Spencer (Spencer was secretary of war when McCoy completed his report), October 25, 1841, and March 30, 1842, McCoy Correspondence.
[34] *Annual Report of the Commissioner of Indian Affairs for 1843*, 390.

to his subjects, and these rights had passed to citizens of the United States in 1776. But now the government had the power to guarantee a perpetual residence for the red man beyond the Mississippi. Almost wistfully he added, "Would our citizens become so corrupt that they would force Indians from their homes without sanction of law?"[35]

John Bell's tenure in the cabinet was brief. Early in 1842, the Commissioner of Indian Affairs informed McCoy, "I am directed by the Secretary of War to inform you that the reasons which induced his predecessor to confide certain special duties to you have ceased."[36] Just prior to this message, the board had indicated its desire to terminate its "nominal" connection with McCoy.[37] Thus McCoy's ties with the two incongruous agencies, the Baptist Board of Foreign Missions and the United States Department of War, which had given direction to his pursuit of an Indian Canaan, were cut. Except for Lykins and Simerwell, he had already become alienated from the Baptist missionaries in the territory. In surreptitious notes to each other they denounced "Father McCoy" for his "popish domineering."[38] In long letters to the board they complained that McCoy and Lykins did not reside in the Indian country, but lived in "handsome and comfortable mansions" at Westport. John C. Pratt, one of the new missionaries, with what he thought to be the most telling criticism, compared Meeker's work with McCoy's. "Our good bro. Meeker . . . had doubtless within the past four years been the instrument in the hands of God, of the conversion of more Indian souls, than ever Mr. McCoy has in his life."[39]

35 McCoy, *Baptist Missions*, 582.
36 T. H. Crawford to McCoy, February 17, 1842, McCoy Correspondence.
37 Solomon Peck (successor to Bolles as corresponding secretary) to McCoy, November 1, 1841, Pratt Collection, MSS in the Kansas State Historical Society Library.
38 Pratt to Meeker, February 5 and September 28, 1842, Meeker Papers.
39 Pratt to Peck, January 15, 1841, John G. Pratt Collection.

Pratt, unwittingly, yet succinctly, described two different missionary philosophies that long had divided the Christian church. Meeker, as a missionary, was almost the complete antithesis of McCoy. He stayed near his mission, content with such mundane duties as setting out "150 cabbage plants."[40] He regarded government relations as incidental, and relied on the board to furnish him his support. His interest in orthography declined, and he increasingly focused his attention on the development of an Indian church of "true believers." Judging from his journal, this church occupied itself almost exclusively with the dismissal of members for moral lapses and their reinstatement after they presented sufficient evidence of reform. Meeker's methods may have seemed extremely narrow to many of his contemporaries, but ironically, the end result drew encomiums from agents and superintendents alike.[41] By the late 1840's the Ottawa reserve had become the showcase of Indian Territory with its comfortable houses and well-cultivated fields. The "Christian party" had emerged the victor in its struggle with the "pagan party" and secured the enactment of tribal temperance regulations and "anti-running-into-debt" laws. In 1852, Meeker wrote, "There has been, the past year, no drunkenness, no dramdrinking, nor has there been a single case of fighting, of stealing, of profane swearing, nor of conjugal infidelity."[42]

In comparison to Meeker's individualistic religious approach, McCoy was primarily a social reformer, and like other reformers of the first half of the nineteenth century, he directed his efforts to the reform of a specific institution. Where some in his genera-

[40] Meeker, Journal, June n.d., 1837.
[41] Thomas H. Harvey (superintendent of Indian affairs at St. Louis) to Meeker, December 12, 1844, Meeker Papers; *Annual Report of the Commissioner of Indian Affairs for 1848*, 436.
[42] Quoted in the *Baptist Missionary Magazine*, Vol. XXXII, (February, 1852), 58.

tion attacked institutions of chattel slavery, war, or legal discriminations against women, McCoy attacked the system of law and custom by which he believed the American Indians had been kept in bondage from the time of their first contact with the white men. His object was to free the Indians from these restraints. McCoy would probably have denied that he had devoted much of his life to reform and not to religion. Yet in none of his later writings did he once mention that he had won an Indian convert to Christianity. He ridiculed missionaries who, because they thought they were among "heathen," took an "avowed stand against all that was heathenish." He objected to the practice of dividing the Indians into "Christian" and "pagan" parties. "Who would think of dividing whites into a heathen or sinful party, and the Christian party."[43]

For McCoy, the goal of Indian reform had been the creation of favorable "circumstances" for the American Indians. In an address delivered in Washington in 1841, McCoy stated,

> If the habits are formed by circumstances surrounding him [the Indian], as they are formed by those which surround us, then the point can be established that a change in circumstances would be followed by a change of habits. Let this change be favorable to civilization and religion.[44]

For good or ill, McCoy had been instrumental in the removal of many Indians to a region where he believed the environment to be more ideal. The federal government had failed to organize the new homeland into a territory, but he could yet work to guarantee its boundaries. He attempted to do so at a time when the United States entered an unprecedented era of western expansion. Had he lived a short while longer, McCoy might have been

[43] McCoy, *Baptist Missions*, 505–506.
[44] From a "Memo" dated April 15, 1841, McCoy Correspondence.

199

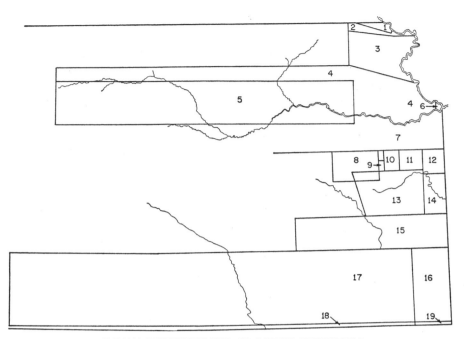

INDIAN RESERVATIONS IN INDIAN TERRITORY
(PRESENT KANSAS), 1846

1. Iowas, 1837
2. Sacs and Foxes of Missouri, 1837
3. Kickapoo Reserve, established under Treaty of 1833
4. Delaware Reserve and Outlet, established under Treaty of 1829
5. Kansa Reserve, established under Treaty of 1825
6. Wyandots, purchased from the Delawares
7. Shawnee Reserve, established by Treaty of 1825
8. Sacs and Foxes of Mississippi, 1843
9. Chippewa Reserve, 1830
10. Ottawa Reserve, 1832
11. Peorias and Kaskaskias, 1833
12. Weas and Piankashaws, 1833
13. Pottawatomie Reserve, established under Treaty of 1837
14. Miami Reserve, 1839 and 1841
15. New York Indian Lands, conveyed under Treaty of 1838
16. Cherokee Neutral Lands, conveyed under Treaty of 1835
17. Osage Reserve, established by Treaty of 1825 (Surveyors arbitrarily extended the western boundary to the old Mexican line.)
18. Cherokee Strip, conveyed under Treaty of 1835
19. Quapaw Strip, 1824

forced to admit that he faced an impossible task. As it was, the activities of his last years indicated a growing realization that the Indians would once more be swamped by white settlers. He became increasingly preoccupied with missionary matters again. His career, so it seemed, had come full circle. But he now had a large enough Baptist following to create his own society. As a missionary executive he could direct others to the mission fields, and did not have to go himself.

In October, 1842, delegates from various western Baptist churches met in Cincinnati to adopt a constitution for the American Indian Mission Association. They appointed McCoy the agent and corresponding secretary,[45] and he moved to Louisville, Kentucky, to set up headquarters for the society. His immediate objective was to get the organization functioning on a scale sufficient to impress the Baptist General Convention, in the hope that it would accept it into the denomination and transfer all Indian missions from the Baptist Board of Foreign Missions to its care. The 1844 Triennial General Convention voted not to adopt the new association, but ruled that the missionaries could decide for themselves whether to change allegiance. Because of the Shawnee Mission's pivotal character and its printing press, Lykins attempted to bring it under the control of McCoy's society. A bitter struggle ensued in which Baptist missionaries excommunicated each other and tried to persuade the few bewildered native converts to take sides.

Removed from the actual scene of conflict, McCoy remained aloof. He advised Lykins to give up the struggle. Meanwhile, he planned new missions and recruited new missionaries. He took up "pen and portfolio" to win support for the American Indian Mission Association. He flirted briefly with the idea of making

---

[45] *Proceedings of the Western Baptist Convention Held in Cincinnati, Ohio, October 27th, 28th, and 29th, 1842,* (Louisville, 1842).

his society part of the Southern Baptist Convention, which broke away from the main body in 1845 because of the slavery issue.[46] John Mason Peck suggested to McCoy that they unite their missions to the pioneers and Indians in a "great Western work."[47] McCoy decided on an independent course.

While promoting missions, McCoy kept watch on the trend of Indian affairs in Washington. As if by habit, he wrote to congressmen and cabinet officers urging them to hold fast on the exterior boundaries of Indian Territory. The last paper that McCoy placed in his files before his death in June, 1846, was a copy of "Document No. 444, A Bill to establish the Territory of Nebraska." The bill did not pass the second session of the Twenty-eighth Congress, but that it came up at all evidently filled McCoy with foreboding.

The Indian State, which Calhoun had hinted at and for which McCoy surveyed a seat of government, of course never materialized. In spite of McCoy's sophistic arguments that the Indians for the first time had a legal claim to the lands they lived on, the titles given in the region beyond the Mississippi proved less substantial than those in the East, for they had no foundation in antiquity. Before the primary removals were completed, the secondary ones had begun. But McCoy's vision of an Indian Canaan cannot be entirely dismissed as chimerical. Eighty-eight years after McCoy's death, President Franklin D. Roosevelt signed the Wheeler-Howard Act, a measure designed to extend to the Indians the right of self-government and the opportunities of education and economic assistance so that they could attain "a wholesome American life." Nor can McCoy's goals and methods be wholly rejected. Much like McCoy's Indian nationalism, a twentieth-century Indian-inspired Pan-Indian movement in the

[46] McCoy, Journal, May 13, 1845.
[47] Peck to McCoy, September 27, 1845, McCoy Correspondence.

United States has de-emphasized tribal distinctions. The federal government of Canada, after sponsoring local schools in Indian and Metis villages in the Mackenzie District for many years, is again encouraging the development of McCoy-type residential schools. Here the students can be given supervision in what is considered a preferable environment.

And yet McCoy's bucolic vision of settled Indian life and his dreams of an organized Indian political state with all the trappings of representative government and written codified laws was typically early-nineteenth-century white America. It should be added that while most contemporary missionaries to the Indians were dispiritedly groping along conventional paths, adding a lone convert here or there to their denomination rolls, McCoy proposed a radical solution for the Indian problem which was only partly religious, and which in its grandiosity was somewhat breathtaking.

Bibliography

PRIMARY REFERENCES

Manuscripts

Francis Barker Collection: "Correspondence" and "Miscellaneous Manuscripts," Kansas State Historical Society Library, Topeka, Kansas.

William Clark Papers, the bulk of which pertains to the United States Superintendency of Indian Affairs at St. Louis. 33 vols. Kansas State Historical Society Library, Topeka, Kansas.

John Dougherty Collection, from typewritten copies of original papers lent to the Kansas State Historical Society, Topeka, Kansas, by O'Fallon Dougherty of Liberty, Missouri, in 1906.

Johnston Lykins Journal, Kansas State Historical Society Library.

Isaac McCoy Collection: "Correspondence," "Journals," "Autobiographical Statement," "Thoughts Respecting the Indian Territory," and "Miscellaneous Papers," Kansas State Historical Society Library, Topeka, Kansas.

Isaac McCoy and Johnston Lykins Letters, from typewritten copies of original manuscripts in the Indiana State Library, Indianapolis. Kansas State Historical Society Library, Topeka, Kansas.

Jotham Meeker Collection: "Journals" and "Correspondence," Kansas State Historical Society Library, Topeka, Kansas.

Bibliography

John G. Pratt Collection: "Correspondence," "Government Papers," and "Miscellaneous Documents," Kansas State Historical Society Library, Topeka, Kansas.
Robert Simerwell Collection: "Journals" and "Correspondence," Kansas State Historical Society Library, Topeka, Kansas.
United States Bureau of Indian Affairs. Records of the Office of Indian Affairs, Washington, D.C. "Letters sent, 1824–1869." Microfilm copies of manuscripts in the National Archives and the State University of Iowa Library, Iowa City, Iowa.

Records of Religious Bodies

"Annual Reports of the American Baptist Missionary Union," *Baptist Missionary Magazine*, 1846–62.
Annual Reports of the American Board of Commissioners for Foreign Missions. Boston, 1810–46.
Documents and Proceedings Relating to the Formation and Progress of a Board in the City of New York, for the Emigration, Preservation, and Improvement, of the Aborigines of America. New York, 1829.
Proceedings of the Board of Managers for the Baptist Mission Society of Kentucky. Louisville, 1818.
Proceedings of the General Missionary Convention of the Baptist Denomination in the United States. Philadelphia and Boston, 1814–32. (The titles also appear variously as *Proceedings of the Triennial Convention* and *Proceedings of the Baptist Convention for Missionary Purposes*.)
Proceedings of the Annual Meetings of the American Indian Mission Association. Louisville, 1842–54.
Proceedings of the Western Baptist Convention Held in Cincinnati, Ohio, October 27th, 28th, and 29th, 1842. Louisville, 1842.
"Two Minute Books of the Kansas Missions in the Forties," [ed. by Kirke Mechem and Lela Barnes], *Kansas Historical Quarterly*, Vol. II (August, 1933), 227–50.

205

Public Documents

Aboriginal Population of the American Indians North of Mexico, The. Smithsonian Miscellaneous Collections, Vol. LXXX, No. 7. Washington, D.C.

American State Papers: Indian Affairs. 2 vols. Washington, D.C., 1832–34.

Annual Reports of the Commissioner of Indian Affairs, 1824–48. Washington, D.C. These reports were published with those of the War Department, and also in separate form after 1838.

Carter, Clarence E., ed. *The Territorial Papers of the United States.* 18 vols. Washington, D.C., 1934–52.

Congressional Globe: Containing the Debates and Proceedings of Congress. Washington, D.C., 1834–46.

Evarts, Jeremiah, ed. *Speeches on the Passage of the Bill for the Removal of the Indians, Delivered in the Congress of the United States, April and May, 1830.* Boston, 1830.

Harrison, James L., comp. *Biographical Directory of the American Congress, 1774–1949.* Washington, D.C., 1950.

Hodge, Frederick W., ed. *Handbook of American Indians North of Mexico.* Bureau of American Ethnology *Bulletin No. 30.* 2 vols. Washington, D.C., 1910.

Kappler, C. J., ed. *Indian Affairs, Laws and Treaties.* 2 vols. Washington, D.C., 1904.

Register of Debates in Congress. 13 vols. Washington, D.C., December, 1824, to March, 1837.

Richardson, James D., ed. *A Compilation of the Messages and Papers of the Presidents.* 10 vols. Washington, 1886–99.

Royce, Charles C., ed. *Indian Land Cessions in the United States.* Bureau of American Ethnology *Eighteenth Annual Report.* Washington, D.C., 1899.

———. *The Cherokee Nation of Indians: A Narrative of Their Official Relations with the Colonial and Federal Govern-*

ments. Bureau of American Ethnology *Fifth Annual Report.* Washington, D.C., 1883–84.

Statutes at Large of the United States of America. Published variously at Boston and Washington, D.C.

Swanton, John R., ed. *The Indian Tribes of North America.* Bureau of American Ethnology *Bulletin No. 145.* Washington, D.C., 1952.

United States House of Representatives, 20 Cong., 2 sess., *House Report 87* (Serial 190), "Removal of Indians Westward."

———. 21 Cong., 1 sess., *House Report 245* (Serial 200), "Memorials of the Inhabitants of the State of Massachusetts"; *House Doc. 246,* "Petition of the Yearly Meeting of Friends"; *House Report 247,* "Memorial of the Board of Managers of the New York Baptist Mission Society."

———. 22 Cong., 1 sess., *House Doc. 2* (Serial 216), "Report of the Secretary of War, November 21, 1831."

———. 22 Cong., 1 sess., *House Doc. 172* (Serial 219), "Country for the Indians West of the Mississippi."

———. 22 Cong., 2 sess., *House Exec. Doc. 2* (Serial 233), "Report of the Secretary of War, November 25, 1832."

———. 22 Cong., 1 sess., *House Exec. Doc. 190* (Serial 220).

———. 23 Cong., 1 sess., *House Report 474* (Serial 263), "Regulating the Indian Department."

———. 25 Cong., 2 sess., *House Doc. 135* (Serial 326), "Statement of All Persons Employed in the Indian Department in the Year 1837."

———. 25 Cong., 3 sess., *House Doc. 174* (Serial 347), "Disbursements to Indians."

———. 26 Cong., 2 sess., *House Exec. Doc. 109* (Serial 384), "Choctaw Treaty at Dancing Rabbit Creek."

———. 39 Cong., 2 sess., *House Misc. Doc. 37,* "Indian Affairs."

United States Senate, 20 Cong., 2 sess., *Sen. Doc. 31* (Serial 181), "Committee Report."

———. 21 Cong., 1 sess., *Sen. Doc. 64* (Serial 193), "Memorial of the

Baptist General Association of Pennsylvania for Missionary Purposes"; *Sen. Doc. 66* (Serial 193), "Memorial of the Ladies of Burlington, New Jersey."

———. 23 Cong., 1 sess., *Sen. Doc. 512* (Serial 244), "Correspondence on the Subject of the Emigration of Indians between 30th November, 1831 and 27th December, 1833 with Abstracts of Expenditures by Disbursing Agents in the Removal and Subsistence of Indians, etc." 5 vols.

———. 24 Cong., 1 sess., *Sen. Doc. 348* (Serial 283), "From the Committee on Indian Affairs."

———. 25 Cong., 2 sess., *Sen. Doc. 395* (Serial 318), "Secretary of War's Letter to the Senate, April 24, 1838."

Reports, Journals, Letters, and Accounts of Missionaries, Agents, Travelers, and Others

Atwater, Calub. "Conjectures Respecting the Origin and History of the Ancient Works in Ohio &c," pp. 102–105 in *The Golden Age of American Anthropology*, ed. by Margaret Mead and Ruth L. Bunzel. New York, 1960.

Barnes, Lela, ed. "Journal of Isaac McCoy for the Exploring Expedition of 1828," *Kansas Historical Quarterly*, Vol. V (August, 1936), 227–77.

———. "Journal of Isaac McCoy for the Exploring Expedition of 1830," *Kansas Historical Quarterly*, Vol. V (November, 1936), 339–77.

Barry, Louise, ed. "William Clark's Diary," *Kansas Historical Quarterly*, Vol. XVI (Spring, 1948), 1–39; Vol. XVI (Summer, 1948), 136–74; Vol. XVI (Fall, 1948), 274–305; Vol. XVI (Winter, 1948), 384–410.

Bauman, Robert F., ed. "The Removal of the Indians from the Maumee Valley: A Selection from the Dresden W. H. Howard Papers," *Northwest Ohio Quarterly*, Vol. XXX (Winter, 1957–58), 10–25.

Berryman, Jerome C. "A Circuit Rider's Frontier Experiences," *Kansas Historical Collections*, Vol. XVI (1923–25), 177–226.

Bliss, Eugene F., ed. *Diary of David Zeisberger: A Moravian Missionary Among the Indians of Ohio*. 2 vols. Cincinnati, 1885.

Catlin, George. *Illustrations of the Manners, Customs, and Conditions of the North American Indians: In a Series of Letters and Notes Written During Eight Years of Travel and Adventure among the Wildest and Most Remarkable Tribes Now Existing*. 7th ed. 2 vols. London. 1848.

[Chouteau, Frederick.] "Reminiscenses of Frederick Choteau: From Notes Taken by Franklin S. Adams, at Westport, Mo., April 24, 1880," *Kansas Historical Collections*, Vol. VIII (1903–1904), 423–34.

Drake, Samuel G. *Biography and History of the Indians of North America from Its First Discovery to the Present Time*. Boston, 1837.

Evarts, Jeremiah (William Penn [pseud.]). *Essay on the Present Crises in the Condition of the American Indians, First Published in the National Intelligencer under the Signature of William Penn*. Boston, 1829.

Faux, William. *Memorable Days in America*, in *Early Western Travels, 1748–1846*, ed. by Reuben Gold Thwaites, XI. Cleveland, 1905.

Foley, John P., ed. *Jeffersonian Cyclopedia*. New York, 1900.

Gipson, Lawrence Henry, ed. *The Moravian Indian Missions on the White River. Diaries and Letters, May 5, 1799 to November 12, 1806*. Indiana Historical Collections, XXIII, (1938).

Goode, William H. *Outposts of Zion*. Cincinnati, 1864.

Gowing, Clara. "Life Among the Delaware Indians," *Kansas Historical Collections*, Vol. XIII (1911–12), 183–94.

Harris, Nellie McCoy. "Memoirs of Old Westport," *Missouri Valley Historical Society Publications*, Vol. IV (October, 1924), 465–75.

Hayward, Elizabeth McCoy, ed. *John M'Coy: His Life and Diaries.* New York, 1948.

Heckewelder, John G. *Narrative of the Mission of the United Brethern Among Delaware and Mohegan Indians.* Philadelphia, 1820.

Hobbs, Wilson. "The Friends' Establishment in Kansas Territory, Personal Recollections of Wilson Hobbs, M.D., Among the Shawnee Indians from November, 1850, to November 1852," *Kansas Historical Collections,* Vol. VIII (1903–1904), 25–271.

Irving, John Treat, Jr. *Indian Sketches.* Ed. by John Francis McDermott. Norman, 1955.

Irving, Washington. *A Tour on the Prairies.* Ed. by John Francis McDermott. Norman, 1956.

Jefferson, Thomas. *The Writings of Thomas Jefferson.* Ed. by H. A. Washington. Vol. V. Washington, D.C., 1871.

"Journal of an Emigrating Party of Pottawattomie Indians, 1838," *Indiana Magazine of History,* Vol. XXI (December, 1925), 315–36.

Keating, William H. *Narrative of an Expedition to the Source of St. Peter's River, Lake Winnepeek, Lake of Woods, and Performed in the Year 1823, by order of the Hon. J. C. Calhoun, Secretary of War, under the Command of Stephen H. Long, U.S.T.E.* 2 vols. Philadelphia, 1824.

Kinzie, Juliette A. "Chicago Indian Chiefs," *Bulletin of the Chicago Historical Society,* Vol. I (August, 1935), 105–16.

Kurz, Rudolph Friederich. *Journal of Rudolph Friederich Kurz.* Trans. by Myrtis Jarrell; ed. by J. N. B. Hewitt. Bureau of American Ethnology *Bulletin No. 115.* Washington, D.C., 1937.

Latrobe, Charles Joseph. *The Rambler in North America.* 2nd ed. 2 vols. London, 1836.

"Letters from the [Methodist] Indian Missions in Kansas," *Kansas Historical Collections,* Vol. XVI (1923–25), 227–71.

McCoy, Isaac. *A Few Observations in Vindication of the Doctrine of the Final Perseverance of the Saints in Answer to Timothy Merritt* (published in approbation of the Regular Baptist Church on Maria Creek, I.T.). Frankfort, Ky., 1811.

———. "Foreign Missionary Intelligence," *American Baptist Magazine and Missionary Intelligencer*, Vol. IV (May, 1824), 330–36.

———. *Remarks on the Practicability of Indian Reform, Embracing Their Colonization.* Boston, 1827.

———. *Remarks on the Practicability of Indian Reform, Embracing Their Colonization, with an Appendix.* New York, 1829.

———. *Address to Philanthropists in the United States Generally: And to Christians in Particular, on the Conditions and Prospects of American Indians.* Surveyor's Camp, Neosho River, Indian Territory, 1 December, 1831.

———. *History of Baptist Indian Missions: Embracing Remarks on the Former and Present Condition of the Aboriginal Tribes: Their Former Settlement Within the Indian Territory, and Their Future Prospects.* Washington, D.C., 1840.

———, ed. *The Annual Register of Indian Affairs Within the Indian (or Western) Territory.* Published at various places by McCoy, 1835–38.

———. *Periodical Account of Baptist Missions Within the Indian Territory, for the Year Ending December 31, 1836.* Westport, Mo., n.d.

M'Coy, John. "Isaac McCoy," in *Annals of the American Pulpit: The Baptists*, ed. by William B. Sprague. Vol. VI. New York, 1865.

McCoy, John C. "Survey of Kansas Indian Lands," *Kansas Historical Collections*, Vol. IV (1886–90), 298–311.

McDermott, John Francis. "A Frontier Library: The Books of Isaac McCoy," *Bibliographical Society of America*, Vol. LII (Second Quarter, 1958), 140–43.

———, ed. "Isaac McCoy's Second Exploring Trip in 1828." *Kansas Historical Quarterly*, Vol. XII (August, 1945), 400–62.

McKee, Irving, ed. *The Trail of Death: Letters of Benjamin Petit.* Indiana Historical Society *Publication*, Indianapolis, 1941.

Mazzuchelli, Samuel C. *Memoirs, Historical and Edifying of a Missionary Apostolic of the Order of St. Dominic among the Various Indian Tribes and among Catholics and Protestants in the United States of America.* Chicago, 1915.

Merrill, Moses. "Extracts from the Diary of Rev. Moses Merrill, a Missionary to the Otoe Indians from 1832–1840." *Transactions and Reports of the Nebraska History Society*, Vol. IV (1892), 160–91.

Morgan, Lewis Henry. *The Indian Journals, 1859–1862.* Ed. by Leslie A. White. Ann Arbor, 1959.

Morse, Jedidiah. *Report to the Secretary of War of the United States on Indian Affairs, Comprising a Narrative of a Tour Performed in the Summer of 1820, under a Commission from the President of the United States, for the Purpose of Ascertaining, for the Use of the Government, the Actual State of the Indian Tribes in Our Country.* New Haven, 1822.

Nevins, Allan, comp. and ed. *American Social History as Recorded by British Travellers.* London, 1937.

Oliphant, J. Orin, ed. "The Report of the Wyandot Exploring Delegation, 1831," *Kansas Historical Quarterly*, Vol. XV (1947), 248–62.

———. *Through the South and West with Jeremiah Evarts, in 1826.* Lewisburg, Pa., 1956.

Parker, Samuel. *Journal of an Exploring Tour Beyond the Rocky Mountains.* Ithaca, 1842.

Peck, John Mason. *Forty Years of Pioneer Life: Memoir of John Mason Peck.* Ed. by Rufus Babcock. Philadelphia, 1864.

Peck, Solomon. "History of the Missions of the Baptist General Convention," pp. 353–620 in *History of American Missions to the Heathen*, ed. by Joseph Tracy. Worcester, 1840.

Perrot, Nicholas. "Memoir of the Manners, Customs, and Religion of the Savages of North America," Vol. I in *Indian Tribes of the Upper Mississippi Valley and Region of the Great Lakes*, trans. and ed. by Emma H. Blair. Cleveland, 1911.

Schermerhorn, John F., and Samuel J. Mills. *A Correct View of That Part of the United States which lies West of the Allegany Mountains, with Regard to Religion and Morals*. Hartford, 1814.

Schoolcraft, Henry R. *Travels in the Central Portions of the Mississippi Valley*. New York, 1825.

———. *Historical and Statistical Information Respecting the History, Condition, and Prospects of the Indian Tribes of the United States*. 5 vols. Philadelphia, 1851.

Smith, Dwight L., ed. "A Continuation of the Journal of an Emigrating Party of Potawatomi Indians, 1838, and Ten William Polke Manuscripts," *Indiana Magazine of History*, Vol. XLIV (December, 1948), 391–408.

———. "An Unsuccessful Negotiation for Removal of the Wyandot Indians from Ohio, 1834," *Ohio State Archaeological and Historical Quarterly*, Vol. LVIII (1949), 305–31.

———. "Jacob Hull's Detachment of the Potawatomi Emigration of 1838," *Indiana Magazine of History*, Vol. XIV (September, 1949), 284–88.

Smith, Timothy. *Missionary Abominations Unmasked; or, A View of Carey Mission Containing an Unmasking of the Missionary Abominations Practiced among the Indians of the St. Joseph Country at the Celebrated Missionary Establishment Known as Carey Mission under the Superintendency of the Rev. Isaac McCoy*. South Bend, Ind., n.d.

Thornbrough, Gayle, ed. *Letter Book of the Indian Agency at Fort Wayne, 1809–1815*. Indiana Historical Society *Publication*, Vol. XXI. Indianapolis, 1961.

Thwaites, Reuben Gold, ed. *The Jesuit Relations and Allied Documents*. Rev. ed. Vols. XXIII and XLIV. New York, 1959.

Tipton, John. *The John Tipton Papers*. Comp. and ed. by Glen A. Blackburn, Nellie A. Robertson, and Dorothy Riker. 3 vols. Indianapolis, 1942.

Tracy, Joseph. "History of the Board of Foreign Missions of the General Assembly of the Presbyterian Church in the United States of America, and of Its Missions," pp. 709–26 in *History of American Missions to the Heathen.* Worcester, 1840.

Trowbridge, Charles C. *Meearmeear Traditions.* Ed. by Vernon Kinietz. Occasional Contributions from the Museum of Anthropology of the University of Michigan, No. 7. Ann Arbor, 1938.

——. *Shawnese Traditions.* Ed. by Vernon Kinietz and Erminie W. Voegelin. Occasional Contributions from the Museum of Anthropology of the University of Michigan, No. 9. Ann Arbor, 1939.

Voegelin, Erminie W., ed. "John Heckewelder to Peter S. Du Ponceau," *Ethnohistory*, Vol. VI (Winter, 1959), 70–81.

Wheelock, Eleazar. *A Plain and Faithful Narrative of the Original Design, Rise, Progress, and Present State of the Indian Charity School at Lebanon in Connecticut.* Boston, 1763.

Williams, Samuel C., ed. *Adair's History of the American Indians.* Johnson City, Tennessee, 1930.

Newspapers and Magazines

American Missionary Register, New York, 1820–25.

American Theological Review, Salem, Mass., 1860.

Baptist Banner and Western Pioneer, Louisville, 1842.

Baptist Missionary Magazine, Boston, 1817–62. Appeared under various titles: *American Baptist Magazine and Missionary Intelligencer*, 1817–24; *American Baptist Magazine*, 1825–35; *Baptist Missionary Magazine*, 1850–62.

Columbian Star and Christian Index, Washington, D.C., 1822–26.

Indian Advocate, Louisville, 1847–55.

Latter Day Luminary, Philadelphia, 1818–25.

Massachusetts Missionary Magazine, Boston, 1803–1808.

Missionary Herald, Boston, 1818–62. Known as the *Panoplist and Missionary Herald*, 1818–20.

Niles' Weekly Register, 1824–40.
North American Review, 1820–40.
Panopolist, Boston, 1805–1807. Known as *Panopolist and Missionary Magazine United*, 1808–16.
St. Louis Beacon, 1830.
Western Monitor (Fayette, Mo.), 1830.

SECONDARY REFERENCES

Books and Monographs

Abel, Annie H. *The History of Events Resulting in Indian Consolidation West of the Mississippi*. Washington, 1906.

Barclay, Wade Crawford. *Early American Methodism, 1769–1884.* 2 vols. New York, 1960.

Berkhofer, Robert F. *Salvation and the Savage*. Lexington, 1965.

Brice, W. A. *History of Fort Wayne, with a Biography of the Late Hon. Samuel Hanna*. Fort Wayne, 1868.

Buley, R. Carlyle. *The Old Northwest: Pioneer Period*. 2 vols. Bloomington, Ind., 1951.

Caldwell, Martha B., comp. *Annals of Shawnee Methodist Mission and Indian Manual Labor School*. Topeka, 1939.

Debo, Angie. *And Still the Waters Run*. Princeton, 1940.

———. *The Road to Disappearance*. Norman, 1941.

Elsbree, Oliver W. *The Rise of the Missionary Spirit in America, 1790–1815*. Williamsport, Pa., 1928.

Faust, Harold S. *The American Indian in Tragedy and Triumph*. Presbyterian Historical Studies No. 1. Philadelphia, 1945.

Foreman, Carolyn Thomas. *Oklahoma Imprints, 1835–1907*. Norman, 1936.

Foreman, Grant. *Indian Removal*. Norman, 1932.

———. *The Five Civilized Tribes*. Norman, 1934.

———. *Indians and Pioneers*. Norman, 1936.

———. *Sequoyah*. Norman, 1938.

———. *The Last Trek of the Indians*. Chicago, 1946.

Frederikson, Otto Frovin. *The Liquor Question Among the Indian Tribes in Kansas, 1804–1881. Bulletin* of the University of Kansas, Vol. XXXIII. Lawrence, 1932.

Gammell, William. *A History of American Baptist Missions.* Boston, 1849.

Garraghan, Gilbert J. *The Jesuits of the Middle United States.* 3 vols. New York, 1938.

Goodykoontz, Colin B. *Home Missions on the American Frontier.* Caldwell, Idaho, 1939.

Graves, W. W. *Annals of the Osage Mission.* St. Paul, Kan., 1935.

———. *The First Protestant Osage Missions, 1820–1837.* Oswego, Kan., 1949.

Hagan, William T. *The Sac and Fox Indians.* Norman, 1958.

———. *American Indians.* Chicago, 1961.

Harmon, George Dewey. *Sixty Years of Indian Affairs: Political, Economic, and Diplomatic, 1789–1850.* Chapel Hill, 1941.

Harvey, Henry. *History of the Shawnee Indians from the Year 1681 to 1854.* Cincinnati, 1855.

Hinsdale, W. B. *Distribution of the Aboriginal Population of Michigan.* Occasional Contributions of the Museum of Anthropology of the University of Michigan, No. 2. Ann Arbor, 1932.

Honig, Louis O. *Westport: Gateway to the Early West.* [Subscriber's edition.] N.p., 1950.

Hunt, Elvid, and W. E. Lorence. *History of Fort Leavenworth.* Leavenworth, Kan., 1937.

Kelsey, Rayner W. *Friends and the Indians, 1665–1917.* Philadelphia, 1917.

Kinietz, W. Vernon. *The Indians of the Western Great Lakes, 1616–1760.* Occasional Contributions from the Museum of Anthropology of the University of Michigan, No. 10. Ann Arbor, 1940.

———. *Delaware Culture Chronology.* Prehistory Research Series, Indiana Historical Society, Vol. III. Indianapolis, 1946.

Kinney, J. P. *A Continent Lost—A Civilization Won: Indian Land Tenure in America.* Baltimore, 1937.

La Farge, Oliver. *As Long as the Grass Shall Grow.* New York, 1940.

Lyons, Emory J. *Isaac McCoy: His Plan of and Work for Indian Colonization.* Fort Hayes Kansas State College *Studies No. 9.* Topeka, 1945.

McCoy, William H. *Notes on the McCoy Family.* Rutland, Vermont, 1939.

McKenney, Thomas L., and James Hall. *The Indian Tribes of North America.* Ed. by Frederick W. Hodge. 3 vols. Edinburgh, 1933.

McMurtrie, Douglas C., and Albert H. Allen. *Jotham Meeker, Pioneer Printer of Kansas.* Chicago, 1930.

Major, Mareem. *Abbreviated Annual Year Book, With the History of the Fort Wayne Baptist Association.* Fort Wayne, 1943.

Malin, James C. *Indian Policy and Westward Expansion. Bulletin* of the University of Kansas *Humanistic Studies,* Vol. II. Lawrence, 1921.

Mathews, John Joseph. *The Osages.* Norman, 1961.

Melville, Herman. *Moby Dick.* New York, 1952.

Meyer, Leland Winfield. *The Life and Times of Colonel Richard M. Johnson of Kentucky.* New York, 1932.

Morrison, William B. *Military Posts and Camps in Oklahoma.* Oklahoma City, 1936.

Pearce, Roy Harvey. *The Savages of America.* Baltimore, 1953.

Phillips, Paul Chrisler. *The Fur Trade.* 2 vols. Norman, 1961.

Posey, Walter B. *The Baptist Church in the Lower Mississippi Valley, 1776–1845.* Lexington, 1957.

Quaife, Milo M. *Lake Michigan.* Indianapolis, 1944.

Quimby, George Irving. *Indian Life in the Upper Great Lakes, 11,000 B.C. to A.D. 1800.* Chicago, 1960.

Reisner, Edward H. *Evolution of the Common School.* New York, 1930.

Rister, Carl Coke. *Baptist Missions Among the American Indians.* Atlanta, 1944.

Schmeckebier, Lawrence F. *The Office of Indian Affairs: Its History, Activities, and Organization.* Johns Hopkins University, Service Monographs of the United States Government, No. 48. Baltimore, 1927.

Seymour, Flora S. *Indian Agents of the Old Frontier.* New York, 1941.

Slobodin, Richard. *Metis of the Mackenzie District.* Ottawa, Canada, 1966.

Smith, Timothy L. *Benevolence and Social Reform in Mid-Nineteenth-Century America.* New York, 1957.

Strong, William E. *The History of the American Board.* Boston, 1910.

Torbet, Robert G. *The Baptist Ministry, Then and Now.* Philadelphia, 1953.

———. *Venture of Faith: The Story of the American Baptist Foreign Mission Society and the Woman's American Baptist Foreign Mission Society, 1814–1954.* Philadelphia, 1955.

Underhill, Ruth. *Red Man's America: A History of the Indians in the United States.* Chicago, 1953.

Winger, Otho. *The Potawatomi Indians.* Elgin, Ill., 1939.

Woodford, Frank B. *Lewis Cass: The Late Jeffersonian.* New Brunswick, N.J., 1950.

Wyeth, Walter N. *Isaac McCoy and Early Indian Missions.* Philadelphia, 1895.

Zornow, William F. *Kansas: A History of the Jayhawk State.* Norman, 1957.

Articles, Essays, and Theses

Abel, Annie H. "Indian Reservations in Kansas, and the Extinguishment of Their Title," *Kansas Historical Collections,* Vol. XIV (1903–1904), 458–83.

———. "Proposals for an Indian State, 1778–1878," *Annual Report of the American Historical Association for the Year 1907*, Vol. I, 87–104.

Anderson, Hattie M. "The Evolution of Frontier Society in Missouri, 1815–1828," *Missouri Historical Review*, Vol. XXXII (July, 1938), 458–83.

Banks, Loy Otis. "The Evening and the Morning Star," *Missouri Historical Review*, Vol. XLIII (July, 1949), 319–33.

Barnes, Lela. "Isaac McCoy and the Treaty of 1821," *Kansas Historical Quarterly*, Vol. V (May, 1836), 122–42.

Barry, Louise, comp. "Kansas Before 1854: A Revised Annals," *Kansas Historical Quarterly*, Vol. XXVII (Winter, 1961), 497–543; Vol. XXVIII (Spring, 1962), 25–59; Vol. XXVIII (Summer, 1962), 167–204; Vol. XXVIII (Autumn, 1962), 317–69; Vol. XXVIII (Winter, 1962), 497–514; Vol. XXIX (Spring, 1963), 41–81.

Bauman, Robert F. "The Migration of the Ottawa Indians from the Maumee Valley to Walpole Island," *Northwest Ohio Quarterly*, Vol. XXI (Summer, 1949), 86–112.

———. "Kansas, Canada, or Starvation," *Michigan History*, Vol. XXXVI (September, 1952), 287–98.

———. "The Ottawas of the Lakes, 1616–1766," *Northwest Ohio Quarterly*, Vol. XXX (Autumn, 1958), 188–93.

Brown, G. Gordon. "Missions and Cultural Diffusion," *American Journal of Sociology*, Vol. L (November, 1944), 214–19.

Cady, John F. "Isaac McCoy's Mission to the Indians of Indiana and Michigan," *Indiana History Bulletin*, Vol. XVI (February, 1939), 100–13.

Chappell, Phil E. "A History of the Missouri River," *Kansas Historical Collections*, Vol. IX (1905–1906), 237–94.

Dewey, Francis A. "A Sketch of the Marine of Lake Erie Previous to the Year 1829," *Michigan Pioneer and Historical Collections*, Vol. IV (1881), 70–81.

Eaton, David. "Echoes of Indian Emigration," *Missouri Historical Quarterly*, Vol. VIII (April, 1914), 142–53.

Ellis, Albert G. "Recollections of Rev. Eleazar Williams," *Wisconsin Historical Collections*, Vol. VIII (1877–79), 322–52.

Edwards, Martha L. "Government Patronage of Indian Missions." Ph.D. dissertation, University of Wisconsin, 1916.

———. "Religious Forces in the United States, 1815–1830," *Mississippi Valley Historical Review*, Vol. V (March, 1919), 434–49.

Fabin, W. W. "Indians of the Tri-State Area: The Potawatomi," *Northwest Ohio Quarterly*, Vol. XXX (Winter, 1957–58), 49–53; Vol. XXX (Spring, 1958), 100–105.

Foreman, Carolyn T. "The Foreign Mission School at Cornwall, Connecticut," *Chronicles of Oklahoma*, Vol. VII (September, 1929), 224–59.

Foreman, Grant. "Missionaries of the Latter Day Saints in the Indian Territory," *Chronicles of Oklahoma*, Vol. XIII (June, 1935), 196–213.

Foster, William O. "The Career of Montfort Stokes in Oklahoma," *Chronicles of Oklahoma*, Vol. XVIII (March, 1940), 35–52.

Gabriel, Ralph H. "Evangelical Religion and Popular Romanticism in Early Nineteenth-Century America," *Church History*, Vol. XIX (March, 1950), 34–47.

Gallaher, Ruth A. "The Indian Agent in the United States Before 1850," *Iowa Journal of History and Politics*, Vol. XIV (January, 1916), 3–55.

Hadley, J. Nixon. "The Demography of the American Indians," *Annals of the American Academy of Political and Social Science*, Vol. CCCXI (May, 1957), 23–30.

Haines, Blanche M. "French and Indian Footprints at Three Rivers on the St. Joseph," *Michigan Pioneer and Historical Collections*, Vol. XXXVIII (1912), 386–97.

Hill, Esther Clark. "The Pratt Collection of Manuscripts," *Kansas Historical Quarterly*, Vol. I (February, 1932), 83–88.

———. "Some Background of Early Baptist Missions in Kansas," *Kansas Historical Quarterly*, Vol. I (February, 1932), 89–103.

Hill, Mabel. "Paul Hill: Removal of the Potawatomi," *Nebraska History Magazine*, Vol. VIII (January-March, 1937), 5–9.

King, Joseph B. "The Ottawa Indians in Kansas and Oklahoma," *Kansas Historical Collections*, Vol. XIII (1915), 373–78.

Kingsbury, Susan M. "A Comparison of the Virginia Company with the Other English Trading Companies of the Sixteenth and Seventeenth Centuries," *Annual Report of the American Historical Association for the Year 1906*, Vol. I, 159–76.

Kinietz, W. Vernon. "European Civilization as a Determinant of Native Indian Customs," *American Anthropologist*, Vol. XLII (January–March, 1940), 116–21.

Klopfenstein, Carl Grover. "The Removal of the Indians from Ohio, 1820–1843." Ph.D. dissertation, Western Reserve University, 1955.

———. "Westward Ho: Removal of Ohio Shawnees, 1832–1833," *Bulletin of the Historical and Philosophical Society of Ohio*, Vol. XV (January, 1957), 3–31.

Lindley, Harlow. "William Clark—The Indian Agent," *Mississippi Valley Historical Association Proceedings*, Vol. II (1908–1909), 63–75.

Lutz, J. J. "The Methodist Missions among the Indian Tribes in Kansas," *Kansas Historical Collections*, Vol. IX (1905–1906), 160–230.

Lynam, Anna Cathryn. "Experiments in Indian Administration, 1824–1871." M.A. thesis, State University of Iowa, 1933.

Mitchell, Kenneth S. "The Migration of the Potawatomi," *Journal of American History*, Vol. XVI (October–December, 1922), 353–60.

Morehouse, George P. "History of the Kansa or Kaw Indians," *Kansas Historical Collections*, Vol. X (1907–1908), 327–68.

Morrison, T. F. "Mission Neosho, the First Kansas Missions," *Kansas Historical Quarterly*, Vol. IV (August, 1935), 227–34.

Murphy, Joseph Francis. "Potawatomi Indians of the West: Origin of the Citizen Band." Ph.D. dissertation, University of Oklahoma, 1961.

"Official Roster of Kansas, 1854–1925," *Kansas Historical Collections*, Vol. XVI (1923–25), 657–775.

Pare, George. "The St. Joseph Mission," *Mississippi Valley Historical Review*, Vol. XVII (June, 1930), 24–54.

Phillips, Clifton Jackson. "Protestant America and the Pagan World." Ph.D. dissertation, Harvard University, 1954.

Polke, James. "Some Memoirs of the Polke, Piety, McCoy, McQuaid, and Mathes Families," *Indiana Magazine of History*, Vol. X (March, 1914), 83–109.

Prucha, Francis Paul. "Thomas L. McKenney and the New York Indian Board," *Mississippi Valley Historical Review*, Vol. XLVIII (March, 1962), 635–55.

———. "Indian Removal and the Great American Desert," *Indiana Magazine of History*, Vol. LIX (December, 1963), 299–322.

Royce, Charles C. "An Inquiry into the Identity and History of the Shawnee Indians," *Magazine of Western History*, Vol. II (May to October, 1885), 38–50.

Smith, Dwight. "The Attempted Potawatomi Emigration of 1839," *Indiana Magazine of History*, Vol. XLV (March, 1949), 51–80.

Smith, Elwyn A. "The Forming of a Modern American Denomination," *Church History*, Vol. XXXI (March, 1962), 74–99.

Spencer, Joab. "The Shawnee Indians: Their Customs, Traditions, and Folk-Lore," *Kansas Historical Collections*, Vol. X (1907–1908), 382–96.

Steiner, Bernard C. "Jackson and the Missionaries," *American Historical Review*, Vol. XXIX (July, 1924), 722–23.

Stuart, Benjamin F. "Transportation of Potawattomies: The Deportation of Menominee and His Tribe of the Pottawattomie Indians," *Indiana Magazine of History*, Vol. XVIII (September, 1922), 255–65.

Thompson, Hildegard. "Education Among American Indians: Institutional Aspects," *Annals of the American Academy of Political and Social Science*, Vol. CCCXI (May, 1957), 95–104.

Underhill, Ruth. "Religion Among American Indians," *Annals of the American Academy of Political and Social Science*, Vol. CCCXI (May, 1957), 127–36.

Wilmeth, Roscoe. "Kansa Village Locations in the Light of Mc-Coy's 1828 Journal," *Kansas Historical Quarterly*, Vol. XXVI (Summer, 1960), 152–57.

Young, James H. "American Medical Quackery in the Age of the Common Man," *Mississippi Valley Historical Review*, Vol. XLVII (March, 1961), 579–93.

Young, Mary E. "Indian Removal and Land Allotment: The Civilized Tribes and Jacksonian Justice," *American Historical Review*, Vol. LXIV (October, 1958), 31–45.

Zerfas, Leon. "Medical Education in Indiana as Influenced by Early Indiana Graduates in Medicine from Transylvania University," *Indiana Magazine of History*, Vol. XXX (1934), 139–48.

Index

Cherokees: 40, 69, 98, 117, 129, 136–
38, 148–51, 154, 178–79, 184, 192ff.;
Cherokee Phoenix, 136; "Cherokee
Strip," 188
Chicago, Treaty of: 18, 54–55, 65, 74
Chickasaws: 98–99, 104, 110–12, 115,
136, 148, 169; *see also* Colbert, Levi
(Chief), 111
Chippewas: 17, 53, 90–91, 154, 159, 188
Choctaws: 67, 81, 98–99, 104, 110–12,
115, 117, 142, 151, 163, 191; Choctaw
Academy, 81, 88, 134ff.; "Hall of
Legislation," 192
Chouteau, Francois: 101, 193
Civilization Fund: 33ff., 73, 134
Clark, Marston G. (General): 128–29
Clark, William (General): 85–86,
100, 104–105, 110, 133, 144, 158, 169,
188
Clark's Grant: 7
Clay, Henry (Senator): 182
Clyde, Peter: 49, 57
Colbert, Levi (Chickasaw chief): 111
Colgate, William: 74
Columbian College: 12, 55, 64, 68, 71,
80–83, 126
Columbian Star and Christian Index:
64, 89, 126
Comanches: 117, 153, 174
Commissioner of Indian Affairs: 142,
173, 197
Cone, Spencer H.: 74
Conway, Henry W.: 79
Creeks: 98–99, 110, 129, 156, 179; Mc-
Intosh faction, 115; William Mc-
Intosh (Chief), 115; "Creek War,"
179
Cushing, Caleb: 194

Davenport, William (Major): 144
Davis, Anthony L.: 177, 183, 186
Davis, John: 149, 156, 158
Delawares: 19, 30ff., 62, 69, 86, 136,
142–45, 159, 163, 167, 174, 183, 191,
195; John Quick (Chief), 143, 145;
William Anderson (Chief), 147,

159; Shawanock (Chief), 167;
Gnadenhutten, 31
Disciples of Christ: 28
"Doctrine of effective occupancy": 95
"Document No. 444, A Bill to Estab-
lish the Territory of Nebraska":
202
"Domestick Missions": 11
Donelson, John: 148–49, 157
Dougherty, John (Major): 111, 145,
152–53, 160

Eaton, John: 128–30, 133, 135, 137–38
"Education families": *see* Jedidiah
Morse
Ellsworth, Henry L.: 139, 161–62, 168,
170, 172, 188
Evans, Alexander: 159, 163
Evarts, Jeremiah: 124, 130–33, 136
Everett, Edward: 173

"Feast of the Dead": 66–67
Fletcher, Richard: 191
Fletcher vs. *Peck*: 95
Foreman, Grant: 152, 172
Fort Dearborn: 53
Fort Gibson: 149
Fort Harrison: 25, 27ff.
Fort Smith: 149
Fort Wayne: 23–24, 32, 36–58, 68, 70,
75, 196; "General Rules for the
Regulation of the Fort Wayne Mis-
sion Family," 57
Foxes: 13, 188; *see also* Sacs
Freylinghuysen, Theodore (Senator):
133, 137
French, Daniel: 170–71

Gardiner, James B. (Colonel): 157
General Missionary Convention of
the Baptist Denominations in the
United States of America for Foreign Missions: 55, 82ff., 126–27, 137,
197, 201; Board of Foreign Missions, 11, 15, 24, 26, 33, 38, 73, 81–82,
98, 151, 165; Triennial General

Index

Tecumseh (Shawnee chief): 22, 24
Tenskwatawa ("The Prophet"): 22,
24, 108, 143
Thomas, John: 89
Thomas Mission: 89–91, 121, 125,
127–28, 159
Thompson, Squire: 77, 92
Tippecanoe, Battle of: 75
Tipton, John (General): 75–76, 86–
88, 91–92, 177–78, 183–85, 188–91,
194
Topenebee (Potawatomi chief): 39,
54, 58–60, 118, 157
"Trail of Tears": 184
Trowbridge, Charles E.: 19, 58
Turner, William (Doctor): 32, 36,
45, 75

Underhill, Ruth: 50
Union Mission: 50
United States Telegraph: 126

Van Buren, Martin: 188

Vincennes: 7ff., 14–15, 24–25, 33, 47,
54, 69

Wabash District Association: 43
Wallace, David (Governor): 184
War Department: 41, 61–62, 65, 67n.,
79, 85, 93, 104, 108ff., 114, 117, 123,
126–29, 135, 148, 156, 176, 179, 183,
187, 197; Civilization Fund, 30–34,
73; *see also* Bureau of Indian Affairs
Wayland, Francis: 74, 137
Weas: 14, 17, 69, 142, 169, 189; Stone-
eater (Chief), 29
Welch, James E.: 12
Wheeler-Howard Act: 202
Wheelock, Eleazer: 40
White Hair (Osage chief): 112
White Plume (Kansa chief): 112
Williams, Eleazer (Reverend): 79
Wilson, Clark E.: 163
Winnebagos: 93
Wolcott, Alexander: 103
Worchester, Samuel A.: 136–37